(

/
/

O

M/

I

A

Perceptual Growth
in
Creativity

Perceptual Growth
in
Creativity

LOUISE DUNN YOCHIM

Supervisor of Art
Chicago Public Schools

INTERNATIONAL TEXTBOOK COMPANY
Scranton, Pennsylvania

This book is dedicated to my son, Jerome, whose scientific achievements exemplify the value of creativity in perceptual growth;

and to

Maurice, my husband, whose steadfast dedication to art, and to the art of teaching art, has been the source of sustaining inspiration to many and particularly to the author of this book.

Preface

This book is intended to serve as a professional reference, as a college-level text, and as a practical guide for teachers of art in the elementary, junior, and senior high schools. It may be of interest also to counselors, principals, supervisors of art, psychologists, and all others who are concerned with fostering growth in visual perception.

This volume deals primarily with the significance of art education, underscoring those factors which enter into the development of perceptual and creative skills. Included in it are topics which relate to the dynamics of visual perception, the nature of the creative process, the nature of the learner, and the role and responsibilities of the teacher of art. Considerable attention is given to the methods of developing "image-forming" skills and "idea-fluency." The achievement of "flexibility" in personality traits is also duly considered.

The special features of this volume are:

1. A critical and detailed analysis and evaluation of paintings which have been selected from 6000 creative expressions painted by students of all grade and age levels in the Chicago Public Schools. These paintings reveal manifestations of gradual growth in perceptual skill. The findings also establish flexible criteria for the evaluation of children's art work, guiding adults in a better understanding of the correlative factors concerning creative performance and physical and mental development.

2. Suggested methods and experiences that can be instrumental in the cultivation of image-forming skills.

3. Approximately 600 image-forming stimuli—ideas for two- and three-dimensional art experiences which are essential in fostering depth in sensory perception—geared to all grade levels.

4. Specific recommendations for classroom organization, procedures relating to the teaching of art and the achievement of perceptual growth.

5. Many illustrations of children's art work, also of art products from various cultures of the past and the present.

6. Illustrations of works of art by contemporary artists and craftsmen.

7. Design processes and how these affect growth in perceptual skill.

8. Basic criteria for viewing and appreciating works of art.

The author's purpose in writing this book has been to record and to share with others the insights, concepts, and findings gained through thirty years of teaching and supervision. It is hoped that this record of empirical and theoretical evidence will in some measure contribute to the recognition of the fact that art experiences play a vital role in fostering growth in visual perception.

LOUISE DUNN YOCHIM

Skokie, Illinois
April, 1967

Acknowledgments

To Bruce Kirk, PhD, Chairman of the Division for Study of Human Personality, Chicago Teachers College, North, I am deeply indebted for his scholarly contribution to this manuscript, Chapter 5, "Psychological Research on Creativity," and for his guidance, criticism, and encouragement at various stages in the development of this manuscript.

To Dr. Italo de Francesco, one of the leading pioneers in the field of art education, educator, author, president of Kutztown Stage College, Pennsylvania, I extend my deepest appreciation for his careful review of the manuscript.

To Dr. Jacob Mandel, psychologist, on the staff of Kutztown State College, I am grateful for his helpful suggestions which led to the enrichment of the psychological concepts developed in the text.

To Velma Miller, Assistant Professor of Art, Department of Art Education, Art Institute of Chicago, and former Supervisor of Art in the Chicago Public Schools, I am particularly grateful for her keen, critical, and professional analysis of the content.

To Samuel Greenburg, Supervisor of Art, Chicago Public Schools, noted painter, author, traveler, and lecturer, I extend my appreciation for his critical reading of this manuscript.

To Maurice, my husband, Assistant Professor of Art, Chicago Teachers College, North, educator, painter, sculptor, and author, I am indebted for his professional advice and his inestimable help in the clarification of details concerning the content of the manuscript.

My gratitude is also extended to many institutions, museums, galleries, collectors, painters, sculptors, artist-designers, teachers, and pupils whose contribution helped to enrich the content of this manuscript.

The Museum of Primitive Art, New York.
Musée de l'Homme, Paris.
Museo Preistorico-Etnographico, Rome.
National Gallery of Art, Washington.
Art Institute of Chicago.
Kunstmuseum, Basel.
The Museum of Modern Art, New York City.
Philadelphia Museum of Art.

The Solomon R. Guggenheim Museum, New York.
Metropolitan Museum of Art, New York.
Cranbrook Academy of Art, Michigan.
University of Illinois.
Montclair Museum of Art, New Jersey.

Collection of Mrs. Julia Feininger, New York.
Collection of the artist, Nahum Gabo, New York.
Collection of Reynolds Morse Foundation, New York.
Collection of A. Mazzota; Milan, Italy.
Collection of Mr. & Mrs. R. Sturgis Ingersoll, Penllyn, Pa.

Pierre Matisse Gallery, New York City.
The Alan Gallery, New York City.
Samuel M. Kootz Gallery, New York City.
The Downtown Gallery, New York City.
The Contemporaries, New York City.
Feingarten Gallery, Chicago.
Richard Feigen Gallery, Chicago

Aaron Bohrod
Lillian Desow-Fishbein
Theodore Frano
Bertrand Goldberg
Samuel Greenburg
Milton Horn

Tim Meier
Harry Mintz
Seymour Rosofsky
William S. Schwartz
Marian Witt
Minori Yamasaki

Frank Las, Photographer
Dorothy Slobodin, Typist

LOUISE DUNN YOCHIM

Contents

Contents

1

Self-assertion, a Vital

Human Need

Very early in the history of human affairs the creative impulses of man found expression in the rudimentary and essential aspects of his daily living. Whether these impulses were directed toward the designing of ceremonial or utilitarian objects or to the building of notable structures—cathedrals, palaces, etc.—they merely suggest the degree of complexity which characterized each successive epoch of civilization. More significant, perhaps, is the clear manifestation of man's desire to improve his destiny and thus insure greater comfort for his physical, moral, and spiritual needs. Although his propensities to intensify life were propelled by technological advances, the creative tendencies of man found expression largely through a compelling desire to assert his individuality. Consequently, he searched, invented, built, and embellished his visual forms and through this process satisfied his love for the novel and the beautiful, as well as his physical needs (Figs. 1-1 to 1-11). To presume that man's ingenuity has been driven purely by practical motives is to give credence only to a partial truth, since historical data clearly support other equally valid assumptions. Visual remnants of ancient cultures, such as those of the Mayan civilization, of Greece, of Rome, of India, of the Gothic and the Renaissance periods, or the well-documented contents of museums the world over, clearly attest to the magnitude of the aesthetic and spiritual proportions in man's creativity which is manifested in the imaginative products of man throughout the centuries. Indeed, it seems rather difficult to conceive that human beings could have long endured living in aesthetically impoverished and chaotic surroundings or to assume that they could dwell in cultures wherein the individual had been, for sundry reasons, deprived of opportunities to express his devotion to the unique, the spiritual, and the beautiful.

ORDER AND MEANING ASCRIBED TO MAN'S EXISTENCE

"Beauty," states Schopenhauer, "gives satisfaction to some dim and underlying demand of our nature." Man must find a release for his

1

FIG. 1-1. The Great Temple at Bhubaneswar, India.
One of the finest examples of Hindu art. It is a true
expression of man's innermost and refined feelings,
rooted in a compelling force—the urge to create and
the need for self-assertion.

imaginative powers in order to have order and meaning ascribed to his
existence; therefore, he creates.   Neither wars nor feudal conflicts have
deterred him from his compulsive urge to reconstruct and to enhance his
surroundings.   Forcibly significant, perhaps, is the fact that men who
lived in remote corners of the earth, who had only limited means of communication, and who lacked technological know-how, despite these deterrent factors, managed to produce not merely functional but also artistically and spiritually gratifying visual forms.   The sculptural forms

FIG. 1-2. Columns in one of the Dilwara Temples in India. The intricate marble carving is 700 years old. Man embellished his environment to satisfy his aesthetic and spiritual needs.

indigenous to Africa, the totem poles and stone carvings of the Americas, the ivory carvings of the Eskimos, or the carvings of the Oriental peoples of the world make us keenly aware of those qualities which characterize and distinguish each civilization. Obviously, neither the difference in cultural orientation nor the lack of intercommunication impeded originality or inventiveness. On the contrary, isolation helped to preserve the genuine and unique qualities of beauty characteristic of each culture. Indeed, these factors underscore the basic truth that in each of us there is that "dim and underlying demand of our nature" which wants to give expression to our imagination and thought (Figs. 1-5, 1-8, and 1-11).

FIG. 1-3. Cathedral of Milan, detail of the upper portion of the façade. Man enriched his visual forms to express his devotion to the unique and the beautiful.

FIG. 1-4. Portion of one of the inner chambers at Mitla. Ancient Mixtec civilization of Mexico. The desire to transcend the mundane and the temporal and to express the vitality and faith of his people was ever strong in man.

FIG. 1-5. Food Vessel; Mali; Dogon, Africa (33¼″ high); The Museum of Primitive Art, New York. "Man finds himself and his happiness in the adornment of life, and in the culture of his imagination"—*Santayana.*

MAN EXPRESSES THE VITALITY AND FAITH OF HIS PEOPLE THROUGH HIS INGENUITY

It seems reasonable to assume that, while man invented to meet his functional and religious needs, he embellished his products to satisfy his aesthetic and spiritual needs as well. And, while his materials and tools have become more numerous and more complex through the ages, his desire nonetheless remained intense to transcend the mundane and the temporal or to express the vitality and faith of his people through the creative process (Figs. 1-1, 1-2, 1-3, and 1-4).

FIG. 1-6. Engraved Gourd, Solomon Islands (Musée de l'Homme, Paris). Despite limited means of communication and technological know-how, through the ages man produced not only functional but also aesthetically satisfying visual forms.

FIG. 1-7. Polychrome Vase, Peru, Civilization of Recuay (Musée de l'Homme, Paris). Man embellished his visual forms to satisfy his love for the novel and to meet his physical needs.

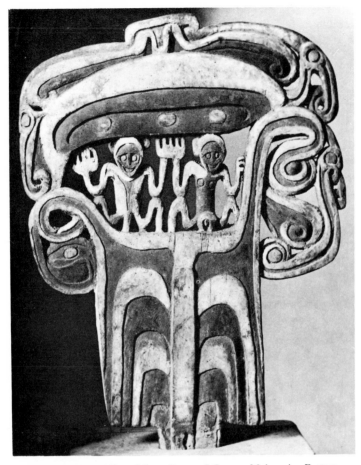

FIG. 1-8. Carved Board from Prow of Canoe, Melanesia, Eastern New Guinea (Wood, Museo Preistorico-Etnografico, Rome). The creative impulses of man find expression through his compelling desire to assert his individuality.

Obviously then, the reasons for creative expression do not lie entirely within the context of technological achievement of a civilization, nor do they exist in its cultural structure. Rather, they are inherent in the powers of a compelling force that is rooted in the innermost and refined feelings of man and in his basic need for self-assertion.

For as this need is met, man realizes the fulfillment of his personal worth and dignity. And thus he attains for himself and for his fellowman the ultimate in happiness. This is expressed in the words of Santayana:

> We may measure the degree of happiness and civilization which any race has attained by the proportion of its energy which is devoted to free and

generous pursuits, to the adornment of life, and the culture of the imagination—for it is in the spontaneous play of his faculties that man finds
himself and his happiness [1].*

FIG. 1-9. Sépik Pillow, New Guinea (Korrigane Collection, Musée de l'Homme,
Paris). A clear manifestation of man's desire to improve his destiny and to insure
greater comfort for his physical needs.

FIG. 1-10. Wood carvings from the Orient which express
the characteristic beauty of creative skill, expressive of
the culture in which the craftsman's talents were
cultivated.

*Numbers enclosed in brackets refer to notes at the end of the chapter.

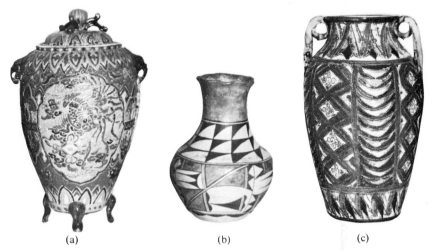

(a) (b) (c)

FIG. 1-11. Ceramic vases which originated in three different cultures: (a) in Japan, (b) in New Mexico, and (c) in Italy. Each of these distinguishes the unique qualities of beauty which characterize the culture in which they were created.

THE EMERGENCE OF HIGHLY SIGNIFICANT AND LASTING VALUES

The basic need for self-assertion, therefore, constitutes a cogent force which ignites the intellectual, emotional, creative, and manipulative powers of man. It brings into synthesis all of the resources that are germane to the development of the human personality. It unfolds the innermost essence of his aesthetic convictions, which crystallize in the emergence of highly significant and lasting values.

SOCIETAL ATTITUDES TOWARD CREATIVITY

Negative Attitudes. While the basic need for self-assertion remains a compelling force which generates self-expression, other operative forces also play a significant role in this process. Among these are the prevalent societal attitudes, which largely determine the extent to which interest is directed toward the pursuit of aesthetic goals. Implicit in this force are far-reaching ramifications which vitally concern the cultural growth of every individual and ultimately the stature of the cultural milieu.

Bearing in mind the hypothesis that self-assertion is a vital human need, it seems pertinent at this point to draw attention to the ways in which society meets this need and to consider the nature and scope of those factors which seem relevant in the development of societal attitudes toward the realization of aesthetic aspirations.

Herbert Read succinctly describes societal attitudes toward art in general:

The symptoms of decadence as they reveal themselves in the art of a country are indifference, vanity, and servitude. Indifference is the absence of appreciations: it is the general attitude towards the arts in an industrial age. ... Indifference is endemic. It is a disease which has spread through our whole civilization, and which is a symptom of a lowered vitality.... Vanity in the patron of art leads to the servitude of the artist. A servile mind is a mind that has committed moral suicide. Art is independence — independence of vision, directness of expression, spiritual detachment.

   ... The economic servitude of the artist is one cause of the death of art, and there is no age which can escape the shame of keeping its artists in poverty [2].

C. P. Snow develops the hypothesis that "western society has become seriously fragmented, and that men educated in different disciplines rarely have any meaningful communication." This state of affairs, he claims, is detrimental to the cultural welfare of a society. Although he compares the "literary intellectuals" and the scientists, this premise holds equally true for men educated in other disciplines, whose attitudes reflect an obvious lack of mutual understanding. He states:

I believe the intellectual life of the whole Western society is increasingly being split into two polar groups. At one pole we have the literary intellectuals, at the other scientists, and as the most representative, the physical scientists. Between the two, exists a gulf of mutual incomprehension — hostility and dislike, but most of all lack of understanding.

   The non-scientists have a rooted impression that the scientists are shallowly optimistic, unaware of man's condition. On the other hand, the scientists believe that literary intellectuals are totally lacking in foresight, peculiarly unconcerned with their brother men, in a deep sense anti-intellectual, anxious to restrict both art and thought to the existential moment. This polarization is sheer loss to us all. To us as people, and to our society. It is at the same time practical and intellectual and creative loss, and I repeat that it is false to imagine that those three considerations are clearly separable.

   ... There is only one way out of all this: it is of course, by rethinking our education. Nearly everyone will agree that our school education is too specialized [3].

The Impact of Material Values. Inasmuch as society places material gains high on the scale of values, attitudes which favor economic and social goals are naturally given priority in the quest for personal fulfillment. As a result, aesthetic and spiritual aspirations are obscured by the glitter of status achieved through material gains. The pursuit of non-traditional avenues of human endeavor is further discouraged by society's tendencies to reward the traditional and conforming member of society, rather than the imaginative, i.e., the poet, the writer, the painter, the sculptor.

   Thus values which seem intangible, but which perhaps are more enduring, are relegated to a minor position in our culture and limited to the interest of a privileged few.

In the educative process, negative attitudes toward art or art education also exist. And this negative attitude exists despite the fact that creative involvement places a high premium upon originality and inventiveness, affords the individual opportunities for uniqueness in self-expression, strengthens his belief in his own capacities to resolve new and novel ideas, and fosters the growth of his perceptual powers.

All of these negative factors tend to inhibit the natural unfolding of the individual's aesthetic convictions and to affect every aspect of his organic functioning.

Impairing the Image-Forming Powers of the Individual. Within this frame of reference, it seems apparent that the persistence of negative attitudes toward aesthetic goals may conceivably impair the development of image-forming skills. "The aesthetic experience is a process, and a process involves activity" [4]. A lack of opportunities to cerebrate and manipulate, to define and illuminate—intellectually, emotionally, creatively, visually, and concretely—may limit the individual's ability to project novel concepts and images, since his abilities have had no activity and no exercise.

It is this writer's belief (which is based on many years of experience with thousands of students) that personal involvement in the visual arts serves to further the growth of the image-forming powers of the individual. For this reason the importance of creative involvement for every individual cannot be ignored.

"Aesthetic education which involves intellectual or cognitive factors, sensation, imagination, and feeling heightens and refines sensitivity to the qualities of experience" [5]. If the experience is limited and poor, the concepts, attitudes, and beliefs will also be poor [6]. The aesthetic experience engages the whole self on the level of perception, all the typical powers and resources of body and mind; and at its best—for example, in an adequate appreciation of a very fine work of art—it engages this self in a way to bring these powers and resources into free and full-orbed and intrinsically rewarding activity, unimpeded by the pressures of ulterior ends [7].

Ignoring the Need to Cultivate the Imaginative Thoughts of All Members in a Democracy. The existence of negative attitudes toward aesthetically oriented goals may be largely attributed to the "cultural lag in a society which is moving out of a tradition-directed system." In a broader sense, the tendency to cling tenaciously to crystallized social forms and to the fanatical belief in educational specialization are two significant factors which adversely affect attitudes concerning aesthetic matters. Unless society reveals a definite concern for each individual's creative potentialities, the imaginative resources of a culture may become limited in nature and narrow in scope.

In view of the phenomenal strides that man has made to date, it may be argued that things are not nearly so critical as they seem to be projected here. But, when we are reminded that most achievements have come about through the properly nurtured creative minds of comparatively few individuals, the need to provide for the imaginative growth of many more becomes increasingly evident. In a democracy, a creatively oriented educational program should serve as a fitting foundation for this worthy purpose.

Positive Attitudes. *Developing Creative Patterns of Behavior Early in Life.* Creative impulses of man must find release through many channels. Those who are cognizant of this particular human need strongly prescribe the provision for outlets which may serve not only to release the creative tendencies of man, but also to relieve the pressures arising from a routine-oriented existence.

While educators appreciate the therapeutic aspects of art activity, the intrinsic values accrued from repeated involvement in art experiences are far greater than those suggested above. This is because art experiences establish creative patterns of behavior in every aspect of human functioning. Established early in life, these patterns of behavior become firmly rooted. They are thus less likely to dissipate later in life. Also, as they become the habitual socially acceptable norm, they become an integral part of the individual's daily functioning. In the words of Thomas Munro:

> The humanistic ideal in aesthetic education is to maintain the fresh spontaneity, enthusiasm, sensitivity, and power of learning which are common in youth, along with greater knowledge and skill of educated maturity [8].

Fostering the Emotional Health of Man. Closely akin to the matter of wholesome outlets for man's creative impulses is the wide concern for his emotional health. Therefore, elaborate art programs and facilities are made available to inmates of prisons and mental institutions. The visual arts are thus used in the rehabilitative process of the emotionally disturbed, the mentally ill, the socially maladjusted, or the mentally handicapped. Implicit in the records of case studies are significant achievements in the realm of readjustment effected through involvement in the visual arts. Inasmuch as society is aware of the rehabilitative facts, it calmly accepts this seemingly unusual approach to mental therapy.

Oddly enough, a similar attitude does not exist outside the rehabilitative institutions. Society is not yet attuned to the values inherent in the visual arts; values which may benefit the normal, the average, the gifted, or the talented individual, as well as the deviate. Consequently, the question arises: if there are valid approaches which seem beneficial in fostering the emotional health and readjustment of deviates, should not these approaches be examined in the light of what they may do for the average, the talented, or the gifted individual? Should anyone be denied the values derived from creative expression? True, many will agree that learning should not be limited to scientific facts and mathematical equations alone, but few will champion the cause that learning must also include those disciplines which promote the humanistic values, values which are derived from, and widely attributed to, the arts. Indeed, society dare not dawdle until the human organism is emotionally and spiritually depraved. The benefits of creative activity should be enjoyed by all.

Showing Concern for the Human Organism in a Complex Environment. Intensive inquiries need to be conducted concerning the preventive aspects of creative involvement. Specifically, what can creative activity do for the human organism which is constantly challenged by a complex and mechanized society? Must he lose contact with reality in order to derive personal satisfaction through art experiences? Rather, should not his life be enriched as the enjoyment derived from creative participation grows and the achievement of tranquility is realized. What seems most unfortunate is that, outside of corrective institutions, creative activity is looked upon with disdain. This attitude permeates our whole society and is not only reflected in the insignificant amount of time devoted to the teaching of art in the schools, but correspondingly in the inadequate funds that are allocated for such purposes. The so-called "frills" of education are generally the first to be deleted, and the last to be added, particularly when funds are low. *Consequently, and unfortunately, the disciplines which vitally affect emotional growth and stability of the individual, namely the arts, often receive the least consideration in times of financial stress.*

Providing Definitive Direction for the Development of the Human Personality. Although the situation is far from ideal, it seems to be slowly reversing itself. Since the advent of Sputnik, many new teaching devices and methods have been injected into the school curriculum. And it is anticipated by some (with tongue in cheek) that progress in all disciplines will be achieved in direct proportion to the number of successful, exploratory rockets thrust into space. While the sciences and languages still claim priority in the classroom, the arts are seemingly elevated to a slightly higher position today than they have been in the past. This has been achieved as a result of the complete realization that *uniqueness, inventiveness,* and *flexibility* are significant by-products of art experiences; also, because of the recognition that these attributes are highly desirable in scientific endeavors.

Still the major concern of all educators is the proper development of every individual's personality; i.e., his achievement of basic skills, understandings, and appreciation. But, in the educative process it is duly recognized that mere development is not enough. There must be a humanistic as well as scientific direction toward which development is aimed, giving impetus to an increasing creative curiosity. The individual must of necessity build for himself a vital reserve for intellectual and creative functioning in all aspects of his culture.

Emphasizing Uniqueness and Selectivity in Perception. The creative life is indisputably a prodigious one, for it excites the innermost feelings of man and brings into synthesis all of his resources. Principally, it is in the creative approach to human functioning that man finds his reward, and certainly it is through creativity that man achieves progress. Mere functioning would reflect neither the zeal nor the initiative which generate his imaginative thoughts. Therefore, it is not presumptuous to assume that a profoundly influential element in any culture should be this emphasis upon uniqueness and selectivity in perception—expecting its scientists, engineers, architects, mathematicians, as well as its artists to be oriented in a balanced framework of aesthetic values. Because our highly complex and technologically oriented culture makes unlimited demands upon its creative thinkers, it must nurture and advance men toward clear vision and imaginative thought. It must provide an environment which is conducive to his development in uniqueness and originality of expression.

Cultivating without Fear the Notional Aspects of the Human Organism. Freedom of expression is, without a doubt, man's greatest heritage since it makes fertile the ground for creative thought. It brings to fruition those elements which comprise his personality as he projects without fear his unconscious fantasies. Given this basic nutriment for self-expression, his notional development finds full sway and brings forth ideas for the welfare and enjoyment of mankind. Though man uses the natural resources of his land in this process, this merely adds uniqueness to his products. He uses these in ingenious ways and thus enriches spiritually and materially his world community.

NOTES

1. George Santayana, "The Sense of Beauty," *The Nature of Beauty.* New York: Dover Publications, Inc., Part 1, 1955.

2. Herbert Read, *To Hell with Culture.* New York: Schocken Books, Inc., 1964, pp. 86–92.

3. C. P. Snow, *Two Cultures: And A Second Look.* New York: Cambridge University Press, 1963, pp. 11–23.

4. D.W. Gotshalk, *Art and the Social Order.* New York: Dover Publications, Inc., 1962, p. 5.

5. Donald Arnstine, *The School Review* (Autumn 1964), University of Chicago Press, p. 261.

6. June McFee, *Preparation for Art.* San Francisco: Wadsworth Publishing Co., 1961, p. 215.

7. D. W. Gotshalk, *Art and the Social Order.* New York: Dover Publications, Inc., 1962, p. 25.

8. Thomas Munro, *Art Education, Its Philosophy and Psychology.* New York: Liberal Arts Press, 1956, p. 8.

READING REFERENCES

Anderson, Harold H., ed., *Creativity and Its Cultivation.* New York: Harper and Brothers, 1959.
_____, *Art in General Education.* Kutztown Pa.: State Teachers' College, Yearbook, 1949.
Barkan, Manuel, *A Foundation for Art Education.* New York: The Ronald Press Co., 1955.
Bettelheim, Bruno, *Love Is Not Enough.* Glencoe, Ill.: The Free Press, 1950, p. 130.
_____, *The Informed Heart.* New York: Free Press of Glencoe, Inc., 1963.
Boulton, J.T., ed., *Edmund Burke—A Phylosophical Enquiry Into the Origin of Our Ideas of the Sublime and Beautiful.* New York: Columbia Press, 1958, Section XVI, pp. 31–49.
Coomaraswamy, Ananda K. *Christian and Oriental Philosophy of Art.* New York: Dover Publications, Inc., 1956, pp. 61, 102.
_____, *The Transformation of Nature in Art.* New York: Dover Publications, Inc., 1934.
D'Harcourt, Raoul, *Primitive Art of the Americas.* New York: Tudor Publishing Co., 1950.
Edman, Irwin, *Arts and the Man.* New York: The American Library, 1949.
Gardner, Helen, *Art Through The Ages*, 4th ed. New York: Harcourt, Brace & Co., Inc., 1958.
Gessell, Arnold L. and Frances L. Ilg. *Infant and Child in The Culture of Today.* New York: Harper and Brothers, 1943.
Gotshalk, D. W., *Art and the Social Order.* New York: Dover Publications, Inc., 1962.
Griaule, Marcel, *Folk Art of Black Africa.* New York: Tudor Publishing Company, 1950.
Guilford, J.P., "The Nature of Creative Thinking," in *Aspects of Creativity*, Eastern Arts Association Research Bulletin, Vol. 5, No. 1, 1954, pp. 5–7.
Haggerty, Melvin E., *Art, A Way of Life.* Minneapolis: University of Minnesota Press, 1935.
Havighurst, Robert, *A Survey of the Education of Gifted Children.* Chicago: University of Chicago Press, 1955, Ch. 1, 6, 13.
Hollingsworth, Leta S., "How Should Gifted Children Be Educated?" *Baltimore Bulletin of Education* (May 1931) Vol. L, p. 195.
"Integrative Function of Art Education," Kutztown, Pa.: State Teachers College, 1950 Yearbook, 1949.
Langer, Susanne K., *Philosophical Sketches.* Baltimore: Johns Hopkins Press, 1962, pp. 83–94.
Larkin, Oliver W., *Art and Life in America.* New York: Rinehart and Company, Inc., 1949.
Leenhardt, Maurice, *Folk Art of Oceania.* New York: Tudor Publishing Co., 1950.
Lem, F.H., *Sudanese Sculpture.* Paris: Arts et Métiers Graphiques, 1949.
_____, The Museum of Primitive Art, New York, *Traditional Art of the African Nations.* New York: University Publishers, Inc., 1961.

Lowenfeld, Viktor, *Creative and Mental Growth*, 3d ed. New York: The Macmillan Co., 1951.

————, *The Nature of Creative Activity*. London: Routledge and Kegan Paul, Ltd., 1939, Ch. 1, 3, 5, 7.

McFee, June, *Preparation for Art*. San Francisco: Wadsworth Publishing Co., 1961.

National Society for the Study of Education, *Art Education*, The Sixty-Fourth Yearbook. Chicago: The University of Chicago Press, 1965.

National Society for the Study of Education, *Art In American Life and Education*, Fortieth Yearbook. Bloomington, Ill.: Public School Publishing Co., 1941.

Read, Herbert, *Education Through Art*, 2d ed. New York: Pantheon Books, Inc., 1945.

————, *To Hell with Culture*. New York: Schocken Books, Inc., 1964.

Santayana, George, *The Sense of Beauty*. New York: Dover Publications, Inc., 1955.

Schaefer-Simmern, Henry, *The Unfolding of Artistic Activity*, 2d ed. Berkeley and Los Angeles: University of California Press, 1950, Ch. 1, 2.

Snow, C. P. *Two Cultures: And A Second Look*. New York: Cambridge University Press, 1963.

Terman, Lewis and others, *Genetic Studies of Genius*, Mental and Physical Traits of A Thousand Gifted Children. Stanford University, Calif.: Stanford University Press, Vol. 1, 1925.

Witty, Paul, ed., *The Gifted Child*. Boston: D.C. Heath and Co., 1951.

Yochim, Louise D., *Building Human Relationships Through Art*. Chicago: L.M. Stein, Publisher, 1954.

CHAPTER

2 An Image of Twentieth Century Man

While it is generally conceded that in many areas of human achievement man has made some impressive inroads, it is also agreed that in other areas he has made only meager advances. To be sure, he discovered some pertinent facts about the human organism, prolonged the life span of man, made vigorous material strides, uncovered some awe-inspiring mysteries of the universe and, thus, rightfully earned for himself a lasting tribute to his ever-probing, curious, and imaginative mind. But, notwithstanding all this, substantiated as these achievements are by an aggregate of facts and well-documented theories concerning the nature of man and the nature of his universe, a harmonious orchestration of the nature of man and the nature of his universe has not yet been fully realized.

PERSONAL FULFILLMENT: A WAY OF LIFE

This is an area in which man must probe much deeper so that he may find and develop useful concepts which will enable him to adapt more readily to his fellow man and to his rapidly changing environment. Thus, he may be able to arrive at a measure of balance in life which will permit the refinement of all of his faculties, placing emphasis upon creativity in the quest for personal fulfillment. This will be a way of life within the framework of values that are humanistic and everlasting and that brings into focus concomitantly a design for living "the good life."

Viktor Lowenfeld appropriately stated, "Scientifically, we can communicate with any part of the globe within split seconds; socially, we cannot even reach our neighbors."

That is to say that, despite the scientific proficiency of man, his ability to reach his neighbor is still in its nebulous stage. To be sure, in this particular area, there is room for vigorous direction. There is a need to recognize that man must be emotionally and intellectually attuned to the needs and values that man everywhere holds dear and that his attainments must be viewed in the light of the benefits that they bring to all of

Fig. 2-1. Developing creative patterns of behavior early in life.

mankind. Unless man is willing to do so, his personal gains will indeed be worthless.

Some frankly admit that the dangers man faces today are inextricably rooted in his assiduous quest for power. Others decry man's obsessive preoccupation with the doctrine of materialism—an objective which they assert widens the gap between man and man and which critically submerges his sensitivities into worthless and sublimated depths. Still others attribute great dangers to the intemperate pace of contemporary life. Be it as it may, and regardless of the thesis subscribed to, the fact remains that all of these factors, in some measure, threaten the equilibrium of thinking and feeling men inasmuch as they forcibly defy the strength of purpose and destroy the moral sinew of a normally functioning society.

Some questions, therefore, arise. Namely, what is the "fortitude quotient" of a many-dimensioned society? How well and how long can a community endure the strain of uncertainty, or withstand the stresses resulting from persistently ominous forces before it reaches the breaking point? What is the limit or the degree of societal tolerance? What mechanisms are there available to man by means of which he can hope to adjust to his inconstant environment (i.e., a life of indeterminate uncertainty) if he must do so in order to survive? And finally, what channels remain open through which he can hope to alleviate anxieties so that he may better expend his energies to ennoble his spirit?

EDUCATING THE HUMAN ORGANISM FOR FLEXIBILITY AND ADAPTABILITY

The importance of resolving these questions cannot be underestimated inasmuch as they suggest a need of paramount importance. Among other human needs, it is the need to educate the human organism for "flexibility" and "adaptability." This must be done in order that man be adequately prepared to meet the challenge of an ever-changing environment and to sustain an emotional and intellectual balance within its framework.

Unless careful consideration is given to this particular need, it is reasonable to assume that the norm in human behavior will reflect the regressive and the neurotic. Collective hysteria or neurosis will permeate every aspect of human endeavor and, in this process, adversely affect human interaction. This has been clearly demonstrated in recent decades, particularly during World War II, as well as during the so called cold-war period. It is not difficult to realize, therefore, how any society can be thrown out of emotional gear despite its technological and scientific proficiency. Through constant infusion of fear and hatred into its structural fiber, a community becomes easily susceptible to negative influences. In its anxiety to maintain the status quo or to improve its existence, it often succumbs to forces which generate aggression. It even yields to relentless behavior.

MAINTAINING AN EMOTIONAL AND INTELLECTUAL EQUILIBRIUM

Bearing in mind the ominous realities of life, therefore, it must be recognized that maintaining an emotional and intellectual equilibrium in every individual is a vital requisite for the sustenance of a stable society. For, as its stability is threatened, its emotional and intellectual vitality can serve to reject and to repel, if necessary, the aggressive and undesirable attitudes of unreasonable men.

Scholars today are duly concerned about the twentieth century image of man. They reason that, while man has made significant strides in many areas of human endeavor, these strides were accomplished largely through the efforts, vision, ingenuity, and persistence of comparatively few individuals. When these achievements are viewed in the light of many centuries of acculturation or civilization, the number of individuals involved is not nearly so impressive as the scope of their achievement. In the main, it is contended that man has inadvertently emerged as a highly compartmentalized human organism, a regimented and conforming member of society, one who surrenders to herd instincts and who is docile and apathetic. Moreover, and perhaps a far greater indictment of him, is the firm conviction of some that man has become insensible, that he lacks compassion for his fellowman, and that all this is largely due to the ebb and flow of his own aggressive attitudes. Therefore, it is reasoned that to him death and misery for his fellows become justified in the light of any political or economic adventure.

Certainly some or all of the above allegations, in the light of historical evidence, exhibit a reasonable measure of truth. They also create a shocking image of man. Unfortunately, this description of man is not well within the framework of popular conviction, inasmuch as he himself is totally unaware of the imperceptibly slow and penetrating process of desensitization which occurs in his obsessive quest for power. Nor is he aware of other demoralizing ramifications which accrue in this process. By some standards man may be considered affluent, today, but he is nonetheless restless and discontented. Although he has enriched his life materially, he has, nevertheless, impoverished himself aesthetically and spiritually. Consequently, he has deprived himself of those values which spur the harmonious integration of his total organism.

Two pertinent questions, therefore, present themselves here: 1) Should not the scientific and technological gains of man be of such magnitude and stature as to encompass all of man's needs—of body and spirit—and thus help him transcend his ideological conflicts? 2) Should not the greatest source of creative energy that is embodied within the infinite bounds of conscious man be stirred, distilled, refined, and purified for man's aesthetic and spiritual consumption?

NURTURING AND SUSTAINING THE WELL-INTEGRATED MAN

To suggest that there are simple solutions to these questions would seem presumptuous; but to identify the problem is a necessary requisite for its solution. Possibly, the current concern for man may stir mankind to resolute and self-assertive action, action which will be designed within an intellectual, creative, and spiritual framework and which will not permit mankind to bow to forces that are governed by fear and collective neurosis.

Perhaps a thoughtful reassessment of values stressed and of methods used in the current educative process may now be in order. Perhaps some educative practices need to be firmly challenged, particularly those which do not allow for the fundamental need for self-assertion and self-affirmation through creativity. Perhaps, the desired goals prescribed for man may be achieved if: *these are simultaneously projected along a well-guided path, reaching a point of confluence at every stage and aspect of the human organism, converging into the apex, that is the human heart, filtered through the mind, and then returned to the heart for affirmation.* Perhaps then creative thought, combined with feeling and compassion for mankind, may reign supreme. Although many may agree that this objective is a lofty one, the methods used to mold the well-integrated man will no doubt vary. To be sure, none will deny that all disciplines play a vital role in the shaping of the human personality. But, unfortunately, few recognize that *the integrative aspect is essentially the function of the arts. For, through the arts, man realizes the harmonious orchestration of all of his faculties— his tastes, his sensibilities, and his skills. Through the arts, he is better able to penetrate the detailed components of his cosmos. Through the arts, he becomes attuned to the differences and similarities of man. And finally, through the arts, he stabilizes his emotions, refines his sensitivities, and develops acuteness of perception in the process.*

"Art is the eugenics of this process," states Herbert Read, "that obeying its discipline we engender, not monsters nor misdeeds, but children of light—grace of living, and beauty of expression."

DIRECTING HUMAN ENERGIES TOWARD HUMANISTIC GOALS

The need for directing human energies toward humanistic goals has never been greater than it is today. It must be met, and it must be given proper emphasis in the scheme of things. The inner resources of man need to be taught to function within a sphere of balanced values and be channeled into constructive avenues to meet the challenge of a many-dimensioned world. The influential elements which guide man's emotional and ideological considerations in the creative process must be nurtured and sustained. "The uniqueness of the individual, his selectivity in perception, and the importance of his own needs and motivations," must be acknowledged and provided for. Only thus may man achieve a state of equilibrium for himself and for his fellow man. Should the reverse be true, as Dewey states, "and man is cowed by fear and dulled by routine," he will no doubt emerge depersonalized and dehumanized, giving way to his penchant for self-destruction. In the words of Bruno Bettleheim:

> Just as democracy requires a more educated and moral population than do more primitive forms of society, so modern man requires a more highly developed emotional sensitivity so as not to succumb to temptations inherent in a machine age. The more mechanized and fragmented the world around us, the more we must develop the humanity of human relations. The more we live in a mass society, the better we must know how to have intimate relations [1].

NOTES

1. Bruno Bettleheim, *The Informed Heart.* New York: Free Press of Glencoe, Inc., 1963, p. 100.

READING REFERENCES

Barkan, Manuel, *A Foundation for Art Education.* New York: The Ronald Press Co., 1955.

_____ , *Through Art to Creativity.* Boston: Allyn and Bacon, Inc., 1960.

Baudelaire, Charles, *The Mirror of Art*, translated and edited by Johnathan Mayne, Garden City, N.Y.: Doubleday & Co., 1956.

Berenson, Bernard, *Aesthetics and History.* New York: Harper and Brothers, 1961.

Bettelheim, Bruno, *The Informed Heart.* New York: Free Press of Glencoe, 1963.

Burke, Edmund, *A Philosophical Enquiry into the Origin of Our Ideas of the Sublime and Beautiful*, J.T. Boulton, ed. New York: Columbia Press, 1958, Part I, Sec. 5, pp. 67–70.

Cary, Joyce, *Art and Reality.* Garden City, N.Y.: Anchor Books, Doubleday & Co., Inc., 1958.

De Francesco, L. Italo, *Art Education, Its Means and Ends.* New York: Harper and Brothers, 1958, pp. 3–59.

Edman, Irwin, *Arts and the Man.* New York: The American Library, 1949.

Ghizelin, Brewster, ed., *The Creative Process.* New York: A Mentor Book, The New American Library, 1963.

Langer, Susanne K., *Philosophical Sketches.* Baltimore: The Johns Hopkins Press, 1962, pp. 95–107.

Ratner, Joseph, ed., *Intelligence In The Modern World*, John Dewey's Philosophy. New York: The Modern Library, Inc., 1939, pp. 405–415.

Read, Herbert, *Education Through Art*, 2d ed. New York: Pantheon Books, Inc., 1945.

Russell, Bertrand, *Unpopular Essays.* New York: Simon and Schuster, Inc., 1950, pp. 34–44.

_____ , "Education Through Art—A Revolutionary Policy," *The Journal of the National Art Education Association*, Vol. 8, 1955.

Smith, J.B., *Art in Today's World.* New York: Related Arts Service, 1952, Vol. 10, No. 1.

White, Morton, *The Age of Analysis.* New York: A Mentor Book, The New American Library, 1961.

Yochim, Louise D., *Building Human Relationships Through Art.* Chicago: L.M. Stein, Publisher, 1954.

Ziegfeld, Ernest, ed., *Human Values In A Democracy*, Art and Human Values, 1953 Yearbook. Kutztown, Pa.: National Art Education Association, 1953, Ch. 1–4.

3

Perception

INTRODUCTION

Having examined some concepts concerning the need for self-assertion, societal attitudes toward creativity, and the current image of man, it seems fitting at this point to consider two other factors which are pertinent to the thesis of this volume; namely, "perception" and "creativity." And, since this manuscript deals principally with the role of creative expression in fostering perceptual growth, considerable thought is given to the definition and to the use of both terms.

This chapter is devoted entirely to a review of the basic concepts concerning perception, i.e., its psychological basis, its definition, and its mechanics. Attention is further focused on the subject of perception in those chapters which deal with the development of perceptual skill and with the teacher's role in understanding the learner through his creative expressions (Chapters 6, 7, and 13).

The subject of creativity, including a review of some basic concepts and a compilation of research on the subject, is treated in the two chapters following this one.

MAN, A REACTING ORGANISM

Man is a living organism whose behavior is determined by any number of important factors. Among these are: his cultural orientation and the physical and mental structure of his organism—its present condition and its past experience. Recall, images, and thoughts all constitute his motivated responses to situations. They are reactions to experiences, the psychological roots of which reside chiefly within the higher neural structures of his organism. When man reacts to his outer world, he perceives it in a frame of reference. He judges what he sees in the light of: 1) what he already knows about that which he sees; 2) what he experienced in the past that is related to what he sees; and 3) how he feels about that which stimulates his vision. His illusional as well as nonillusory perception of a form, color, or shape depends upon the orientation of which these are a part. Gradually man learns to see parts of his world, not as a jumble of pieces, but in their functional relationships with one another. This awareness of functional relationships adds greatly to the efficacy of his own functioning, for he gains insights and understandings which serve as guides to his behavior.

Through the process of perceiving, man learns to believe what he perceives—to know and to feel keenly and sensitively about his outer world—which is to say that perception may end in action, meaning, or belief. While "man gains knowledge by observation, his observations are best when he brings knowledge to them" [1].

As has been often pointed out, what an individual sees is not determined solely by the images that fall on the retina but by many factors which influence his perception of color, form, and shape. Not all of these factors, however, are inherent in the process of perceiving. Some are due to the habits established by past experience. A child who wants his red toy on the table does not see it as a stimulus, but as an object. It takes a much more sophisticated and artificial approach to see stimuli in redness, roundness, or squareness, abstractly and apart from their presence in the unified pattern of the whole object [2].

Perception, therefore, is not merely a sensing of stimuli. It is indeed a set of extremely elaborate processes through which we organize our sensory impressions received from our internal or external environment. While perception cannot be directly observed, it must be inferred from observable behavior (including what the person says) and a knowledge of the stimulus situation. When a child is engaged in a creative activity, his behavior is observable. But what the child tells about his painting or clay form is equally important. He reveals additional clues to his frame of reference, i.e., his past experience, his newly acquired impressions, his stimulus situation, and his perceptual needs which require additional guidance.

Generally, perception is defined as the faculty of receiving knowledge of internal or external things by means of all of one's senses. This simple definition of perception has particular meaning in the planning of art experiences for the learner. Consequently, art experiences are designed to involve all of the learner's sensory powers and, in the process, to engage his intellectual, emotional, creative, and manipulative capacities.

PSYCHOLOGICAL DEFINITION OF PERCEPTION

Perception according to Gotshalk is a complex operation which involves intellectual or cognitive factors and sensation, imagination, and feeling. It involves an operation with two major aspects, a *mechanical* and a *telic* (that which is purposely directed toward ends). The mechanical aspect consists of the powers of apprehension which operate in the perceptual act. In ordinary alert perception these powers, at a minimum, are three. The first is *sensation*, or awareness of objects in their sensory features: their colors, pitches, timbers, textures, masses, bulks, weights, etc. The second is *intuition* in the Kantian, not in the Crocean, sense, primarily the awareness of objects in their spatial and temporal order and arrangement. The third is *intellect*, in minimum cases the usually effortless and variously muted interpretations both of the type of the object being perceived and of the type of its detail, such as its sensory and spatiotemporal features. Suppose, for example, one is perceiving a blue vase. Sensations, chiefly sight and touch, disclose the object as exhibiting color, texture, solidity, etc. Intuition discloses it as exhibiting spatial position and arrangement. Intellect interprets its color as turquoise blue, its texture as smooth glaze texture, its spatial pattern as Chinese, and the intellect applied to the total object interprets it as an imitation oriental vase. It is true, of course, that even in very alert ordinary perception, different persons often perceive objects differently. But this is due to differences in a common perceptual equipment, particularly differences in the capacity of their sense organs and in the character of the symbols acquired from the past and available for interpreting entities. Ordinary alert perception of objects usually contains more than these three minimum mechanical factors. The chief additional factors, are feeling and imagination [3].

Max Wertheimer presents his concept of perception in the following:

> Perception must be treated from the point of view of stimulus—constallations on the one side and actually given mental Gestalt phenomena on the other. And this leads in physiological theory to the assumption of whole processes. The cells of an organism are "parts" of the whole and excitation occurring in them are theirs to be viewed as part-processes functionally related to whole-processes of the entire organism. This does not mean, however, a rejection of the psychological approach.... Thus the comprehension of whole-properties and whole-conditions *must* precede consideration of the real significance of "parts." ... Hence we may say in general that a whole is meaningful when concrete mutual dependency obtains among its parts [4].

Kurt Lewin describes perception in four stages: The perception of an object or event may 1) give rise to a certain physical tension (e.g., a desire), or 2) it may communicate with a state of tension already existing (as a result of some intention or need) in such a way that this tension system thereupon assumes control over motor behavior. In such cases we say that the object in question possesses a "valence." 3) Valences act as environmental forces "steering" subsequent behavior. Finally, 4) this behavior leads to satiation or to a resolution of tension so that a state of equilibrium is approached [5].

Wolfgang Koeler presents a psychological formula for vision. In vision, for instance, the organism tends to respond to millions of stimuli at once; and the first step of this response is organization within a correspondingly large field. In many cases reactions of the effect on organs which carry out the response of the organism will begin soon; but often even the first of these reactions depend upon the organization of the field as it develops at that time. Take eye movements as an example. The laws of visually determined eye movements refer to the boundaries of segregated entities, to the location of these entities in the field, and so forth. Apart from eye movements, a man's actions are commonly related to a well-structured field, most often to particular thing-units. The right psychological formula is therefore: *pattern of stimulation-organization-response to the products of organization.*

Prolonged inspection of any specific visual object tends to change its organization. Moreover, other objects which are afterwards shown in the same region of the field are also affected, namely, displaced or distorted [6].

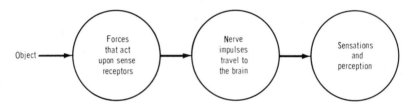

FIG. 3-1. Perception in sequence.

THE DYNAMICS OF VISUAL PERCEPTION

The receiving apparatus for vision is the eye. It consists of elaborate accessory mechanisms, which bring an image to focus, and the retina, which contains the sensitive nerve endings or receptors proper. The forms of objects are perceived by the projection of images upon the retina. Since the retina consists of a number of small but separate receptors, the image is really a mosaic of tiny dots of perceived gray, white, or color. The eye is a system of convex lenses, and therefore, like a camera, it projects an image that is inverted and also transposed as to right and left [7].

We do not perceive everything at once; rather we select certain objects while ignoring others. We have a tendency to combine the elements of experience into groups—"wholes" or "configurations"—so that the number of separate things that we can see at once is very limited.

Perception is determined jointly by outer (stimulus) and by inner (personal) factors. What is perceived depends as much on the perceiver as on that which is to be perceived. The two factors working together determine perception [8]. (See Fig. 3-1.)

An intense stimulus is more likely to demand attention than one that is less intense. But when we perceive an object, or stimulus, one part tends to come forward, while the rest seems to remain in the background. (The part which stands out in art is referred to as "subject-matter," "content," or "figure"; while the rest of the stimulus pattern is called background). Sometimes the content and background relationships seem ambiguous [9], that is, reversible or interchangeable as Figs. 3-2 and 3-3 and in Figs. 3-4 and 3-5.

SIMILARITY

Stimuli that are similar tend to be perceived as a group rather than individually. This illustrates the *theory of similarity*, as in Figs. 3-4 and 3-5.

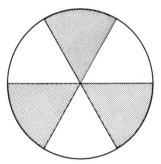

FIG. 3-3. Is it a black three-leaf clover, or a white three-leaf clover? The two are interchangeable.

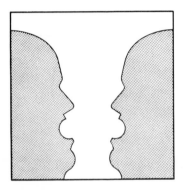

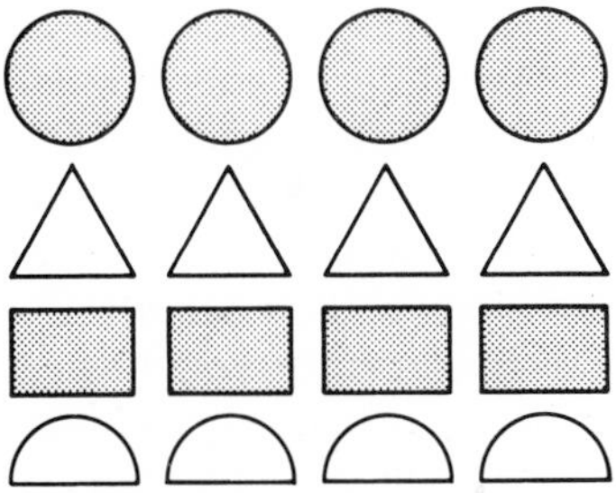

FIG. 3-4. Shapes are seen as horizontal rows rather than as vertical columns.

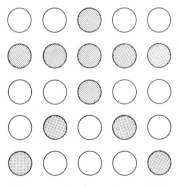

FIG. 3-5. The similarity of the filled-in circles helps us perceive a human form.

FIG. 3-2. Is it a white vase, or are they two screaming profiles? The two are interchangeable.

PROXIMITY

Stimuli which are close together in space tend to be perceived as entities, or as groups, as in Fig. 3-6. This theory is called *proximity*.

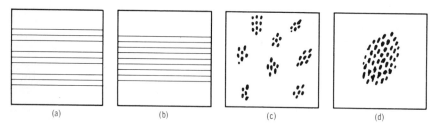

(a)   (b)   (c)   (d)

FIG. 3-6. In (a) the nine lines are seen as *three distinct groups* because of the proximity of lines in each and because each unit of three is separated by wide spaces. In (b) the nine lines are seen as *one group* because of their proximity. In (c) the dots appear as *eight distinct groups* because of their proximity in each group and because of the wide spaces between each group. In (d) the dots appear as *one group* because of their proximity.

THE LAW OF PRÄGNANZ—A THEORY OF PERCEPTION

The most general law underlying all change is the Law of Prägnanz, according to which every gestalt [10] becomes as "good" as possible. In perception, the "possible" is strongly determined by the stimulus complex. When freed from this influence "the engram" (a lasting trace left in memory) is able to change in ways prescribed by the Law of Prägnanz. It is for this reason that memorial gestalten tend towards unique forms. From this it is also possible now to understand the normalizing effect. Well-known forms (structures) are themselves already stable. If the structure given in perception is such as to initiate processes proceeding along the same lines as those of already stable forms, they will eventuate in the same forms as their predecessors. The significant factor is not how frequently a form has been experienced, but whether its structure is stabilized in accordance with gestalt laws [11]. See Fig. 3-7.

Perhaps more than anyone else, the artist utilizes the law of Prägnanz in the process of delineating his creative configurations. The law of Prägnanz refers primarily to certain "stable," "normal" forms toward which our perceptions (and memories) tend to lean; that is to say, that when viewing slightly distorted or broken images that closely resemble the stable forms, the tendency is to perceive them as though they are stable forms; e.g., broken circles tend to be perceived as complete circles; an ellipse, which is in some respects similar to a circle, is perceived as more nearly circular, etc., the tendency being to fill in gaps perceptually when the stimulus is incomplete [12]. Figure 3-7(a) and (b) illustrate the point (see also Fig. 3-8).

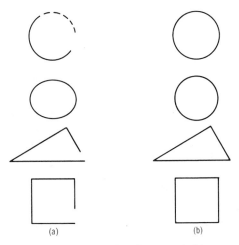

FIG. 3-7. (a) Incomplete forms and (b) complete forms. (Modified from A. Q. Sartain, A. J. North, J. R. Strange, and H. M. Chapman, *Psychology, Understanding Human Behavior*. New York: McGraw-Hill Book Company, 1962.)

FIG. 3-8. "Carousel" (Theodore Frano, egg tempera, 42″ × 61″). In this painting the artist used incomplete forms to create the illusion of complete architectural structures in the background. The painting illustrates how the Law of Prägnanz, a theory of perception, is utilized by the artist to give the impression of completeness to the viewer.

When the artist creates incomplete forms or resorts to distortion, intuitively or consciously, he utilizes the law of Prägnanz. He reasons: "I leave these images broken, or distorted, because I feel that through this means I can intensify my statement and at the same time leave something to the imagination of the viewer, engaging his intellect and stimulating his emotions in the process."

A simple illustration may bear out this point. Examine the graphic treatment of an eye belonging to a human or to an animal form. Generally, an eye is drawn by three curved lines—two concave, one convex—representing the eyelids which circumscribe a large dot, i.e., the pupil of the eye. Often, only one convex line is used to represent the upper eyelid, while the concave line which represents the lower eyelid, is omitted entirely. Nonetheless, and despite this deletion, the image is retained because the omitted lines are filled in perceptually by the observer. See Fig. 3-9(a) and (b).

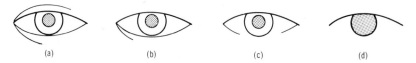

(a)   (b)   (c)   (d)

FIG. 3-9. Although some lines which are present in (a) and (b) are omitted in (c), the image of the eye is nevertheless left intact in the latter. This is due to the fact that a sufficient number of lines have been retained in (c) to validify the statement perceptually. This is apparent also in (d), where a line and dot are used, the symbolic method of depicting an eye which is often used by children.

Distortion, a familiar device, is often used by the artist to strengthen or to weaken the emotional impact of a work of art. It is used to create an illusion, a mood, or a spiritual quality in the organization of visual images. The works of El Greco, Picasso, Rodin, Mattisse, and others poignantly illustrate the use of distortion. For instance, in the painting "St. Martin and the Beggar" (Fig. 3-10), El Greco disproportionately elongates the human forms in order to intensify the feeling of compassion. In the painting, "The Old Guitarist" (Fig. 3-11), Picasso elongates the form to create a similar mood, but perhaps more intensely. In it, the old guitarist seems lean and indigent. In both instances the feelings have been intensified through distortion. However, the viewer perceives these images as though they are "stable" or "normal" in proportion.

While it is true that not all works of art may illustrate the law of Prägnanz, nevertheless it is safe to assume that in most paintings distortion plays a vital role in the intensification of feelings.

FIG. 3-10. "St. Martin and The Beggar"
(El Greco, 1597–1599, National Gallery
of Art, Washington, Widener Collection).
Distortion, a familiar device, is used by
the artist to evoke an emotional response
from the viewer.

THE GESTALT THEORY OF PERCEPTION

The gestalt [10] theory of perception, which was founded by Max
Wertheimer together with Kurt Koffka and Wolfgang Kohler, is also of
particular interest to creative individuals. They, perhaps, are more appreciative of the theory than others, who are less concerned with problems
which arise in the creative process. In essence, the theory is that the
whole is significantly greater than the sum of its parts. Most painters,
sculptors, writers, poets, and musicians are well aware of this truth, since

FIG. 3-11. "The Old Guitarist" (Picasso, oil, 1903,
Art Institute of Chicago, Helen Birch Bartlett Memorial Collection). In this painting the human form
has been elongated to intensify the mood and to evoke
a feeling of compassion.

they are forever grappling with the problem of achieving a unified whole
through the organization both of component parts and often of totally
unrelated elements in a work of art. They also recognize the significance
of the intangible and the interactive elements in a creative scheme
which make the whole far greater than the sum of its parts.

"The ability of the individual to perceive a series of fragments as
the whole object, depends upon many factors. The intelligence of the perceiving individual and his mental set are extremely important among
these" [13].

As Rudolph Arnheim states: "Vision is not a mechanical recording of elements, but the grasping of significant structural patterns. ... Every act of seeing is a visual judgment" [14].

NOTES

1. Floyd L. Ruch, *Psychology and Life*. Chicago: Scott, Foresman & Co., 1941, p. 254.

2. L. Shaffer, B. Gilmer, and M. Schoen, *Psychology*. New York: Harper and Brothers, 1940, p. 30.

3. D. W. Gotshalk, *Art and the Social Order*. New York: Dover Publications, Inc., 1962, pp. 3–28.

4. Max Wertheimer, "The General Theoretical Situation," Selection 2 from *The Source Book of Gestalt Psychology* (prepared by Willis D. Ellis). London: Routledge and Kegan Paul, Ltd., 1955, p. 15, par. 54–57.

5. Kurt Lewin, "Will and Needs," Selection 24 from *The Source Book of Gestalt Psychology* (prepared by Willis D. Ellis), London: Routledge and Kegan Paul, Ltd., 1955, p. 288.

6. Wolfgang Koehler, *Gestalt Psychology*. New York: A Mentor Book, The New American Library, 1962, pp. 96, 97.

7. L. Shaffer, B. Gilmer, and M. Schoen, *Psychology*. New York: Harper and Brothers, 1940, pp. 234–249.

8. A. Q. Sartain, A. J. North, J. R. Strange, and H. M. Chapman, *Psychology, Understanding Human Behavior*. New York: McGraw-Hill Book Co., 1962, pp. 232–253.

9. G. Murphy, *Personality: A Biosocial Approach to Origins and Structure*. New York: Harper and Brothers, 1947, pp. 331–361.

10. The term "gestalt" (*German*) means form or organized pattern.

11. Frederich Wulf, "Tendencies in Figural Variations," *The Source Book of Gestalt Psychology* (prepared by Willis D. Ellis). London: Routledge and Kegan Paul Ltd., 1955, p. 148.

12. A. Q. Sartain, A. J. North, J. R. Strange, and H. M. Chapman, *Psychology, Understanding Human Behavior*. New York: McGraw-Hill Book Co., 1962, p. 244.

13. Floyd L. Ruch, *Psychology and Life*. Chicago: Scott, Foresman & Co., 1941, p. 267.

14. Rudolph Arnheim, *Art and Visual Perception*. Berkeley and Los Angeles: University of California Press, 1954, pp. 1–26.

READING REFERENCES

Arnheim, Rudolph, *Art and Visual Perception*. Berkeley and Los Angeles: University of California Press, 1954.

Beardsley, D. C. and Wertheimer, M., eds., *Readings in Perception*. New York: D. Van Nostrand Co., Inc., 1958.

Blake, R. R. and Ramsey, G. V., eds., *Perception: An Approach to Personality*. New York: The Ronald Press Co., 1951.

Boring, E. G., *Sensation and Perception in the History of Experimental Psychology*. New York: Appleton-Century-Crofts, 1942.

Bruner, J. S., Goodnow, J., and Austin, G. A., *A Study of Thinking*. New York: John Wiley & Sons, 1956.

Ellis, Willis D., ed., *A Source Book of Gestalt Psychology*. London: Routledge and Kegan Paul Ltd., 1955.

Fallico, Arturo B., *Art & Existentialism.* Englewood Cliffs, N. J.: Prentice-Hall, Inc., 1962.

Gibson, J. J., *The Perception of the Visual World.* Boston: Houghton Mifflin Co., 1950.

Gotshalk, D. W., *Art and the Social Order.* New York: Dover Publications, Inc., 1962.

Kohler, W., *Gestalt Psychology,* 3d ed. New York: Liveright Publishing Corp.

Morgan, Clifford, *Introduction to Psychology.* New York: McGraw-Hill Book Co., 1956.

Murphy, G., *Personality, A Biosocial Approach to Origins and Structure.* New York: Harper and Brothers, 1947.

Ruch, Floyd L., *Psychology and Life.* Chicago: Scott, Foresman & Co., 1941.

Sartain, A. Q., North, A. J., Strange, J. R., and Chapman, H. M., *Psychology, Understanding Human Behavior.* New York: McGraw-Hill Book Co., 1962.

Shaffer, L., Gilmer, B., and Schoen, M., *Psychology.* New York: Harper and Brothers, 1940.

4 Some Basic Concepts Concerning Creativity

To understand the dynamics of the creative process—the role that it plays in fostering perceptual growth—and to appreciate more fully creative functioning as it relates to the whole complex of the human organism, it is essential to bear in mind some existing concepts, theories, and hypotheses concerning the subject of creativity. For these reasons, among others, Chapter 4 will be devoted to a general orientation to creativity, while Chapter 5 will include a comprehensive compilation of psychological data on the subject, gathered by Dr. R. Bruce Kirk, an eminent psychologist.

DIVERGENT THINKING AND CREATIVITY

In his recent studies on traits of creativity, J. P. Guilford, an experimental psychologist and a leader in research on creativity, identified two significant patterns in the thinking process. They are "convergent" and "divergent" thinking [1]. Convergent thinking is explained as the intellectual process of gathering and organizing data, while divergent thinking relates more clearly to the creative process in that it involves the use of unique abilities to improvise, to invent, to expand the range of relationships, the use of image-forming skills, and a talent for rearranging established concepts into new and novel systems [2]. There is general agreement, however, that both patterns in the thinking process are essential to creative production. In the process of experimentation or exploration of any number of possible solutions to a specific problem, *divergent* thinking seems most useful. But in the organization and synthesis of the findings resultant from experimentation and exploration, *convergent* thinking is useful.

It is also Guilford's contention that most educational experiences prescribed by curricula today are geared to convergent thinking, the emphasis being placed upon the accumulation of data which has been transmitted from generation to generation, which the student is expected to absorb. Consequently, a great deal of attention is devoted to those areas of

Fig. 4-1. Art experiences serve as an index to
the learner's imaginative and inventive skills.

the curriculum which deal with facts and figures, and less attention is
given to those in which the primary emphasis is the development of individual differences, special talents, and creative skills. However, if the
development of creative skills is to become a major objective in the education of the individual, the implication of Guilford's findings should prove
to be extremely useful.

TRAITS OF CREATIVITY

It should be borne in mind that one has to be very careful when
handling factor-analytic data such as Guilford used. The "results" one
gets out of the mathematical manipulations are a function of the variables
fed into equations and the sample tested with variables. Moreover, there
is good reason to believe that what we are reading in Guilford's list is not
a list of psychological findings but, rather, an itemized definition of creativity based on a factor analysis of data which implicitly specify these
things to begin with [3].

Nevertheless, it may be of interest to think about the briefly described, and possibly oversimplified statements concerning traits of creativity identified by J. P. Guilford. They are:

1) A creative person is a fluent thinker.
2) A creative person is an elaborate thinker.
3) A creative person is a reflective thinker.
4) A creative person is tolerant of ambiguity.
5) A creative person is inclined to be on the impulsive side.
6) A creative person is self-assertive and self-sufficient.
7) A creative person appreciates beauty as well as order.

More often than not the above qualities tend to be associated with creativity, but *faithful application to the creative task* seems to be the most common attribute of creative individuals [4].

GENERAL THEORIES ABOUT CREATIVITY

Fundamentally, there have been some basic but general theories about creativity which have guided the art educator in the active pursuit of educational goals. Among these are the beliefs that:

1) Creative activity plays a vital role in the development of personality.
2) Creative skill is a matter of import to all and not merely to those individuals whose interests lie in the field of art.
3) Creative activity affects not only the whole complex of the human personality but, most of all, the coordination of human functioning.
4) Creativity flourishes in a sympathetic environment.
5) Creativity is achieved best through goal-directed activities.
6) "Creative activity cannot be separated from the nature of man, and ... it must grow out of him as a unified process"—*Dewey*.
7) Creative activity involves not only factual knowledge, but also attitudes, standards, and skills which can be acquired best and quickest through active participation.
8) The phenomena which influence creative growth of an individual also affect every aspect of his overt behavior.
9) Imagination and inventiveness are products of deep-rooted and *habitual practice* in creative thinking. (See Fig. 4-1.)
10) Creative involvement offers a means of identifying the extent to which sensitivity of perception has been developed.
11) Creative activity breaks down barriers to the individual's sensual, emotional, and intellectual growth.

MOTIVATIONS OF CREATIVITY

The causes of creativity have been viewed from various orientations, projected in the light of philosophy, psychology, sociology, and anthropology. For our purpose, however, the examination of a few should be sufficient. They are quoted briefly in the following paragraphs.

Sir Herbert Read, the eminent British aesthetician made an interesting observation concerning one of the strongest impulses of man, i.e., creativity. He stated:

> From antiquity to our time, it has been the habit of philosophers and moralists to frown on innovation in religion or in art. It is only in science and technology that innovation or invention has been recognized as a principle of life itself. And yet, an unconscious desire for novelty is one of the strongest impulses in the average man or woman: a desire for new fashions in clothes or furnishings, for strange food and exotic scenery; and, is not the instinct of procreation the expression of a desire for the most original of all things,—a new human being, a recognizable member of the species,—but not, we pray, a duplicate of ourselves or of any one else?" [5]

John Dewey reflected upon the motivations of creativity when he stated:

> The live creature demands order in his living, but he also demands novelty ... the process of organic life is variation.... Demand for variety is the manifestation of the fact that being alive we seek to live, until we are cowed by fear or dulled by routine. The need of life itself pushes us out into the unknown.... Aesthetic recurrence, in short, is vital, physiological, functional [6].

Plato made reference to what he called "indigence" as being the first cause of production. Ananda Coomaraswamy, the art historian, philosopher, and orientalist, remarked that:

> Everyone is naturally a doer, patron and consumer; and at the same time an artist, that is to say a maker of art in some specialized sense, for example, either a painter, carpenter or farmer [7].

John Dewey felt that the natural impulses of man motivated creative activity. He stated:

> Natural impulses and desires constitute in any case the starting point. But, there is no intellectual growth without some reconstruction, some remaking of impulses and desires in the form in which they first show themselves. Thinking is a postponement of immediate action, while it affects internal control of impulse through a union of observation and memory—this union being the heart of reflection.
> ... No experience is educative that does not tend both to knowledge of more facts and entertaining of more ideas and to a better, a more orderly arrangement of them. It is not so generally recognized that a similar transformation takes place on the side of "inner" materials, images, observation, memories and emotions. [See Fig. 4-2.] They are also pro-

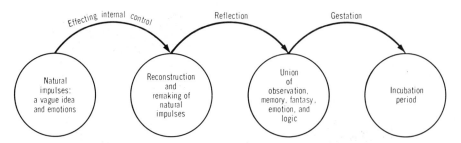

FIG. 4-2. John Dewey's concept of the birth of an idea.

gressively reformed; they too must be administered. *This modification is the building up of a truly expressive act.* We should find that it assumed definite shape only as it worked itself through a series of changes in imagined material. What most of us lack in order to be artists is not the inceptive emotion, nor yet merely technical skill in execution. *It is the capacity to work a vague idea and emotion over in terms of some definite medium....* Between conception and bringing to birth there lies a long period of gestation. During this period the inner material of emotion and idea is as much transformed through acting and being acted upon by objective material as the latter undergoes modification when it becomes a medium of expression. *It is precisely this transformation that changes the character of the original emotion, altering its quality so that it becomes distinctively aesthetic in nature....* Perception and imagination are the basic mental processes involved in art expression, but all faculties of thought, namely,—logic, memory, sensibility, and intellect are utilized in the production of a creative idea. [8. See also Fig. 4-3.]

The creative urge is at first extremely vague and indeterminate. The creator possesses a restlessness and an inordinate appetite for invention and discovery. Only through his diligent efforts does he bring about an aesthetic fulfillment. Though the creative process is thought to be an organic development, the fact remains that the mind, in creation, nearly always requires some conscious management. According to Ghiselin;

It is essential to remember that the creative end is never in full sight at the beginning, and it is brought wholly into view only when the process of creation is completed.... The creative process is not only the concern of specialists however; it is not limited to the arts and to thought, but is as wide as life itself. Or perhaps, it would be more correct to say that invention in the arts and in thought is a part of the invention of life, and that this invention is essentially a single process [9].

Concerning artistic activity Dewey commented:

It is not something possessed by a few persons and setting them apart from the rest of mankind, but is the normal or natural human heritage. Its spontaneity is not a gush, but is the naturalness proper to all or-organized energies of the live creature. Persons differ greatly in their respective measures. But there is something the matter, something ab-

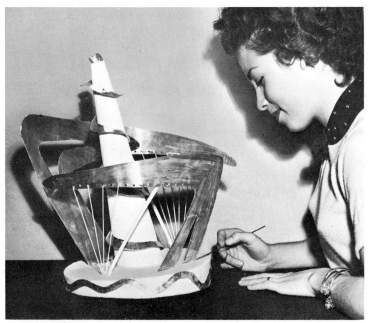

Fig. 4-3. "Perception and imagination are the basic mental processes involved in art expression, but all faculties of thought, namely,—logic, memory, sensibility, and intellect are utilized in the production of a creative idea"—*John Dewey.*

normal, when a human being is forbidden by external conditions from engaging in that fullness according to his own measure, and when he finds it diverted by these conditions into unhealthy physical excitement and appetitive indulgence [10].

Normally and naturally, artistic activity is the way in which one may "gain in strength and stature, the belief in his own powers, and the self-respect which make artistic activity constructive in the growth of personality [11].

R. W. Gerard's concept showed the relation of psychological phenomena to neural mechanisms. About imagination, he had this to say:

Imagination, creative imagination, is an action of the mind that produces a new idea or insight. The thing comes unheralded, as a flash, full-formed.... It is to social inheritance what mutation is to biological inheritance.... Clearly then, pursuit of imagination leads us into the unconscious and its mechanisms.

He further explained:

Ordinary talent produces artistically by means of rational selection and combination, guided by its aesthetic judgment.... *A good insight is likely to recognize the universal in the particular and in the strange* [12].

Wertheimer defined creative thinking as the process of destroying one gestalt (or pattern) in favor of a better one.

Italo De Francesco's theory of creative growth is: "The conceptual powers of a pupil adequately and progressively expressed through the art form with growing control over material through processes, and with evidence of deepened insights and broadened outlook [13].

A FEW CONCLUSIONS

A few conclusions are relevant at this point. First, if it is true that the pursuit of imagination leads one to the unconscious and its mechanism, then it stands to reason that every human being can pursue imaginative thought, having access to the same source—namely, the unconscious and its mechanism.

Secondly, if rational selection and combination, guided by aesthetic judgment are essential in the creative process, then this procedure does not preclude anyone with the ability to make rational selection and combination from developing a reasonable degree of aesthetic judgment—an essential tool in the creative process.

Thirdly, if all faculties of thought—namely, logic, memory, sensibility, and intellect—are utilized in the production of a creative idea, it stands to reason that everyone possessing these faculties of thought can "according to his own measure" produce creative ideas. Thomas Munro states:

Developing of the artistic and aesthetic strains in personality is not a purely subjective, mental process. It should involve increasing control of hands, arms, limbs, voice and other parts of the body in executing artistic techniques, under the direction of a controlling mind, imagination, and purpose [14].

The psychological research in the following chapter has been compiled by Dr. R. Bruce Kirk, an eminent psychologist and educator whose interest in creativity has been keenly profound. He is chairman of the Division for Study of the Human Personality, Chicago Teachers College, North. For his scholarly contribution to this manuscript, this writer is deeply grateful.

The inclusion of psychological findings on creativity is intended to serve a distinct purpose. Fundamentally, it is to confirm and to give added zest to the theories and deeply felt convictions which emanate from the field of art education, and which are based, to a great extent, on empirical evidence, experimentation, and keen observation. It is hoped that the reader will find this compilation of data helpful in developing new insights into the dynamic nature of the creative process and its relevance to the functioning of the living organism.

NOTES

1. J.P. Guilford, "Traits of Creativity" in *Creativity and Its Cultivation*, Harold H. Anderson, ed. New York: Harper and Brothers, 1959, pp. 151 ff.

2. Guilford, *op. cit.*, pp. 142–161.

3. These comments have been suggested by a reviewer.

4. J. P. Guilford, *Creative Crafts*, Vol. 1, No. 1, April 1960, published by Fred de Liden, Los Angeles, California.

5. Sir Herbert Read, "Originality," *Eastern Arts Association Research Bulletin*, Vol. V, March 1954.

6. John Dewey, *Art as Experience*. New York: Minton, Balch & Co., 1934, pp. 167–172.

7. Ananda Coomaraswamy, *Christian and Oriental Philosophy of Art*. New York: Dover Publications, Inc., 1956, Ch. 2.

8. John Dewey, *Experience & Education*. New York: The Macmillan Company, 1954, p. 28.

9. Brewster Ghiselin, ed., *The Creative Process*. Berkeley and Los Angeles: University of California Press, 1954, pp. 1–21.

10. John Dewey, Foreword to *The Unfolding of Artistic Activity*, 2d ed., by Henry Schaefer-Simmern. Berkeley and Los Angeles: University of California Press, 1950.

11. Henry Schaefer-Simmern, *The Unfolding of Artistic Activity*, 2d ed. Berkeley and Los Angeles: University of California Press, 1950, Ch. 1.

12. R.W. Gerard, *The Creative Process-Biological Basis of Imagination*. Berkeley and Los Angeles: University of California Press, 1954, pp. 236–259.

13. Italo L. de Francesco, *Art Education—Its Means and Ends*. New York: Harper and Brothers, 1958, pp. 196–229.

14. Thomas Munro, *Art Education, Its Philosophy and Psychology*. New York: The Liberal Arts Press, 1956, p. 8.

READING REFERENCES

Anderson, Harold H., ed., *Creativity and Its Cultivation*. New York: Harper and Brothers, 1959.

Barkan, Manuel, *A Foundation for Art Education*. New York: The Ronald Press Co., 1955.

Bruner, Jerome S., *On Knowing*. Cambridge, Mass.: Harvard University Press, 1962.

_____ , *The Process of Education*. Cambridge, Mass.: Harvard University Press, 1963.

Cruickshank, William M., ed., *Exceptional Children and Youth*. Englewood Cliffs, N.J.: Prentice-Hall, Inc., 1961.

Dewey, John, *Art as Experience*. New York: Minton, Balch & Co., 1934.

Ghiselin, Brewster, *The Creative Process*. New York: A Mentor Book, The New American Library, 1963.

Lowenfeld, Viktor, *The Nature of Creative Activity*. London: Routledge and Kegan Paul, Ltd., 1939.

McFee, June King, *Preparation for Art*. San Francisco: Wadsworth Publishing Co., Inc., 1961.

Munro, Thomas, *Art Education, Its Philosophy and Psychology*. New York: The Liberal Arts Press, 1956.

Read, Herbert, *Education Through Art*. New York: Pantheon Books, Inc., 1945.

Torrance, Paul E., *Guiding Creative Talent*. Englewood Cliffs, N.J.: Prentice-Hall, Inc., 1962.

5

Psychological
Research on
Creativity

by R. Bruce Kirk, Ph. D.

WHAT IS CREATIVITY?—AN EARLY ANSWER

Genius was the subject of a study by Francis Galton. Implicit in his study was an answer to the question, "What is creativity?" The answer was found in his *Hereditary Genius*, published in 1869. His sources were world statesmen, poets, musicians, painters, and other men of genius. The concentration was on family relationship. The implicit answer was, "Genius is that which leads an individual to rise above his fellows, by his own creative effort." And the creativity was attested to by the meeting and mastering of obstacles, in whatever field one found his interests. Galton's basic concern had not been in defining creativity; that was a side issue. He was anxious to establish that "... a man's natural abilities are derived by inheritance, under exactly the same limitations as are the form and physical features of the whole organic world." His studies took him into *accomplishment*, the final test. His summation was, "It points to the conclusion that all life is single in its essence, but various, ever varying, and interactive in its manifestations, and that men and all other living animals are active workers and sharers in a vastly more extended system of cosmic action than any of ourselves, much less of them, can possibly comprehend."

Galton had seen that the individual who had genius could profit within an interacting society and could make an outstanding contribution to that society. He pioneered the study of creativity.

It is interesting to note that this early explorer of genius was not a psychologist. At that time Wundt was investigating individual differences, experiment, physiology; James was finding the pragmatic truth in his dynamic psychology; Freud was making his way into the understanding of human personality; no psychologists were studying genius or creativity as such. Later Ribot, almost alone in Europe and America, turned his attention to creativity. He found the creative process to be like a plant: its germ a desire to solve a problem, its incubation a long, painful period of work, its flowering a sudden solution, its completion, more long, hard work. His study was interesting and productive. But others were concentrating on the study of *intelligence.*

THE QUESTION: OBSCURED BY AN ASSUMPTION

Binet's great work in finding a measurement of intelligence had tremendous practical implications. Intelligence testing, the IQ classification, factoring and relating of intelligence, provided several insights into the work of learning and teaching. Industry, education, social work, diagnosis, therapy, the study of the retarded, all, were influenced by the research on intelligence. However, in one area there was a less happy effect: in the area of the gifted, the creative.

The early work of Terman [37, 38] and of Hollingworth [18] was predicated on the assumption that a high IQ was the equivalent of a high creativity quotient. The creative and gifted were "chosen" for study on the basis of their being among the upper two or three percent in terms of IQ scores.

Terman [37] who with Oden and others studied the careers of over a thousand "gifted" children, found that through life they were on the average physically stronger, healthier, more stable emotionally and better adjusted psychologically than normal children. Hollingworth [18], also relying on IQ, as the criterion, found that there were early recognizable signs of giftedness, ability to use and interpret abstract symbols, precocity in reading and in talking.

They set a pattern for the hundreds who did similar and related studies. In nearly all these cases, there was an assumption that the IQ as measured (mostly by the Stanford-Binet) would be the key by which the gifted would be discovered. This assumption was not entirely unreasonable. The IQ was being used for schoolroom classification; it was being used in all kinds of research and as a basis for all kinds of studies: personality, sociological, motivational, and others. However, there had been no proof that the gifted were the high IQ students or that creativity equaled high intelligence. Later research was to suggest that the two qualities are quite different.

ANSWERS BY INDIVIDUALS: COMMENT

The phenomenon of creativity is such that any attempt to capture it in a definition seems a kind of paradox. It is easier to say, "Creativity has been here" or "Creativity flourishes in these surroundings" or "He is a creative person" than it is to say "This and this constitute creativity." It presents a problem like that given to Job. "Where is the way to the dwelling place of light, and where is the place of darkness, that you may take it to its territory and that you may discern the paths to its home?" Modern Job would be inclined to say that he knew more of the *signs* of creativity than he did of "the dwelling place," its source. Yet signs there are, and they are seen in and out of the classroom, suggesting, pointing, intimating that here is creativity in this individual. Many today feel that creativity is not an esoteric ability, but a common characteristic, shared in some degree by all, but with a few having great amounts of it. Some social factors have interfered with its discovery.

Cultural enrichment and deprivation, motivation or the lack of it, social class, the problem of practical, as against academic, achievers, all these concepts called into question the basis upon which the gifted were being "discovered." Davis [6] and Dollard, to name but two, indicated the need for "culture-fair" tests. These tests were needed to correct for bias inherent in the earlier IQ measures. The bias existed in the selection of items, in assumptions about motivation, in emphasis on exclusively academic skills. With a new need for finding and utilizing all the best talent available, there was a new urgency to find the best means of discovering it. Means are being found, and definitions improved.

One definition may be used, with the recognition that perhaps no definition is completely adequate. English [8] and English define creativity as "ability to find new solutions to a problem or new modes of artistic expression; bringing into existence a product new to the individual (not necessarily new to others)." There are implicit: levels of creativity; artistic output; problem solving.

Hans Sachs [27] describes creativity as the interaction between the individual, his needs, and his expression. The artist involves others, the spectators, in his solution of the conflict between his unspoken, unacceptable needs and the action, the creation which leads to an acceptable and satisfying product.

In 1950, Guilford [15] reporting in the *American Psychologist* identified the following as factors of creative thinking: free flow of ideas; fluency of thought; originality; adaptive and spontaneous flexibility; logical evaluation.

Led by the spectacle of creative genius in process, Ghiselin [13] reported on the actual self-description of the creative mind at work. Thirty-eight of the world's most noted creators are caught in self-revelation. The best-known, perhaps, is Poincare's Caen journey, "At the moment when I put my foot on the step the idea came to me, without anything in my former thoughts seeming to have paved the way for it, that the transformations I had used to define the Fuchsian functions were identical with those of non-Euclidean geometry...." The suddenness, the apparent unrelatedness is referred to again and again. This seems a significant part of the creative process, and it takes into account the functioning of the unconscious; he speaks of conscious work done as a preliminary, followed by this sudden, apparently unrelated idea, a solution or a significant step forward. Mozart, Coleridge, Nietzsche, Jung (to name a few) indicate aloneness, "all-at-once-ness" clear imagery, acting as a medium, obscurity of the sources of material, as being among the many facets of the creative process. Ghiselin, the collector and analyst of this varied description, comments, "I have emphasized the value of understanding, discipline, and hard work in the creative process. High and sustained achievement demands even more, the concentration of a life. And even that is not all ... we must always listen to the world.... We must expect to live the orderly ways we have invented continually conscious of the imminence of change."

Drevdahl [7] in looking at a group of fifty college students and using scales developed by Guilford, Cattell, and Thurstone, discovered that the creative were more verbal, more flexible, more individual, more original, more nonconforming, more radical (but also more withdrawn) than were the average students.

Lowenfeld [19], looking at gifted children, discovered them to be fluent in imagination and expression, highly sensitive, direct in expression, and highly intuitive in imagination.

Schoelin [29] discovered that the creative person exercises choice, does not depend on retrospective logic, has already shown creative ability, sees beyond the immediate problem, and is willing to be different.

Henry [17], using the technique of allowing first grade children to be spontaneous in their letter writing, found that creativity begins as an accidental response which eludes cultural controls and finally appears undetected within the cultural stereotypes.

"Professional creativity," the work of the "idea man" in industry, is described by Von Fange [40]. To him creativity is a "new association of existing elements, as far as the creator himself is concerned." Obstacles to creativity are: fixed thinking, following, conformity. Ways to overcome these obstacles of the creator in the industrial surrounding include, notably, "brainstorming." This takes into account the following suggestions:

1) state the problem in basic terms;
2) have only one focal point;
3) do not stop to criticize or explore any idea;
4) reach for any idea, no matter if it may seem remote at the time;
5) provide the support and encouragement so necessary to free the restrictive attitude.

In addition to brainstorming (proposed by Alex Osborne of Batten, Barton, Durstine and Osborne) there is also the "Gordon technique."

This was devised by William J.J. Gordon of Arthur D. Little, Inc. It stresses three points:

1) the group attacks the underlying concept of the problem, rather than the problem itself;
2) the group encourages radical applications of old techniques;
3) the solution is held off, to prevent premature "closure."

Von Fange includes also a speech by Charles F. Kettering, "How Can We Develop Invention?" One part of that speech is very apposite to educators:

> Some years ago a survey was made in which it was shown that if a person had an engineering or scientific education, the probability of his making an invention was only about half as great as if he did not have that specialized training.
>
> Now that is very interesting, and I have spent a great deal of time wondering why it is so. As a result, I have arrived at a definition of what an inventor is. An inventor is simply a fellow who *doesn't take his education too seriously.* You see, from the time a boy is six years old until he graduates from college he has to take three or four examinations a year. If he flunks once, he is out. *But an inventor is almost always failing.* He tries and fails maybe a thousand times. If he succeeds once, he is in. *These two things are diametrically opposite.* [Italics added.]

This is a comment on what our educational "succeed-fail" demand may be doing to creativity.

Osborne [20] describes more fully the technique of brainstorming. Criticism is precluded; freewheeling is encouraged; large quantities of ideas are desired; mutual approval of ideas is sought.

(It might be noted here that industry has made use of many devices to encourage creative thinking by and in groups: buzz sessions; case studies; communication models; analysis of social action; incomplete film showings, etc. The basic principle seems to be: arouse people in a free environment to attack problems from a new direction.)

In a specific field, that of science, Porterfield [21] traced the creative factors in scientific research. Tracing the work of Galileo, Charles Darwin, and Auguste Comte, he also (as others have done) stresses the "flash," the insight, the imagination. Whether in physical science, biological science, or social science, the implication of the cathedral's swinging lamp, of the depth to which the coral polyp might go and survive, or of Comte's "stages" of the human mind all provided in a moment a field of investigation which it would take years to explore.

Lack of suggestibility, a presence of tolerance of the ambiguous and of tolerance of structural disorderliness, and the presence of originality marked the highly creative people studied by Barron [2].

Bronowski [4] finds that innovation, discovery, and creation in art are paralleled in the field of science. The meaning of giftedness for 25 creative pupils is reported by Getzels [10] and Jackson. The pupils had

wider out-of-class interests than their fellow students, and they emphasized far less the customary topics of grades and teachers' attitudes. Also,
their humor was related to a broader field than the confines of the classroom.

Three dimensions of intellect are described by Guilford [16]. These
are identified as operations, products, and contents. These result from
another application of factor analysis to the product and process of creative thinking. Out of this, as well as many other studies, Guilford has
derived *divergent* thinking as an essential part of creativity.

Seventh graders were investigated by Reid [22], King, and Wickwire.
Twenty-four creative and twenty-four noncreative pupils were nominated
by their peers. The creative were more sociable, warmhearted, and less
anxious than the noncreative. Boys from the lower socioeconomic level
were significantly more confident and self-sufficient when creative than
were the noncreative; upper-class creative boys were significantly more
stable than the noncreative.

Riers [23] gave seven Guilford creativity tests to 114 junior high
students of above-average IQ. The results were compared with teacher
ratings of creativity and with each other. Tests of originality correlated
more highly with other tests and with teacher ratings of the students than
did tests of ideational fluency.

Schmadel's [28] study of 403 sixth graders revealed that:
   a) creative thinking ability contributed to school achievement;
   b) traditional intelligence tests do not reveal this creative thinking
      ability.

Torrance [39] shows that in the language arts there is revealed, as in
other areas, a composite of fluency, flexibility, curiosity, and originality,
making up part of creativity. Torrance suggests the need to:
   a) help children recognize the value of their ideas;
   b) provide activities which give practice in or which exercise creative
      thinking;
   c) reward creative thinking in the classroom.

Getzels [12] and Jackson have done an outstanding job of looking at
the similarities and differences between "intelligence" and "creativity."
A sketch of their work follows.

They discovered four (out of thirteen) basic personality and other
factors as being significant aspects of outstanding students. These four
were intelligence, creativity, morality, and psychological adjustment. They
decided to study in depth the similarities and contrasts between intelligence and creativity. These two had "theoretical and practical significance." Five tests of creativity were given: word association; uses for
things; hidden shapes; fables, and make-up problems. A notable difference was discovered in outlook; the creative students were *divergent* in

their thinking (Guilford's term), *open* and looked for *growth*; the non-creatives were *convergent* in their thinking, *defensive* and looked for *safety*.

The comparison was made between students in a private school in the Chicago area, "the one group high in intelligence as represented by the conventional IQ metric but not as high in the cognitive functions represented by tests of creativity, the other group high in the cognitive functions represented by the same tests of creativity but not as high in intelligence as represented by the conventional IQ metric" [12, p. 15].

It must be noted here that these students, from the sixth grade through the senior year of high school, were part of a population whose mean IQ was 132, SD of 15. Even the sample chosen as being creative (rather than intelligent) would therefore be operating at a high level of intelligence.

The authors report many findings, related to family, school performance, acceptance in home and school, approach to problems and to life in general, kinds of thinking, kinds of personality, point of view.

Some of the main findings may be summarized: there is a difference between intelligent thinking, as measured by the IQ, and creative thinking. Creative persons are intelligent; intelligence is not their most salient characteristic.

The authors have done a service in making much clearer the distinc-between intelligence and creativity. Another look at creativity may be in order.

SUMMARY: INDIVIDUALS

As the individual research reports are examined, some elements of creativity are identified: for Sachs, the unconscious; for Guilford, fluency of thought, originality, flexibility, spontaneity, logical evaluation, divergent thinking; Ghiselin finds the suddenness; Drevdahl sees verbal facility, originality, lack of conformity; Lowenfeld stresses sensitivity and intuition; Bronowski, discovery. Barron finds that creative people are not suggestible, though they are flexible; Schoelin finds that they are able to see beyond the immediate problem, willing to be different. None seem to disagree with the stages discovered by Wallas [41] preparation, incubation, illumination, verification. However, unusual energy output and perseverance as functions of the individual are reported by Roe [24], who studied living painters, scientists, psychologists, and anthropologists.

In summary, we find that the elements are varied, but there seems to emerge a pattern. The pattern includes:
   1) for adults:
        a) willingness to be different, opposite, and firm;
        b) ability to adapt to new ideas which come from within;

    c) perseverance, planning, and hard work;

    d) sensitivity to people, sensitivity to challenge, sensitivity to media;

    e) suddenness—a flash (after much hard work and preparation);

    f) a sense of freshness; discovery.

2) for children:

    a) accidental discovery is part of the process;

    b) sociability marks the creative child;

    c) originality comes "naturally";

    d) creative children do not emphasize rules, tests, or the teachers' opinions;

    e) intelligence is part of creativity, not the salient part;

    f) schools will do a greater service if they understand the distinction between creativity and (traditionally measured) intelligence.

ANSWERS FROM CONFERENCES: COMMENT

In recent years, symposia have been held over the whole country. The following are brief reports of some of the proceedings at a few of these symposia: a) Syracuse University, b) University of Colorado, c) Los Angeles State College, d) University of Utah. Symposia such as these have cut across a wide coverage of creativity:

    a) its meaning, its origins, its unique characteristics;

    b) its wide application, from art to science to medicine to engineering, etc.;

    c) personality traits and creativity;

    d) the discovery of creativity;

    e) the encouragement of, or provision for, creativity.

The Syracuse Conference. Michael Andrews, introducing the Syracuse Conference [1, p. vi] says:

> For a fair consideration of this publication, the reader is invited to recognize creativity as a positive self-integrating force and to set aside his predominant concern for the creation of aesthetic forms. Where once creativity was greeted with derisive laughter, scorn and suspicion, it is today considered a professional interest and treated with the respect it deserves even among engineers, inventors and medical personnel.

Pitirim Sorokin develops a "general theory of creativity" in his contribution. He denies the value of the unconscious in creativity; insists, however that there is a "supraconscious" which has touched the great creative geniuses of the ages, religious, artistic, inventive, musical, philosophical. "Contrary to the prevalent Freudian, Jungian, Hartmann's, Janet's or other claims, the unconscious cannot and does not create anything" [1, p. 5]. "In behavioral terms, a truly creative activity represents an *adequate* and *constructive* response to the old situation" [1, p. 1]. For him, the three stages of creative accomplishment are: conception of the essentials of a new discovery, materialization (painting, writing, etc.), and making available the objective of creative achievement. He stresses the specificity and fluctuation of creativity.

In the same symposium, Fliegler defines the dimensions of the creative process as: simple habit creativity, simple selective creativity, complex selective creativity, problem-solving creativity, and projected creativity. Two other levels exist, but they are the concern of the universals: the creation of life and the creation of the universe [1, p. 24]. He then points out that "If more creative people are to be developed it is only through *process* that this can be accomplished. The biological factors are inherently set, but creativeness or lack of it is determined by the kind of processes which are evolved in the life space of the individual. As a consequence it is important to recognize that control over process is feasible and desirable since the destiny of man is changed only through process." Here is stressed the function of the *teacher*; similarly there is an implicit emphasis of the same kind in the following work, that of Ojemann [1, p. 25].

Taking the main theme, mental health, as his topic, Ojemann traces the story of three "greats" whose lives were anything but calm and stable: Beethoven, Van Gogh, and (in the field of medicine) Semmelweiss. He emphasizes the conflict between the individual and the demands made on him by people and conditions surrounding him. In one other case, the subject was stable and steady, but he was aware of the terrible pressures put on him by steady opposition to his every new proposal.

Ojemann points out that when the environment (or the people in it) provide no support, if "the budding artist, the creative mechanic or the highly intellectual child is not appreciated in a community which values athletic ability or physique or conformity above all else, and if he is given no help in understanding how these forces came about or how to react to them constructively there will be many threats to adequacy and security and much difficulty in adjustment. If children and teachers in the elementary school have difficulty in accepting the child with peculiar or different interests or different ideas, such children with high special ability will have a difficult time. If schools and universities give more credit to conformity than they do to originality, new ideas, unusual sensitivity or insight, then creativity and mental health are incompatible" [1, p. 34].

Ojemann then goes on to point out an answer or suggestion: the need for teaching a causal orientation to the social environment, a reasoned view, a view which traces the behavior to its source (and allows for differences—knowing that these may be symptoms of different surroundings and could be signs of creativity). Terman's work, which indicated that the gifted were also healthier, more stable, more contributing than the average sets a counterpoint; if the background is supportive (or at least not too much in conflict), then the individual who is outstanding may grow up with his potential fulfilled.

Andrews, the editor, has designed a dialectics of creativity and mental health [1, p. 95]. His definitions are clear and interesting, both of general themes in art and of specific processes and techniques. It is in the area of mental health as related to art, however, that his definitions are most interesting. They indicate the place of creativity in maintaining mental health:

> "Does art lead to mental health?" Some art does and some does not. Art may be a flight from reality or it may be an endeavor to understand reality a little better. It would depend on whether it increases or decreases independence.
> "What is the role of art expression in mental health?" The role of art is to reflect deviate behavior. It reveals the individual's efforts to overcome obstruction to his normal development and difficulties in social relationships. It may be called a corrective or therapeutic effort.
> "How can the teacher cultivate and promote good mental health?" The teacher can cultivate good health by:
>   a) possessing the personal stature and human attributes worthy of respect of all;
>   b) establishing a favorable climate which challenges and allows for creative experiences;
>   c) setting up conditions of inquiry and self-actualization;
>   d) allocating enough time for experimentation, exploration, discovery, and the inculcation of thoughts;
>   e) encouraging the learner to find the true, the beautiful, and the good with himself;
>   f) fostering a feeling of security, freedom, confidence, belonging, courage, independence, and integrity;
>   g) accepting and respecting individual differences in others.

This contribution of question and answers which relate art to mental health is followed by a discussion by Ordway Tead of the healthy person's creative outlets. Three creative outlets are described: the creation of the individual's own personality; the creation of an ongoing process of interpersonal relations; or the more familiar creation of an artistic product.

The last article in this symposium report is that of the late Viktor Lowenfeld. He had planned to attend the symposium; his friend and colleague, Kenneth Beittel, presented the address. Lowenfeld, in writing on creative teaching, stressed the following as essential for the teacher of art: perceptual sensitivity, intellectual sensitivity, and aesthetic sensitivity (involving intense personal relationships and utmost sincerity). In addition, the teacher must adjust to the changing situation and be able to penetrate into an experience and encourage pupils and students to do the same. The essential and the unessential must be distinguished for the pupil; the time will come when he can do this himself.

The University of Colorado Symposium. This symposium [14] includes such participants as Bruner, Henle, MacLeod, and Newell. Participants at the symposium were concerned with research on process and product; the marks of creativity in such groups as theologians, military officers, college alumnae, research workers; the tracing of creative thought in the individual and the group; and the computing machines which ap-proach human thought in their handling of problems posed. Bruner's emphasis on creativity and education, and on the need to unite the two, is apparent here. Bruner speaks [14, p. 1] on the conditions of creativity. He describes the hallmark of a creative enterprise as being *effective surprise*. This creativity contains predictive effectiveness, formal effective-ness, and metaphorical effectiveness. There are two paradoxes in the creative process: one must have passion and decorum; he must also have detachment and commitment. In the first case, the artistic product must be a living thing, yet it must be within the bonds required to make it acceptable. In the second case, one must be able to see the process as a thing apart, yet one must be completely dedicated to its successful func-tioning. In addition one must be free to surrender to the domination by the object (the art object, for example). Bruner's description of a highly creative *work group* in operation throws much light: there is a feeling of the effective support of the members of the group noticeably lacking when one leaves the group.

Newell, Shaw, and Simon [14, p. 116] give a full description of "thinking machines" which simulate human thought. They are useful as models which can help us trace more accurately the steps and process of thinking; they can be subjected to different stimuli or to the same stimuli repetitively; something which cannot be done with the human counter-part. These authors describe the success in synthesizing mechanisms that solve difficult problems in the same manner as humans do. They provide a theory of problem solving that is highly specific and operational. They then draw out some of the implications of this theory for creative think-ing. Fields such as symbolic logic, chess playing, or musical composition have been programmed for the computer. Some elements of "creativity" seem to be indicated in computers already designed; the prediction is that, within ten years, a machine will be able to produce original composition of aesthetically significant music or discover and prove an important mathematical theory.

Mary Henle's work on gestalt psychology and on the Lewinian ap-proach is well known. Henle emphasizes [14, p. 31], as did Bruner (and many others), the unknown origin of creative ideas. She quotes Helm-holtz: "they crept quietly into my thinking"; Poincare: "the idea came to me though nothing in my former thoughts seemed to have prepared me for it." Certain characteristics are involved in creativeness for Henle: correctness (there must not be mere unchecked fantasy); novelty (which does not guarantee creativeness, but must be related to freedom); freedom is the essence of creative thinking. There is a danger to creativity in "knowing" something, for when we "know" it, we will not pursue it further. We must be free from our own assumptions; harmony, the last characteristic listed by Henle, is close to what is termed "elegance" in a solution. It clarifies the structure, emphasizes the essentials, places the subordinate parts in proper order. How do we induce creativity? Henle suggests that we:

   a) be receptive to creative ideas (as Gertrude Stein suggests, "Let it come; it will come");
   b) be immersed in the material—be aware not only of what has been done but of the problems which still remain;
   c) see the questions which matter;
   d) use the errors for improvement.

Finally, according to Henle, ideas must die, giving place to the newer, sharper or sometimes broader idea.

Robert B. MacLeod [14, p. 175] says: "The Creativity was experimental and empirical; all were affected by Wertheimer. They were not Freudian, not mystics, not testers." Some intuition was used; one Freudian hypothesis. Three questions were raised: 1) Is it possible to study creativity by thinking scientifically? 2) What are the criteria of creative thinking? 3) In what conditions do people become creative?

1) If science is disciplined curiosity, then creativity can be studied scientifically. The science of science is an attitude of disciplined curiosity. Experimental psychology is our main basis, but it probably leaves much undone. Problem solving is the best example of the creative mind in action, and properly instructed machines can solve problems much as humans do (often more efficiently). There is a need to adapt the tools to the fuzzy problems that exist.

2) For present purposes, we know that experience is the starting point of an inquiry. An attempt is made to remove the bias of the culture and the individual. Phenomenology is not a science, but an approach to science.

3) Introspection and retrospection give us intuitions derived from direct experience. These are memories, and they indicate some of the characteristics of creativity. There are four situations to be studied: a) creative periods in history; b) creative groups; c) creative persons, and d) creative acts. If there is something in common between these four, we are moving toward a criterion of creativity.

The creative period in history is usually left to the literary historian: Athens, the Italian Renaissance, the American Revolution, and the present technological revolution. Psychologists have not done much in this problem.

Group Activity: Groups can be creative or uncreative. As we get more records of natural groups, we can look back on what made them creative.

Creative Persons: McClelland has said that Nobel prize winners are creative. The Institute for Personality Assessment and Research has listed many creative individuals. However, there is the question of accidental discovery and discovery by design, between the developing inventor and the inventor who really presents something new. Two facts stand out clearly. Creative people are not uniformly creative. Acts of creation may emerge from people who are considered uncreative.

The Creative Act: The Wurzburgers were able to report a discovery. Kohler and others who studied apes (as well as those who studied children) found that, although these subjects often behave stupidly, they could *see into* a situation, apprehend things in a new relation, and open up new possibilities. Another distinction is that between thinking that is merely repetitive and the kind that goes to the heart of the problem and grasps inner structural relations.

Are creative thinking and problem solving the same? It depends on the meaning of "problem." This may be too broad or too narrow, as at present. The most nearly satisfactory criterion is novelty. The discovery must be new to the thinker, and the context must be the world as he understands it. It must not be accidental, and it must not be trivial. The experience must be in relation to a search situation. The creative act is truly creation when it demonstrates how and within what limits it has yielded something new.

The conditions of creativity require that the creator be detached yet committed, free yet ensnared, concerned but not too much so. There must be motivation from within, yet there must not be a blinding influence.

MacLeod refers (in summarizing the symposium) to the creator as revealed by Bruner and Henle as both dominating and receiving. He also reports that it is not yet known whether there is a creative type or a trait of creativity.

Los Angeles State College Conference: Implications of Creativity Research. This one-day conference [30] brought together (among others) J. P. Guilford, J. C. Flanagan, and I. A. Taylor. Guilford pointed out that to him creativity has at least these characteristics:

1) All individuals have some degree of potential for creativity.

2) Creativity is not a uniform or unitary commodity.

3) Creativity is an aspect of intelligence, not something apart from intelligence. (However, there is a difference between creativity and creative productivity).

Guilford also emphasized that even those in the field of the arts could be or become far from creative; attitude is important. In our society, compared to American Indians, Japanese, or Mexicans, our art teachers have induced relatively few into the production of art objects. We must learn to live with increased creativity.

John C. Flanagan emphasizes the many dimensions of intellect, as Guilford also does. To discover ingenuity or creativity, the people at (Flanagan's) American Institute for Research used as the main technique a large number of specific situations which could be solved at the rate of about one a minute. These situations demanded originality, insight, and a practical outlook. One of the difficulties with current education, Dr. Flanagan feels, is that it is often designed to prevent people from being creative.

For Dr. Taylor, creativity falls into five levels: expressive; productive; inventive; innovative; and, the highest level, emergentive. In this last, there is the emergence of a new and different set of properties, as water emerges from hydrogen and oxygen. This type of creativity is achieved by very few: Einstein, Freud, Darwin, Marx, Picasso, and Wright in our generation. They are the nonaristotelians, the nonnewtonians, the noneuclidians, challenging the established. He believes that the history of thought has come from single absolutes (the Roman *virtus*) through two-point references (stimulus-response) and into three-point references (thesis-antithesis-synthesis). We are ready, he says, for a four-point reference; the fourth point will be human participation in and control of the phenomena of the universe. In this era, creativity will demand to be recognized.

(It is useful to note that there is included in this conference report an excellent bibliography on creativity—general, art, music, literature, education, and science—about 550 articles, books, and references.)

Utah Conferences. The editor of the reports of these conferences, C. W. Taylor, indicates some of these findings [33, 34, 35] as a result of the search for creative scientific talent: In the creative individual, there is a tolerance for the unstructured, the undefined. The creative personality is original and able to endure ambiguity. He is not suggestible, however.

SUMMARY OF SYMPOSIA

The symposia and conferences have brought together varying attacks on the question of creativity. They have sparked the contributions of people like Bruner, Guilford, Lowenfeld, Ojemann, Witty [43] and others. To summarize, in this case as in the case of individual contributors, is to oversimplify and to omit important findings. Some findings, however, should be mentioned:

    a) Creativity and mental health are related: there is much more to be investigated in this field.

b) Some of the paradoxes in creativity are discovered: one must be committed yet detached, ready to give oneself to the activity, passionate yet restrained.

c) Machines already are available which perform creatively.

d) "Correctness," novelty, and immersion in the medium are all parts of creativity.

e) Creativity is not uniform. The creative person is not steadily creative; some noncreative persons will at times (perhaps only once) show themselves to be genuinely creative.

f) Tolerance for the unstructured and undefined does not imply that the creative person is weak, suggestible. The contrary is indicated: firmness and the impressing of one's own ideas on the medium.

MEASURES OF CREATIVITY

As we mentioned earlier, there is difficulty in pinning down the creative talent, analyzing it or predicting it. The value of earlier IQ measures is called into question. Some of these newer tests have been mentioned in connection with research. Guilford's work, Thurstone's, Cattell's have all employed tests. Factors in these tests are: a) uncommonness of response; b) remoteness of association; c) "cleverness" as a sign of originality. Factors known for some time have been put into tests: verbal comprehension; numerical facility; perceptual speed; visualization; general reasoning; word fluency; association fluency; ideational fluency; closure. Newer factors which may be tested for are: a) originality, the ability to produce uncommon, clever, or remote responses; b) redefinition, the ability to shift attack and use objects in a new way; c) adaptive flexibility, the ability to change "set" where changes are unrestricted; and e) sensitivity to problems, the ability to recognize practical problems. Open-end tests also provide a means for discovering originality: plot titles, work association, and remoteness tests were good types. In all these tests there is a trend away from the culture-bound tests and an attempt to provide for freedom of choice, originality, and a sense of humor as indicators of creativity.

TEACHERS' DECISION

As Louise Dunn Yochim has pointed out repeatedly in this book, the teacher has a responsibility to the potentially creative. In the field of art preeminently, there is the place for discovery and nurture of creativity. However, practical considerations enter. Time is limited; space is not available; facilities are inadequate—at least, in many schools. What does the teacher do? Apparently, what good teachers of art have been doing for years, not relying on traditional tests, traditional methods, or traditional emphases. By their own individual attention and encouragement, teachers have already anticipated much that the research would suggest. They have listened, they have evaluated, they have encouraged, they have perceived. The result has been the discovery and promotion of talents which would have been lost. Now that society is about to move toward rather than against creativity, perhaps the hand of these teachers will be much strengthened.

SOME REFERENCES

The bibliographies included in the symposia listed are excellent guides to the many studies done on creativity. Also Ruth Strang [31] has given an excellent listing (for teachers) of practical suggestions for aiding in creativity nurture. A hundred-page pamphlet useful for teachers has been provided by L. Rubin [25], and there are also many annotated bibliographies published by NEA guidance and counseling associations, etc.

NOTES

1. Michael F. Andrews, ed., *Creativity and Psychological Health: a Symposium.* Syracuse, N.Y.; Syracuse University Press, 1961.
2. F. Barron, "The Disposition Toward Originality," *Research Conference on Identification of Creative Scientific Talent*, C. W. Taylor, ed. Salt Lake City: University of Utah Press, 1955, pp. 156–170.
3. F. Barron, "The Psychology of Imagination," *Scientific American* 199: 150–170 (Sept) 1958.
4. J. Bronowski, "The Creative Process," *Scientific American* 199: 58–65 (Sept) 1958.
5. O. K. Buros, *The Fifth Mental Measurements Yearbook.* Highland Park, N.J.: Gryphon Press, 1959 (also 1953, 1949, 1940 yearbooks).
6. Allison Davis and John Dollard, *Children of Bondage.* Washington, D.C.: American Council on Education, 1940.
7. J. E. Drevdahl, "Factors of Importance for Creativity," *J. Clinic Psych.* 12: 21–26 (Jan) 1956.
8. H. B. English and C. A. English, *A Comprehensive Dictionary of Psychological and Psychoanalytical Terms.* New York: Longmans, Green, 1958.
9. Adele Franklin and others, "The Teachers' Role in Creativity," *Psych. Abstracts* 34: 473, 1960.
10. J. W. Getzels and P. W. Jackson, "The Meaning of Giftedness," *Phi Delta Kappan* 40: 75–77 (Nov) 1958.
11. J. W. Getzels and P. W. Jackson, "The Study of Giftedness," *The Gifted Students.* U.S. Dept. of Health, Education and Welfare, 1960.
12. J. W. Getzels and P. W. Jackson, *Creativity and Intelligence.* New York: John Wiley & Sons, 1961.
13. Brewster Ghiselin, *The Creative Process.* Berkeley and Los Angeles: University of California Press, 1954.
14. Howard E. Gruber, Glenn Teyrell, and Michael Wertheimer, eds., *Contemporary Approaches to Creative Thinking: a Symposium.* Boulder: University of Colorado Press, 1962.

15. J. P. Guilford, "The Nature of Creative Thinking," *The American Psychologist* 5: 444–454 (Sept) 1950.

16. J. P. Guilford, "Three Faces of Intellect," *The American Psychologist* 14: 469–479 (Aug) 1959.

17. J. Henry, "Working Paper on Creativity," *Harvard Education Review* 27: 148–155 (Spring) 1957.

18. Leta S. Hollingworth, *Gifted Children: Their Nature and Nurture.* New York: The Macmillan Company, 1926.

19. Viktor Lowenfeld, "Care of the Gifted," *School Arts* 55: 13–18 (April) 1956.

20. A. F. Osborne, *Applied Imagination: Principles and Practices of Creative Thinking.* New York: Charles Scribner's Sons, 1957.

21. Austin L. Porterfield, *Creative Factors in Scientific Research.* Durham, N.C.: Duke University Press, 1941.

22. J. B. Reid, F. J. King, and P. Wickwire, "Cognitive and Other Personality Characteristics of Gifted Children," *Psychological Reports* 5: 729–737, 1959.

23. Ellen Riers and others, "The Identification of Creativity in Adolescence," *J. Ed. Psych.* 51: 346–351 (Dec) 1960.

24. Anne Roe, "The Personality of Artists," *Ed. Psych. Meas.* 6: 401–408, 1946.

25. L. Rubin, *Nurturing Classroom Creativity.* Ventura, Calif.: Ventura County Schools, 1960.

26. David H. Russell, "Higher Mental Processes," *Encyclopedia of Educational Research,* Chester W. Harris, ed. New York: The Macmillan Company, 1960, pp. 645–657.

27. Hans Sachs, *The Creative Unconscious.* Cambridge, Mass.: Sci-Art Publishers, 1951.

28. Elnora Schmadel, "The Relation of Creative Thinking Abilities to School Achievement," unpublished Ed.D. thesis. Los Angeles: University of Southern California, 1960.

29. J. Schoelin, "Creativity and Psychological Health," *American Management Association Personal Services* 168: 12–21, 1956.

30. J. Leonard Steinberg, coordinator, *The Future Implications of Creativity Research.* Los Angeles: Los Angeles State College, 1962.

31. Ruth Strang, "Developing Creative Power of Gifted Children," *Creativity of Gifted and Talented Children.* New York: Teachers College, Columbia University, 1959, pp. 20–31.

32. J. R. Suchman, "Inquiry Training in the Elementary School," *Science Teacher* 27: 42–47.

33. C. W. Taylor, ed., *The 1955 University of Utah Research Conference on the Identification of Creative Scientific Talent.* Salt Lake City: University of Utah Press, 1956.

34. C. W. Taylor, ed., *The Second (1957) University of Utah Research Conference on the Identification of Creative Scientific Talent.* Salt Lake City: University of Utah Press, 1958.

35. C. W. Taylor, ed., *The Third (1959) University of Utah Research Conference on the Identification of Creative Scientific Talent.* Salt Lake City: University of Utah Press, 1959.

36. C. W. Taylor, "A Tentative Description of the Creative Individual," *Educational Leadership* 18: 7–12 (Oct) 1960.

37. Lewis M. Terman, and others, *Mental and Physical Traits of a Thousand Gifted Children,* Genetic Studies of Genius, Vol. I.   Stanford, Calif.: Stanford University Press, 1925.

38. Lewis M. Terman and Melita H. Oden, *The Gifted Child Grows Up,* Genetic Studies of Children, Vol. IV. Stanford, Calif.: Stanford University Press, 1947.

39. E. P. Torrance, "Creative Thinking in the Language Arts," *Educational Leadership* 18: 13–18 (Oct) 1960.

40. Eugene K. Von Fange, *Professional Creativity.* Englewood Cliffs, N.J.: Prentice-Hall, Inc., 1959.

41. Graham Wallas, *The Art of Thought.* New York: Harcourt, Brace & Co., Inc., 1926.

42. Pauline Williamson, secretary, *Creativity of Gifted and Talented Children.* New York: Teachers College, Columbia University, 1959.

43. Paul Witty, *Creativity of Gifted and Talented Children.* New York: Teachers College, Columbia University, 1959.

6

Understanding the Learner in the Creative Process

The complex mechanism of the human organism and its variant aspects of action, reaction, and interaction, as it is affected by external and internal stimuli, represents a tremendous reservoir of substance which is cultivated by an aggregate of human experience. *But the conversion of the notional essence of human experience into concrete forms, through any medium, constitutes the sum and substance of the creative process.* This process involves the individual's conceptual, perceptual, and intuitive powers and the cultivation of aesthetic sensibilities—the basis for artistic behavior. An uncritical acceptance of the theory that imitation of nature provides this basis is faulty. Moreover, it is, in every respect, detrimental to the development of one's own image-forming skills. In the words of Fiedler: "*How can objects in nature have an artistic substance if the essence of artistic substance owes its origin to the spiritual powers of man?*"[1]

The theory that all children are endowed with creative impulses is not a new one. It has its roots in the extensive and laborious investigations of many eminent scholars among whom a few are William James, George Santayana, Conrad Fiedler, John Dewey, Thomas Munro, Viktor Lowenfeld. They not only confirm this theory but also suggest the urgency for careful consideration, as this theory concerns all individuals and not merely a privileged few. The implications for teaching children, therefore, are unmistakably clear. The task of the art educator is to channel those powers and intuitive feelings into vistas through which each child can discover for himself, can discipline, and can fully express his individuality. The approach to this process must be logical, well structured, and sequential in nature. Moreover, it must encompass the conscious and less conscious motivations of the child—the instinctive and the subconscious as well.

FIG. 6-1. The budding artist at the easel. The author's son at the age of seven. "Creative ability can develop and grow under proper stimulation and guidance, particularly during the child's early years"—*Cecil V. Millard.*

FIG. 6-2. "Spring." Crayon drawing by six-year-old girl. The notional essence of human experience converted into concrete forms constitutes the sum and substance of the creative process.

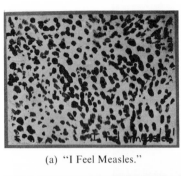

(a) "I Feel Measles."

(b) "I Feel Sleepy."

(c) "I Feel Like a Dunce."

(d) "I Feel Dizzy."

(e) "I Feel Like Going Back to Bed."

(f) "I Feel Upside Down."

FIG. 6-3. "How I Feel on the First Day of School." The above illustrations are a result of a teacher's request to paint a picture of "How You Feel on the First Day at School." The paintings were done by boys and girls in the first grade on the first day of school in September.

UNDERSTANDING AND APPRECIATING THE CREATIVE NEEDS OF THE LEARNER

In the foregoing chapters, the essence of creative expression and its significance in the life of every individual have been discussed. Much more has been said, of course, than needs to be repeated here. But an awareness of the basic need for self-assertion and of the fundamental views concerning creativity suggests the recognition of other correlative

FIG. 6-4. Tempera painting by five-year-old girl showing a decided interest in details—revealing a high degree of perceptual skill.

FIG. 6-5. Watercolor painting by five and a half-year-old girl, indicating an awareness of line, form, movement, and pattern in a natural setting.

factors. These must be taken into account in the planning of creative experiences for the learner. An art program which is designed to foster aesthetic and perceptual growth should take into account all factors which may possibly influence the scope and sequence of its content. Moreover, it should allow for flexibility in its implementation. Consequently, this requires a plan which is structured within the framework of variability, showing a decided concern for the diverse aspects of the human organism, and the diverse patterns of human behavior. For example, growth in the aesthetic and perceptual realm needs to be viewed in relation to, and in the light of, the physical, intellectual, creative, and emotional makeup of the learner. (See Chart 1 at the end of Chapter 8.) His experiential background, his abilities, his interests, his dominant drives and needs at every level of development must be assessed in order to insure the proper unfolding and growth of his unique and creative powers at each level. Significant in this process also is information derived from biographical data, observation, case studies, and spontaneous conversation. Facts about the socioeconomic status of the community and the environmental factors of the home offer valuable clues to the experiential background of the learner and may profoundly influence the nature and the content of the art program that is planned for him. These sources of information facilitate the understanding of the learner and his environment. Moreover, they provide significant clues to his basic needs.

In the planning of an art program, therefore, three major considerations must be born in mind. First, it is necessary to identify and analyze the motivating factors behind the learner's existing understandings, appreciations, attitudes, and patterns of behavior. Secondly, it is essential to provide experiences which modify and foster the proper development of them; that is to say, experiences which discipline and condition the learner's emotions, intellect, attitudes, aesthetic, and perceptual powers and, consequently, his overt behavior. Thirdly, the content of an art program must be reevaluated periodically in the light of the above and of newly discovered factors, and the program must be restructured within a framework of experiences which will induce desirable intellective and emotional integration within the learner.

PROVIDING STIMULI TO PROMOTE DESIRABLE LEARNING PATTERNS

Although the multiple outcomes derived from creative involvement do not become apparent at first, even to a trained observer, in time, it is possible to identify them with a reasonable degree of accuracy. This is especially true in determining aesthetic and perceptual growth through visual experiences. Specific stimuli which are designed to generate particular art learnings do produce desirable learning patterns. These become clearly apparent in the visual interpretations of the learner's

FIG. 6-6. Tempera painting by eight-year-old girl expressing a joyous reaction to summer vacation. The abundance of detail reveals her perceptual and imaginative skill in the delineation of natural forms.

FIG. 6-7. Tempera painting by twelve-year-old girl, a recent arrival from Puerto Rico. The student reveals a cultural influence in the treatment of natural forms; i.e., an inclination to enrich the flat surfaces with decorative pattern.

FIG. 6-8. Eight- and nine-year-old boys and girls portray themselves in their Halloween costumes, using varied materials—paper, crayons, felt, yarn, buttons, and sequins. The portraits represent unique interpretations of the self, revealing varying levels of perceptual and imaginative skill.

notional concepts, whether delineated or constructed. As the learner acquires skills in projecting his ideas visually, his learnings increase. When he utilizes his newly acquired learnings in more complex situations, it is evident that these are an integral part of his overt behavior.

Unquestionably it is the teacher's task to provide the kind of experiences which spur and stimulate a desire to think and to act creatively at all times. The resourceful teacher of art can meet this challenge by providing stimuli which promote desirable learning patterns.

DEVELOPING DEPTH IN SENSORY PERCEPTION

The frequency of creative involvement in guided activities which challenge the learner's aesthetic, perceptual, and manipulative judgment determines to a great extent the degree to which his sensory perception is developed. The lack of opportunities to express imaginative thoughts definitely curbs the development of his image-forming skills. This also adversely affects his perceptual growth. Because art experiences involve all of the learner's abilities, it is important to provide him with challenging opportunities which engage his skills early in life and which continue to do so in later years. It is well to bear in mind that *imagination* and *inventiveness are products of deep-rooted and habitual practice in creative thinking and acting.* In the words of Cecil V. Millard:

> Creative ability can develop and grow under proper stimulation and guidance, particularly during the child's early years. Creative skill, like any other, lends itself to improvement. There can be little doubt that had a tradition of inventiveness been in vogue in place of the tradition of

FIG. 6-9. "We Made Portraits of our Teacher." Second grade students convey a sensitivity to the various moods of their teacher.

FIG. 6-10. "I Feed the Chickens on Grandpa's Farm" (age seven, second grade). Student's reaction to responsibility.

FIG. 6-11. "Mother Takes Care of Me When I Am Sick" (age ten, fourth grade). Student expresses her feelings of comfort, warmth, and security.

mastery, schools today would be far better able to serve the needs of children and adults [2].

OBSERVING THE BEHAVIOR PATTERNS OF THE LEARNER IN THE CREATIVE PROCESS

It should be noted that, in the things that the learner creates, he discovers his own and new worlds in which his sphere of influence is boundless. In this process he brings into play his fantasies and his manipulative skills. He utilizes the learnings he acquired, including the use of tools, materials, and processes. He projects insights and concepts in the syntax of ideas which he creates. He invents his own graphic symbols for self-expression, and he structures these in two- or three-dimensional space. As he matures, his symbols increase in number. His ideas become more complex. His skill in structuring ideas increases. His ability to utilize new media and new techniques also develops.

RECOGNIZING INSTABILITIES AND EMOTIONAL CONFLICTS THROUGH THE CREATIVE PROCESS

While art experiences serve as an index to the learner's imaginative and inventive skills, in the creative process, they also communicate his innermost thoughts and feelings to others. These not only express his

FIG. 6-12. "We Visited the Cemetery on Armistice Day" (age six, second grade). Student expresses his reaction to a national holiday.

Fig. 6-13. "The Little Dog Made Tricks in the Circus" (sixth grade). A twelve-year-old boy expresses his sensitivity to animal forms and an appreciation for animal skill in performance.

reactions to his environment or to his personal fantasies, but also divulge instabilities, emotional conflicts, and often unwholesome attitudes. To the trained observer, this is a source of communicative value [3]. A person's artistic product constitutes an inexhaustible reservoir for penetrating judgment concerning the learner's personality. Close observation of the learner in the creative process may also reveal pertinent data concerning his working habits, particularly as he develops his ideas, step by step, through the initiating, developing, and culminating stages of an art experience. Insight into his creative thought processes may be gained by observing the manner of approach which he chooses in order to resolve the problem at hand, i.e., the plan of action, the symbols he selects to articulate his ideas, and the methods he employs to organize his tangible and intangible thoughts. All of these are elements of interest which offer implicit data for critical assessment of the learner's perceptual growth and the growth of creative learning patterns.

The concepts the learner has about himself, his environment, his interests, and motivations, his fears and joys, his needs and desires, his reactions to his peers, to adults, to his own and to community activities, to imagined and contrived ideas, and to every aspect of life often become clearly apparent through his art experiences. As the learner matures, other manifestations of his conscious world appear. Among these are: an increased interest in social events, a critical awareness of the adult world and adult behavior, a desire to achieve technical skill in the solution of creative problems, and an eager responsiveness to new and varied media, methods, and processes.

Figures 6-2 through 6-13 suggest a number of clues which may be of interest and of value in appreciating the learner's reactions to his world. These represent varied stages of perceptual development.

NOTES

1. Conrad Fiedler, *On Judging Works of Visual Art.* Berkeley and Los Angeles: University of California Press, 1949, pp. 1–26.

2. Cecil V. Millard, *Child Growth and Development in the Elementary School Years.* Boston: D. C. Heath & Co., 1958, pp. 174–206.

3. Warning: One has to be very careful not to read too much into a few of one individual's art works. Clinical psychology students learn this the hard way in projective testing courses and during their clinical practicums and internships, by finding that their interpretations of a few observations more often than not lead in the wrong therapeutic directions. Unfortunately, artists do not have this sobering experience and are liable to overinterpret a limited sample of a person's art work.

READING REFERENCES

Alschuler, Rose H., and Hattwick, Laberta W., *A Study of Painting and Personality of Young Children.* Chicago: University of Chicago Press, 2 vols, 1947.

Barkan, Manuel, *A Foundation for Art Education.* New York: The Ronald Press Co., 1955.

———, *Through Art to Creativity.* Boston: Allyn and Bacon, Inc., 1960.

Conant, Howard, and Randall, Arne, *Art in Education.* Peoria, Ill.: Charles A. Bennett Company, Inc., 1959.

DeFrancesco, Italo L., *Art Education, Its Means and Ends.* New York: Harper and Brothers, 1958.

Dewey, John, *Experience and Education.* New York: The Macmillan Co., 1954.

Fiedler, Conrad, *On Judging Works of Visual Art.* Berkeley and Los Angeles: University of California Press, 1949.

Gaitskell, Charles D., *Children and Their Art.* Harcourt, Brace & Co., Inc., 1958.

Jefferson, Blanche, *Teaching Art to Children.* Boston: Allyn and Bacon, Inc., 1959.

Lowenfeld, Viktor, *The Nature of Creative Activity.* London: Routledge and Kegan Paul, Ltd., 1939.

Millard, Cecil V., *Child Growth and Development in the Elementary School Years.* Boston: D. C. Heath & Co., 1958.

Munro, Thomas, *Art Education, Its Philosophy and Psychology.* New York: The Liberal Arts Press, 1956.

Read, Herbert, *Education Through Art.* New York: Pantheon Books, Inc., 1945.

Schaefer-Simmern, Henry, *The Unfolding of Artistic Activity*, 2d ed. Berkeley and Los Angeles: University of California Press, 1950.

Yochim, Louise Dunn, *Building Human Relationships Through Art.* Chicago: L. M. Stein, Publisher, 1954.

7 Attitudes and Values are Revealed to the Perceptive Teacher

How frequently in the never-ending discussions about the relative merits of environment and heredity in the life of man has it been said that "no man is born into a vacuum." And how often the errors and the achievements of man have been attributed to one or to both of these forces. Few have questioned the fact that external circumstances play a dynamic role in the shaping of the human personality. It is reasoned that an individual is born into a world which is structured by doctrines, practices, and customs—long established and transmitted from generation to generation. To these he is expected to comply and to conform to the traditionally prescribed patterns of behavior. He is also expected to make adjustments to his ever-present and ever-changing environment. Indeed, his very survival depends upon his skill in maintaining an equilibrium between the conflicting forces which persistently harass him. But this is no less true of any other living organism. Certainly, "one of the basic generalizations of the biological sciences is that the activities of a living organism tend to vary in response to the changing conditions of its environment. It must modify its response to meet the changes brought about by its environment. As long as it continues to adjust, it survives. But if it fails to adjust in some degree, its existence is imperiled"[1].

In matters of adjustment, however, man's problems are inconceivably greater than those of other living organisms. All too often, his metamorphosis occurs through self-imposed restraint of impulses with which he was endowed at birth. And, while these restraints generate internal strife, in this process they also help to mold the human personality. For as man's problems are ultimately and rationally resolved, he gains in significant values. For instance, a child at first is puzzled, but soon he learns to function in a world of contradictions, of divergent and incongruous forces, which somehow operate and manage to coexist. It

FIG. 7-1. Through creative expression J.A.'s fears and tensions found a release and gave way to self-confidence and personal fulfillment.

cannot be denied that the magnitude of self-restraint is often overwhelming. Indeed, it places extraordinary stress upon the human being as he is struggling to grow and particularly when internal drives enter into the process of self-adjustment. But, despite the difficulties involved, it must be recognized that these forces constitute life itself, and, as such, they are necessary elements that normally condition the individual to all facets of life.

What are the major areas of life to which it is necessary to adjust? A child is born into a family to which he must adjust. He is also born into a community of which he must become an integral part. He inherits a religion to which he must adhere, and by its precepts he must live. He inherits a form of government, and, finally, a universe. Admittedly, these are areas which call for unfailing and consistent attention on the part of the child and most certainly on the part of those who are concerned with his development. How then does the child react to the life into which he is born and to which he is expected to adjust? What are his ideas about his role in a strange world? How does he react to the incongruities which permeate his culture? What values seem significant to him? How does he view the adult and adult values?

THE PERCEPTIVE TEACHER

Insights into these questions about adjustment, and many other vital questions concerning the learner, may be gained through a careful study of his creative expressions. But it must be firmly stated here that the highly developed perceptual skill of the classroom teacher is a significant

Fig. 7-2. In time, J.A.'s work revealed a spark of freshness and spontaneity, expressive of the inner freedom
that he himself had begun to feel.

and indispensable factor in the process of achieving an understanding of the learner.

It might be interesting to recall a situation which illustrates this point. In a fourth grade room of an urban elementary school, a class of nine-year-olds was asked to draw some of the things which they did during

FIG. 7-3. "Celebrating Christmas in Mexico" (tempera
painting by Mexican boy aged fourteen). An adolescent's
account of his cultural heritage.

the past weekend. Having been exposed to the usual process of motivation or stimulation, the children recorded their experiences. At the end of
the lesson they displayed their drawings in front of the room. Some
drawings were done in paint, while others were done in chalk on manila
paper. In studying these paintings, it was noticed that most of the children
recorded experiences such as: bicycle riding, picnicking, going to the zoo,
the farm, the art museum, the flower conservatory, the woods, to church,
to a wedding, riding in daddy's new car, watching television, roller skating, and visiting grandmother—all of which represented happy experiences. But this observer's interest was particularly drawn to one painting
which was contrasting in mood and unusually drab in color. It represented an area painted in black upon which lay an elongated mass of white
color, which faintly suggested a human form. The classroom teacher had
completely ignored this painting. She felt that it lacked interest, that it
was just a mass of color, and drab color at that. She also felt that it said
nothing. The youngster was then called upon to tell the story which

FIG. 7-4. "We Take Turns on the Playground" (tempera painting, second grade). Painting reveals a seven-year old's awareness of his social responsibility, indicative of wholesome attitudes that are developing early in life.

FIG. 7-5. "Friendliness at Lake Street and Western Avenue" (tempera painting). A seven-year-old boy reveals a sensitivity to human relations.

inspired the painting, and she did. "That is a coffin, and this is my Mom," the little girl explained tearfully as she pointed to the painting. "She died Saturday."

One did not dare to ask much more. "I had no idea," said the teacher, rather shocked, "that this had happened to her. She has been moody all day, wouldn't recite and wouldn't do her seatwork. I was too busy with the other children to be able to find out, though I wondered why she acted that way."

Then, turning to the girl, the teacher inquired, "Why didn't you tell us about it, Gloria?" The little girl shrugged her shoulders and silently returned to her seat [2].

Aside from revealing the deeply felt emotions of children, creative experiences often divulge information about the environmental factors of a community. These factors, if utilized in the planning of a well-integrated school program, can be of inestimable value in determining the causes of attitudes and behavior patterns of children. They can also reveal the interests, and the needs of the children in a community. For instance, from this art lesson, it was possible to conclude that these children came from a middleclass socioeconomic level; that their parents were interested in exposing them to cultural and recreational activities; that they were financially able to purchase cars, television sets, and bicycles; that they attended elaborate weddings and had enough leisure

FIG. 7-6. "With Liberty and Justice for All" (tempera painting). An eight-year-old boy expresses a democratic ideal.

FIG. 7-7. "My Neighborhood from the School Window" (tempera painting, age fourteen, eighth grade). A student's sensitive reaction to her drab and colorless environment.

FIG. 7-8. "An Evening at Home" (tempera painting, age thirteen, eighth grade). A student's reaction to family life at home.

FIG. 7-9. "I Hate to Clean House" (tempera painting, age thirteen, eighth grade). A student's expression of a negative attitude toward home responsibility.

time to enjoy museums, flower shows, picnics, and other cultural and social events. Apparently, emphasis was placed upon wholesome family living through participation in activities involving the whole family. The home environment, in general, was such that it provided an atmosphere conducive to the building of admirable social behavior patterns. Those were general observations. Upon closer analysis of each drawing, however, it was possible to determine more about the children's individual personalities.

Some youngsters seemed highly inhibited in their attempts at pictorial expression. Whether it was the fear of the medium or the fear of failure that thwarted them in their efforts was hard to tell. Their drawings were tight, small, meticulous, and precise. As the teacher later revealed, these youngsters came from very strict homes where rigid discipline was constantly enforced. Drawings from other classes communicated a freedom of expression, uninhibited, creative, and exciting. The latter groups of children were exposed to a number of after-school activities.   They studied dancing, music, and art.   They were also permitted to travel long distances by themselves.   Being accustomed to performance, they seemed self-sufficient, confident, and generally more expressive.

It is not difficult, therefore, to imagine what the results could bring if this type of painting lesson were presented to students whose experiences were rather limited in scope, and whose unfortunate circumstances constituted misery, hunger, and ill health.   They would be less inclined to tell about "going to the museum" or "riding in daddy's new car."   Their creative expressions would probably include episodes such as "fighting in the alley," "shooting dice," "stealing food," or "running away from the cops."   A great deal can be learned about students from paintings such as these.   Insights thus gained into the established patterns of student behavior and into the environmental influences in personality development can be most valuable in understanding the pupil and his individual needs.

ART EXPERIENCES; VALUABLE CLUES TO PUPIL GUIDANCE

The processes involved in personality development are indeed complex.   Admittedly, they are contingent upon many contributing factors among which heredity and environment play a dominant role.   Learning experiences, however, constitute an extremely significant and dynamic

Fig. 7-10. "The Family Picnic" (tempera painting, age thirteen, eighth grade).   A student's reaction to a leisure-time activity involving the whole family.

FIG. 7-11. "We Visited the Art Museum" (tempera painting, age thirteen, seventh grade). A student's reaction to a cultural activity and to contemporary trends in art.

FIG. 7-12. "Skating Is Fun" (tempera painting, age thirteen, eighth grade). A student's reaction to a leisure-time activity involving his peers.

Fig. 7-13. "At the Ball Game" (tempera painting, age thirteen, seventh grade). A student's reaction to a sport activity. Attention is focused upon food rather than the game.

force which acts upon and helps to mold the learner's personality. Through learning experiences, the learner's individual differences in abilities, skills, and capacities are cultivated. In the educative process, therefore, individual differences are fundamental, and they demand special consideration. In the realm of art education in particular, individual differences are fully recognized, primarily because *art education is dedicated to the preservation of the distinctly unique qualities inherent in each human being.* Because a great deal about the learner is revealed through creative experiences, this information becomes an infinite source of clues to the understanding of his innermost feelings, attitudes, values, hopes, and aspirations and therefore a valuable aid to guidance.

The following case studies illustrate poignantly how creative expressions of students can offer clues to their most intimate feelings, and correspondingly to their overt behavior, as well as their needs.

Case Study of A.B.   A.B. was a boy of sixteen whose drawings, time after time, portrayed the sensuous types of women. He frequently exaggerated the form of the female figure to such a degree that it made little difference whether it was clothed or not. Invariably, he included men with guns shooting at one another or shooting at policemen. Physically, A.B. seemed more mature than his classmates were; his drawings disclosed a great interest in the opposite sex, in crime, and in sordid matters.

Because of the nature of his art work, and the fact that he had been out of school for a few weeks, it became necessary to consult with him. One of the things brought out in the consultation was that he had been in jail some time ago. He would not admit why he had been there, but he did say that it was because of some girl. "It was all her fault. I hate cops, and dames," he asserted.

A.B. also admitted that he disliked school; that the only reason he came to school once in a while was because he "liked to draw." He would rather draw than do anything else, he said. He had no use for his other subjects, and, to avoid having unpleasant incidents with his teachers, he decided to stay away from their classes.

Fig. 7-14. "Getting Ready for the Race" (tempera painting, age twelve, seventh grade). A sensitive rendering of animal forms by a twelve-year-old boy who is deeply impressed with the size and beauty of the horses.

Notwithstanding all this, it was interesting to learn that there was something A.B. *did* like among the many things which he professed to dislike intensely.

The character of his art work, his hostile attitude toward the police, the opposite sex, and the school authorities, presented ample evidence that A.B. was in need of immediate help. But, in view of the fact that he expressed an interest in art, his art teacher was designated to handle the situation. She therefore proceeded to use A.B.'s interest as a point of departure. His program was so arranged that he could be under her supervision four periods daily. During these periods, A.B. designed stage scenery for all school performances. He painted large streamers and posters which were displayed in the halls to publicize the sport events of the year. He constructed props and booths and stands for art displays. In brief, he painted profusely and also gave help to others upon request.

It seemed that through these projects, A.B. received a great deal of personal satisfaction. His skill was frequently admired by his friends. His work was highly publicized in the school and community newspapers. As he gained in prestige, he realized that his efforts contributed immeasurably to the welfare of the school, and his daily presence in school was of utmost importance. Gradually his attendance improved. In time, his school work, and his attitude toward school authority also improved. Consequently, he became a much happier individual than he had been in the past. His hatred for "cops" and "dames" was seldom mentioned again.

FIG. 7-15. "Those Big Shears Looked Dangerous" (age thirteen, seventh grade). A student reveals her concern for pet.

It would not have been possible to achieve these results without first becoming aware of the nature of A.B.'s art work. Through it was realized the need for redirecting his energies and guiding his thinking toward wholesome interests. His drawings, unlike his verbal or written attempts at expression, provided A.B. with an excellent medium for communicating his thoughts and feelings to others without the fear of being reprimanded. Indeed, there are some things about which every adolescent is concerned and which he hesitates to disclose to those in authority.

Case Study of B.C.   B.C. was a girl of sixteen who kept to herself

FIG. 7-16. "I Told the Police Where I Saw My Boyfriend Drown" (tempera painting, age thirteen, seventh grade). A student's sensitive account of tragedy.

and seldom mingled with her classmates. She was extremely quiet and reticent. She drew very well, but was unusually slow in completing her work. That in itself would not have been a disturbing factor, but she kept going over her drawings, again and again, adding little or nothing toward their improvement. Her approach to pictorial expression led one to believe that she was deeply concerned about some problem. To be sure it was not her art work. Since she did not divulge her feelings to the teacher, she simply withdrew into her own little world, daydreaming and "pushing" her pencil aimlessly about.

B.C.'s unexerted efforts in the art class, however, led the teacher to arrange for a conference with her in order to investigate the reasons behind her passive behavior. The conference disclosed: 1) that B.C. was not working up to her usual capacity, not only in the art class, but also not in any of her other classes, and 2) that she was thinking seriously of leaving school in order to go to work. She stated that she wanted to be "independent."

"I don't care for school, anyway! I am tired of being bossed around by everyone, even at home; and I'm sick of it all!" she concluded.

B.C.'s unexpected outburst startled the teacher. It was in strong contrast to her usual retiring and quiet manner in the classroom. This "pouring out" of her feelings, however, seemed good. It released her pent-up emotions. It also paved the way for further discussion. Suddenly she seemed ready and willing to receive the sympathetic counsel of her teacher. It was then agreed to call B.C.'s parents in for an interview in order to help bring about a satisfactory solution to her problems. Since B.C.'s father worked during the day, the mother came to school.

"I want my daughter to go to work," she stated firmly. "My daughter is causing me too much trouble. She runs around with boys 'til all hours of the night and acts like a tramp. She wouldn't have time for them bums if she got a fulltime job during the day and went to evening school after work."

Though mother's reaction seemed justifiable, obviously, her approach caused resentment on the part of B.C. To the teacher it became clearly apparent that any successful solution to this problem would have to overcome the mutually expressed hostilities of both mother and daughter.

The teacher than proceeded to give the mother many reasons why it would be unwise for B.C. to leave school, particularly at this time when she lacked only one year toward graduation. Instead, the teacher suggested that B.C. find part-time employment after school. This, she explained, would enable B.C. to graduate with her friends and would result in giving her the desired "independence" as well. After much discussion, both mother and daughter agreed to accept the teacher's advice, and the conference finally ended satisfactorily.

Fig. 7-17. "My Dog Spilled Ink on Our New Rug" (age thirteen, seventh grade). A student's sensitive reaction to the feelings of her pet.

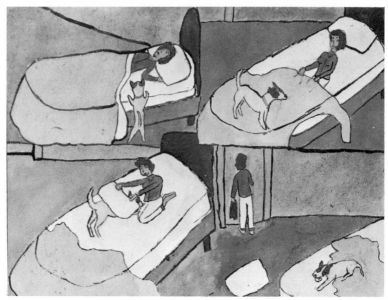

FIG. 7-18. "How I Awaken Each Morning" (tempera painting by thirteen-year-old). A student's account of a "rude" awakening.

With the help of the art teacher, B.C. found part-time employment, coloring photographs of lamps. As B.C. had little experience in this field, she was given additional help during study periods and after school hours daily. Through this help, she acquired greater confidence in her ability and the self-assurance which she needed badly. With added courage and faith in herself, she began to demonstrate greater enthusiasm for her work in school. Her interest in her personal appearance also increased, since her income permitted her to dress more attractively.   She gracefully acknowledged the admiring remarks of her classmates and developed friendly relationships with them.   As a result of the newly developed friendships, she became a sociable individual.   She appeared no longer dissatisfied with school.

Case Study of J.A.   J.A., a Japanese boy of fifteen, came to the art class one day, selected the last seat in the last row, and proceeded to draw. He was a clean-cut boy and appeared very shy and frightened.   He seldom spoke to anyone and left the impression that he did not wish to be disturbed. Since he usually did more work than was required of him, he demanded little of the teacher's attention.   However, a month elapsed and still J.A. had said nothing more than "Yes, ma'am" or "No, ma'am" to his teacher.   He seldom asked questions.   He never got out of his seat, unless to get some water for his painting.   Although teachers are often thankful for quiet pupils such as J.A., nevertheless, it seemed strange for a normal and healthy adolescent to behave that way, because, after children had been in an art class for one month, they had come to realize that a certain amount of freedom was generally permissible.

One day J.A. was asked by his teacher why he did not request help when he felt that he needed it. His reply was direct, "I'm afraid," he said. "But why are you afraid?" she inquired. "I don't know," was his answer.

It became obvious then that J.A. was imbued with certain fears and inhibitions. He did not dare to be like others. But, knowing something of the rigidly disciplined culture of his people, it seemed natural to attribute his behavior to that. However, J.A. had been born in the United States. Therefore, it seemed inconceivable that he should not wish to exercise the freedom which was rightfully his.

Subsequently, a study of J.A.'s paintings was made in the hope of finding some clues to the underlying causes for his fears. It was found that in most of his paintings he included beautiful sunsets. Whatever he painted revealed an unusual rendering of textures. He painted the desert

FIG. 7-19. "My Grandmother at Prayer." Religious and moving, a deeply moving portrayal of poverty and prayer, rendered by a fifteen-year-old boy.

FIG. 7-20. "My Father Enjoys Fishing" (by a four-teen-year-old). A student's reaction to adult be-havior is clearly manifested in this rather sketchy but highly perceptual rendering of an idea.

profusely, including mountains and all types of desert growth. He seemed to be very familiar with the structure of these things and painted them with the intimate knowledge of one who might have lived in the West. Upon further inquiry, of course, it was discovered that he came from Arizona, where he experienced many hardships. Unfortunately, his had been one of many Japanese families interned in camps during World War II.

When the family came to Chicago, J.A. enrolled in a public high school. At first, as one might gather, he appeared tense and confused, not knowing exactly how to accept the friendliness which was extended to him. He seemed cautious and fearful and very difficult to reach. Obviously, he needed to gain the assurance that here he had found friends who wished to guide and to help him. The deeply rooted barriers which prevented the teacher from reaching him needed to be broken.

He was, therefore, given many opportunities to participate in social and creative activities. He was encouraged to take an active part in the art council, art assemblies, and art exhibits. On these occasions, he was able to socialize in a creative atmosphere to which he contributed much of his own talent. Through these and other art experiences, he learned to have confidence in himself and in others. He gradually released his fears and inhibitions. He became more talkative and asked for advice more frequently. In time, his behavior in class was more nearly like the behavior of other adolescents of his age. Before long, his tensions gave way to free and unrestrained expression. His work began to show a spontaneity and freshness expressive of the freedom which he himself was beginning to feel.

J.A. was later graduated from school with honors and was awarded a scholarship to the Art Institute of Chicago.

Case Study of M.N. Pan-Americanism was stressed in the schools a number of years ago. In the art class many discussions were held about the people of the South and Central Americas in order to acquaint the students with the customs and cultural contributions of these countries. The acquired information was intended to build a general background for painting experiences which were to follow later.

M.N., a boy of fourteen, was called upon to tell the class what he thought were the cultural contributions of his people. He rose and made a simple statement which left the class in an uproar. "The Mexicans," he said, "are dumb. I hate them. They don't know nothin'."

"Are you serious about your answer?" M.N. was asked. In a very positive manner, he replied, "Yes, they're dumb because all they do is work on the peanut plantations, on the potato farms, in coal mines, or in gasoline stations. What could they contribute?" he concluded with vehemence.

This was obviously the kind of an answer none expected from M.N. Apparently, he felt very unhappy about being of Mexican origin. By belittling himself and his people, he hoped to gain some sympathy from his classmates. Judging from the outburst of laughter which he provoked by his statements, however, the contrary was being achieved. His classmates thought it was rather peculiar and very amusing that M.N., of all people, should come forth with a statement such as this.

In the light of this uproar, it became evident that quick action was needed. The class was immediately divided into committees to do research on the cultural contributions of Mexico. Each of the committees was given time to prepare and to bring clippings, prints, and literature on the painting, sculpture, architecture, and minor arts of Mexico. Serapes, jewelry, glassware, masks, woodcarvings, and pottery were to be borrowed for class use.

When all of the material was finally gathered, many students from other classes came to view the display. In the classroom much discussion

FIG. 7-21. "This Is the Life" (tempera painting, by a fifteen-year old).
An adolescent student portrays a leisure activity against a background
of detail, disclosing his keen perceptual skill. He also reveals a wholesome attitude toward the use of leisure time.

was given to the beauty and color of the land, its architecture, its mag-
nificent churches, its museums, its universities, its art schools, its murals
and paintings, its minor arts, and its great artists, Diego Rivera, José
Clemente Orozco, and Siqueiros.

Later, movies were shown on the land of Mexico and its craftsmen at
work. It was interesting to note the reactions of M.N. during this learning
experience. Although he said nothing, his eyes were sparkling with
genuine pride. At the end of the vicarious trip to Mexico, he was heard
to say: "You know, I never knew so much about my people. It sure was
interesting!" Just then, a very pleasant and satisfied smile appeared on
his face. His head was turned to a side as if to say, "That was quite a
revelation." As he stood there when the bell rang, one of his classmates
approached him with, "Well M.N., what do you think of Mexicans now?"
M.N. replied by placing his thumbs under his armpits, sticking his chest
out proudly, "I guess we Mexicans are pretty good! It's not a bad idea to
get acquainted with yourself, once in a while." The painting lesson
followed the next period, and M.N., like the other students, gave a good
account of himself.

Thus ended the lesson on Mexico. One had the feeling that this
class gained much in terms of appreciation for the accomplishments of the
Mexican people. Moreover, to M.N. was given that much needed feeling

of belonging to, or being associated with, a group which was admired and appreciated by all.

Volumes can be written about the analysis of conflicts of maladjusted pupils through art, but that is not the aim at this point.   Attention is merely being directed to the existing possibilities for human understanding made available through art experiences. This method of tapping the source of personal material has not as yet been fully explored by educators. Psychologists, however, are well aware of the importance of this medium of expression. They often employ this means of obtaining additional information about the needs of children or adults.

NOTES

1. Louise Dunn Yochim, *Building Human Relationships Through Art.* Chicago: L. M. Stein, Publisher, 1954, p. 138.
2. *Ibid.*, pp. 2–16.
3. *Ibid.*, Chapters II and IV, pp. 63–98.

READING REFERENCES

Alschuler, Rose H., and Hattwick, Laberta W., *A Study of Painting and Personality of Young Children.* Chicago: University of Chicago Press, 2 vols., 1947.

Bannon, Laura, *Mind Your Child's Art.* New York: Pelligrini and Cudahy, 1952.

Cane, Florence, *The Artist in Each of Us.* New York: Pantheon Books, Inc., 1951.

Dewey, John, *Art as Experience.* New York: Minton, Balch & Co., 1934.

Dunnett, Ruth, *Art and Child Personality.* London: Methuen & Co., Ltd., 1940, p. 45.

Gaitskell, Charles D., *Children and Their Pictures.* Toronto: The Ryerson Press, 1951.

Gessell, Arnold L., and Ilg, Frances L., *The Infant and Child in the Culture of Today.* New York: Harper and Brothers, 1943.

Goodenough, Florence L., *Children's Drawings, A Handbook of Child Psychology.* Worcester, Mass.: Clark University Press, 1931.

Lowenfeld, Viktor, *Creative and Mental Growth*, 3d ed. New York: The Macmillan Co., 1957.

———, *Your Child and His Art.* New York: The Macmillan Co., 1954.

Mendelowitz, Daniel M., *Children Are Artists.*   Stanford, Calif.: Stanford University Press, 1954.

Munro, Thomas, *Art Education, Its Philosophy and Psychology.* New York: The Liberal Arts Press, 1956.

Schaefer-Simmern, Henry, *The Unfolding of Artistic Activity*, 2d ed. Berkeley and Los Angeles: University of California Press, 1950.

Yochim, Louise Dunn, *Building Human Relationships Through Art.* Chicago: L. M. Stein, Publisher, 1954.

Ziegfeld, Ernest, ed., *Human Values in A Democracy*, Art and Human Values, 1953 Yearbook. Kutztown, Pa.: National Art Education Association, 1953.

8

A Critical Study of Children's Paintings in Terms of Perceptual Growth

This chapter is devoted entirely to a critical investigation of fifteen paintings which were done by children of all ages and grade levels. The paintings are representative selections from more than six thousand creative expressions which have been carefully examined, screened, classified, analyzed, and assessed by the author. The total number of paintings examined were painted by children of different ethnic, racial, religious, and cultural origins; also, of varied socioeconomic levels. These paintings were collected by the author in the process of improving instruction in art throughout the varied school districts in an urban community. More than two hundred elementary and high schools were thus represented.

As a result of this critical screening of paintings some seemingly pertinent conclusions were drawn:

1) In those schools where a tradition of creative activity has been firmly established, from kindergarten through high school, the level of perceptual skill and artistic performance was usually high. In those schools where there was a lack of interest on the part of the administration and teachers, the level of performance was very low, or practically nil.

2) It is possible to establish general criteria which serve to identify the norm in perceptual growth at any developmental stage.

3) There is a high degree of correlation between academic achievement and creative "thinking" and "doing." In 90% of the cases checked during a period of fifteen years, the "gifted" art student performed well in Science, Social Studies, and Language Arts, but not necessarily so well in mathematics or other highly disciplined areas of the curriculum which required mathematical skill.

EVALUATIVE CRITERIA USED IN THIS STUDY

1) Was the student's creative expression highly imaginative or un-imaginative or imaginative?

2) Did the student express concepts and visual forms in his environment in depth or superficially?

3) Has a conscious effort been made to express emotions, feelings, and reactions to external and internal stimuli or to problems of life that are uniquely significant to the student, to his peers, and to the adult world?

4) Did the painting reveal a keen sensitivity to line, form, color, texture, and space relationships in the resolution of creative thoughts?

5) Was the delineation of notional concepts unusual, average, or poor in its rendering?

With the above criteria in mind, the collected paintings were classified.

PROCEDURE IN CONDUCTING THE STUDY

All paintings which were collected for this study were placed into four major, but general, categories; namely, primary, intermediate, upper grades, and high school. The paintings in each of these categories were also classified into three distinct groups such as: the "perceptually above average," "perceptually average," and "perceptually poor."

The "perceptually poor" paintings were so designated because they showed a decided lack of thought or imagination. They were devoid of detail, lacked feeling and sensitivity to form, color, line, texture, space, or to environmental factors.

The "perceptually average," which constituted the largest group of paintings, showed a decided interest in expressing action, feelings, and reactions to visual forms and to the surrounding environment. Not in-frequently, thought-provoking ideas were expressed which revealed the students' awareness of visual images in a related setting. These were not necessarily delineated with exceptional skill, i.e., the kind that is usually attributed to the "gifted" student.

Paintings which were classified in the "perceptually above average" group were undoubtedly representative of the "gifted" students. They were indicative of the students' unusual conceptual ability and of their skill in organizing thoughts visually in a given space. They expressed a keen awareness of environmental factors. They reflected technical skill in the depicted images. They showed a genuine concern for detail and a decided interest in filling the space with carefully delineated and well thought-out ideas.

For the purpose of this study, however, it was decided to examine critically the largest group of paintings, i.e., the art work which has been classified as "perceptually average." Subsequently, this group of paintings was divided according to grade and age levels. This was done in order to enable the author to identify more accurately those characteristics which typified aesthetic and perceptual growth at each age and grade level. From each level, several paintings were then selected for critical study in this chapter.

It should be noted also that, with the exception of the last one, "Moving into a New Apartment," none of the paintings selected for this study fall into the category of the so-called gifted. They simply point to a growing maturity in conceptual thinking, as well as in visual perception. The last painting, however, done by a "gifted" student, was included for the purpose of comparison and for contrast.

The detailed study of the following paintings, therefore, reveals some significant findings. These include thought processes, feelings, reactions, emotions, and thematic schemes which "average" students expressed. Allowances were made for individual temperament. But, the paintings selected for this study represent what is generally accepted by art educators as the norm in artistic performance; i.e., the paintings are not necessarily unusual. This choice was made in order to enable the author to establish, and to relate with some degree of accuracy, the aesthetic and the perceptual qualities found in each painting; also, to see how and where these characteristics paralleled each stage of physical and mental development.

To those who have great faith in the scientific method of measuring progressive performance in art, it may be stated that artistic skill, in this author's opinion, is best judged visually by competent observers. Few tests have yet been devised which can measure successfully those intangible values that emanate from the never-ending interaction between the very essence of a living organism and its ever-changing experiential and physical world. Many intuitive factors enter into the creative process which cannot be adequately measured or explained by laws of science alone. If that were possible and if art were as exacting as other disciplines, the chances are that it would be less desirable as an area of expression through which man can give free play to his emotional, experimental, probing, inventive, and imaginative thoughts. True, intellectual variance significantly affects creative growth to a lesser or greater extent, but it is also a fact that excessive intellectualism in a work of art often defeats its original purpose. It amounts to an overextended and overly eloquent rationalization which destroys the spontaneity and dims the spark of an inherently disciplined intuitiveness which characterizes a truly imaginative statement.

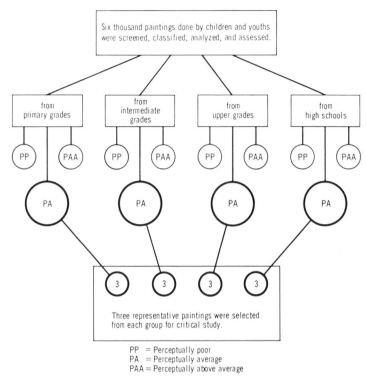

FIG. 8-1. A graphic representation of the procedure followed in the study of "growth in visual perception through painting experiences."

Other values which cannot be adequately measured can, nevertheless, be identified from empirical evidence. Worthy of note, for example, are the humanistic values, i.e., those which constitute the sensibilities, sensitivities, and feelings of compassion. Though intangible, these values are nevertheless important. They are made visible through art experiences perhaps more often than through any other learning experiences to which the learner is exposed. In the creative process, it must be recognized that competent observers can pinpoint, with a high degree of objectivity, evidence pertinent to value judgments and to conceptual and perceptual maturity. Under overly scientific methods of evaluation, these values can be easily overlooked. Often, this occurs at the expense of the individual's loss of opportunity to develop these intangible values through the only skill with which he has been endowed in life.

"**I Am Catching the Ball**" **(age five).**   In the painting, "I Am Catching the Ball" (Fig. 8-2), the child exaggerates the size of the arms; she stresses the importance of the function of the arms. The young artist is not yet conscious of the environment in which the picture takes place.

Random strokes in the background indicate an awareness of the need for filling the space to complete the statement but not necessarily with a particular setting.

The symbolic use of the figure (i.e., the use of a circle for the head, dots for the eyes, and line for the mouth, a triangle or square attached to a head for a female figure or long legs attached to the head for a male figure) is a typical representation of a human form by children in the primary grades (kindergarten, 1, and 2). The symbols change frequently and are not necessarily an attempt to imitate natural forms, i.e., people or animals. Rather, they are symbols which stand for a human form or animal.

The painting "I Am Catching the Ball" is not unusually creative. Some children at the age of five are more expressive; others are less so, having poor control of the brush and paint. But in the main, this painting is representative of the perceptual, manipulative, and imaginative skill at the early age of five. It should be noted, also, that here there is a definite attempt to introduce details, including facial expression, i.e., the smile and the buttons on the dress. The random strokes in the background could be birds or simple decorative strokes to fill the otherwise empty space in the background. The child is still unaware of a horizon line or a base line representing the foreground.

"Boats on Lake Michigan" (age six). In the painting "Boats on Lake Michigan" (Fig. 8-3), the child introduces the horizon line into the picture. This is not usually done at this age level. Variations in the sizes and shapes and details of boats, and the airplane flying above the boats, reveal a keen sense of observation on the part of this young child.

In this painting the child expresses a view which indicates relative distance. The boats in the foreground have been painted larger than those on the horizon line. Even the size, the color, or the number of portholes is varied. Some boats have chimneys; others do not. Only one boat in the background has smoke emanating from its chimney. Those boats which do not have chimneys indicate the child's awareness of structural differences in boats and in their particular functions. This kind of observation is usually attributed to boys who possess a variety of toy boats at home who become intimately familiar with the details of different types of boats through continuous involvement in play with them.

"Boats On Lake Michigan" indicates a growing sense of awareness of the child's environment and particularly of forms which appeal to his interests.

"The Nice Clown I Saw in the Circus" (age six). The child paints best the things which grow out of his personal experiences. In the painting "The Nice Clown I Saw in the Circus" (Fig. 8-4), the message is clearly conveyed. To this child the clown is the big, stout, jovial, and

FIG. 8-2. "I Am Catching the Ball" (age five).

FIG. 8-3. "Boats on Lake Michigan" (age six).

exciting personality—sympathetic and amusing. In this painting little concern is shown for the background because the child is fascinated by the details of the subject which is of utmost importance to him, namely, the clown. The facial features (the eyes, the bulbous nose, the heavy eyebrows, the cheeks, the broad smile); the small, pointed clown's hat perched on his bald head; the amusing patches of red hair on both sides of the clown's face; the striped pattern of his costume; the fingers (four) on the right hand holding balloons; and an umbrella in the left hand—all are indicative of a growing perceptual maturity and of the importance that the child attaches to a very essential character in his life. It will be noted that the ears have been completely ignored; they are obviously unessential in the child's concept of a clown.

The heavy area of color at the base of the painting represents the foreground, while the scalloped edges around the clown form, represent the stage. This child is obviously aware of a need for some sort of setting to surround the clown. It will also be noted that the arms of the clown are properly located. These do not emerge from the neck, as did those seen in an earlier illustration.

"I Am Going Home" (age six). In the painting "I Am Going Home" (Fig. 8-5), the child reveals the importance of the self in relation to his environment. Although conscious of some details in the figure, he seems more concerned with the things which he sees on his way home. Consequently, he gives a great deal of attention to those forms which seem significant to his story. He skillfully depicts the divided and the dotted roads to the right of his painting, one of which leads to his home. The dots may well represent stones, bricks, pebbles, or automobiles. The closed door, and the dark window in the background seem to float in the air, but these may be symbolic of objects which he passes on his way.

By contrast, his own house, beside which he stands as tall as the house itself, has well lighted windows. In the extreme lower left of this house is a rectangular space which he painted yellow. This may suggest that the door is wide open, and is well lit for him. The lamp in front of the house is also lit, implying the importance of that particular area near his home.

The self is symbolically interpreted. The neck, and the waistline were omitted. Stubs were used to indicate arms, which are seemingly unimportant in a walking activity. The legs were attached to the oval-shaped body and were somewhat more realistically painted than the arms. The feet were turned toward the house (in early Egyptian fashion). They suggest a walking position which function may account for the realistic representation of them.

The sun appears in the extreme upper right-hand corner, as it does in most paintings done by children at this age. Its massive rays, and one

FIG. 8-4. "The Nice Clown I Saw in the Circus" (age six).

FIG. 8-5. "I Am Going Home" (age six).

eye (for lack of space) typify the human qualities which children attribute to the sun.

"I Am Cleaning House" (age seven).   The painting "I Am Cleaning House" (Fig. 8-6), reveals the child's conceptual growth in the development of the figure, and its relationship to the environment in which the figure finds itself. A growing consciousness of detail is evident in the figure and in the background. The use of a correct number of fingers on the hands, a neck between shoulders and head, a waistline about the middle of the figure, a bow in the hair, and in the background the tables, the vases, the flowerpot and one blossom, the window with its curtains, as well as the decorative scallops which frame the composition—all are indicative of the child's growing perceptual ability and the skill in interpreting what she sees. Motion, another dimension important in the creative process, has been introduced in the exaggerated arms of the girl. Exaggerations are frequently manifestations of the importance which the child attaches to the function of particular parts of the human or animal form. This is especially true at the "early childhood" stage of physical development.

The space has been well filled with sufficient content, indicating a growing awareness of the self and the manner in which the self relates to its environmental setting.

"My Friend and I" (age seven).   The animal is "the friend" pictured in a massive and elongated manner in the painting "My Friend and I" (Fig. 8-7). Teacher guidance is clearly apparent here. The stress was laid upon space filling. This was interpreted by the child to mean "tall" from "baseline" to "skyline." At the primary level, children often express these by two lines of color—blue for the sky, and green for the grass or brown for ground. It may be of interest to note that in this particular class, all children drew their figures, animals and trees in elongated rubberlike fashion. Obviously, there had been an overemphasis upon the word "tall."

However, the tender, gentle, and happy expression on the face of the slightly tilted head of the figure is expressive of the warm feelings that most children have for their pets. The frightened looking figure in the background may be a younger playmate who seems overwhelmed by the size of the animal.

The clouds, the trees, and the flowers are details which reveal an awareness of the setting in which the episode takes place and a clear manifestation of growth in visual perception.

"My Sister Is Riding on My Bike" (age eight).   The painting "My Sister is Riding On My Bike" (Fig. 8-8), represents a spirited interpretation of an activity which projects a feeling that the "big brother" has complete control of the situation. The "kid sister" is clinging close to him

FIG. 8-6. "I Am Cleaning House" (age seven).

FIG. 8-7. "My Friend and I" (age seven).

as usual. The heavy brush strokes emanating from his head represent his blowing hair, since he is seemingly riding very fast. Mother and father are following but not interfering. One senses a pride of achievement in the sitting position of the "big brother." In this painting, as in others previously described, the sun assumes the smiling characteristics of a human being. The tree is abounding with apples. Altogether, the painting reflects the spirit of a happy family relationship. It also reveals a growing sense of observation on the part of the student.

In this painting a great amount of detail has been added. A keen understanding of the bicycle's structure is revealed here; also, an unusual skill in the rendering of the tree form. The human forms are far less maturely expressed than the tree and the bicycle.

"Praying in Church" (age nine). In the painting "Praying In Church" (Fig. 8-9), the student obviously arrived at a definite concept in the handling of the figure, which she used repeatedly with confidence throughout her composition. She has also captured the essence of movement as indicated by the kneeling rubberlike legs and the raised encircling arms, showing little concern for realism in either case. Here, too, the observer has been given an unusual view of the church interior; particularly as one looks down at the altar, upon the kneeling figures, the stairs, and the flickering lights of the candles at the extreme right. This student's rendition of the church is rather unique in that it does not express the somber, spiritual concept which an adult would generally associate with the interior of a church. Rather, it expresses a happy and colorful experience, judging from the playful patterns in the clothes of the worshipers, and the smiling priest in the background. Abstract patterns of stained-glass windows and crosses create interest in the background and in the skillfully broken spatial areas of the stairs which lead to the altar. These represent different levels of height and varied decorative treatment of surfaces.

One is deeply impressed with this nine-year-old's perceptual ability, and, at the same time, one is aware of the fact that she is very much a part of the function which she has so skillfully depicted in the painting. This student was a recent arrival from Puerto Rico.

"Christmas Morning" (age ten). The painting "Christmas Morning" (Fig. 8-10) is delightful in its treatment of the Christmas theme. It conveys with childish enthusiasm the excitement of Christmas morning. The amount of detail recorded by this ten-year-old is a clear manifestation of a high degree of perceptual skill. The drawing is particularly good in the position of the arms and in the rendering of hands since, to this student, these apparently play an important role in the process of giving gifts. Exaggerated emphasis is placed upon the smiles of those who are actively engaged in giving as well as of those who are eagerly awaiting

Fig. 8-8. "My Sister Is Riding on My Bike" (age eight).

Fig. 8-9. "Praying in Church" (age nine).

the receiving of gifts.   The background areas are given considerable thought.   Bricks are suggested in the treatment of the fireplace holding three logs.   Stockings adorn its facade, while candleholders with candles and bells appear above it.   Through the window one sees heavily falling snow, leaving no doubt in the observer's mind as to what the season of the year might be.   Suspended in the air, upon the window, is the symbolic wreath bespeckled with mistletoe.   A large Christmas tree stands on the floor, and a small one is placed upon what appears to be a piano.

The family unit seems most significant to this child, judging from the size and placement of the group.   Dad stands smiling in the background.   The oldest child in the family distributes the gifts to her sisters and brothers.   The restless baby brother is held by its mother, who is also standing in the background.   Everyone seems to be smiling with the exception of the second child from the left, who appears overwhelmed and surprised by the number of gifts she has received from the entire family.   The expression in her eyes betrays her feelings.   The younger sister and brother eagerly await their turn in line.   All arms are busily engaged— legs less so, although they are drawn in an active position.   Each figure expresses the excitement and the joy which this particular morning brings to the whole family.

"Do We Have Fun Skating!" (age eleven).   Uninhibited and with unusual vigor and gusto, this youngster expresses in Fig. 8-11 her idea of skating.   Action, movement, and speed are depicted with an amazing amount of feeling, and almost violent handling of brush strokes.   The excitement of skating penetrates the very soul of the observer.   It is revealed in every inch of painted space—in the swinging arms and legs, in the wind-blown hair and scarfs and skirts, in the wild-eyed expressions on the girls' faces, in the mounds of soiled snow in the foreground, and in the exploding branches of the corner bush.   Even the sky is moving rapidly. The groove marks engraved upon the ice are suggestive of movement which literally leaves the observer dazed and clearly conscious of that overabundance of energy which is characteristic of most children at this age.   One has the feeling that this student may have been an active participant in many such skating experiences.   Emphasis here has been placed upon the rhythm, movement, and speed and upon the strong emotional reaction to a most enjoyable experience in the life of an eleven-year-old. Emotion, rather than visual reality, appears to have been her concern in the delineation of this skating activity.

"Our Assembly Program" (age eleven).   In contrast to the skating activity depicted in the previously discussed painting, Fig. 8-12 is seemingly flat, placid, and impersonal, but charming.   The student seems more inhibited and reserved; nonetheless, she is keenly observant.   She appears to be conscious of the decorative qualities on the backdrop, on the clothes

Fig. 8-10. "Christmas Morning" (age ten).

Fig. 8-11. "Do We Have Fun Skating!" (age eleven).

of the performers, on the stage floor, and on the stage curtains. Interest is shown in flat, rather than shaded, areas. Some action is indicated in the performing figures, but without any manifestation of personal feeling about the performance or the performers. It occurs to the observer that this child is completely detached from the activity itself, being a passive onlooker rather than an active participant. In the delineation of the idea, the young student arrived at a rather expedient formula in the representation of the figures. For example, all the heads have a squarelike contour. Necks and waistlines are well defined, faces are dotted with features that are expressionless, unmoved, and disinterested. None of the dancers have eyebrows. Shoulders are also angular and stiff. Some variety has been achieved in the treatment of the hair, headdresses, costumes, and positions of the arms and legs. A rubberlike flexibility expressing action has been achieved in the representation of arms and legs. Although the feet have been painted fairly well, the hands appear to be less important in this dance activity.

The flowers and the flowerboxes in the foreground and on the stage have been varied in size and in color. The palm trees, the huts, and the dotted treatment of the backdrop indicate the child's interest in enriching flat surfaces through decorative means.

The painting "Our Assembly Program" is a fine example of what a perceptually oriented student can do to express a personal reaction to an idea. Although it is less dynamic than the preceding painting of skaters, nonetheless, it is a sincere expression of a student's passive response to an experience.

"Polish Dancers" (age twelve). In Fig. 8-13 the viewer is made aware of an early adolescent's impersonal impression of dancing performed by her own peers in an assembly program of an elementary school. From the amount and the type of detail in this painting, it is evident that she is well acquainted with the Polish dance, with the kind of costumes that are most frequently worn in this type of dance, and with the kind and placement of ornamental detail on these costumes. All of these factors point to a reasonable assumption that her knowledge of details is rooted in a subcultural background, which reveals an intimate relationship with an experience such as this one.

Despite this fact, however, there seems to be little or no emotional involvement manifested in connection with the activity. Rather, the idea is delineated as a docile, static, emotionless experience, with primary emphasis upon decorative pattern. This is evident in the uniquely designed overall patterns of the sashes and blouses worn by boy dancers and in the bejeweled crowns, sleeves, skirts, and vests worn by the girl dancers. There is very little action in this painting aside from that of the dancing figure in the foreground and the accordion player in the back-

FIG. 8-12. "Our Assembly Program" (age eleven).

FIG. 8-13. "Polish Dancers" (age twelve).

ground. Other figures are simply standing at ease, supposedly resting as the solo performance is going on. Upon closer scrutiny of the figures, however, one realizes that the young artist's treatment of the human form is showing signs of maturity. Lack of proportion and other graphic inadequacies, which frustrate some adolescents, are by no means a deterrent factor in this student's determination to communicate an idea. On the contrary, her use of line and form express a vigor and confidence in her ability to relate and to interpret experiences—real or imagined—with forceful conviction. While features and facial expressions are more timidly expressed and not necessarily well defined, there is an obvious attempt to achieve variety. This may be noted in her use of profile and front-view positions of faces and figures alike and in the varied positions of legs, arms, and shoulders respectively. A decided concern is shown for linear and spatial relationships and for contrast in values. For instance, a heavy outline is utilized to circumscribe the contours of the legs and skirts of the figures, while a thinner line is used in the detail of the clothes. Apparently, the student felt it necessary to emphasize, with force, those elements which had a direct bearing upon the activity, namely, the booted legs and skirts and trousers. Moreover, this was for this individual an expedient way of resolving the contrast between the figures and the foreground. Bold details were also used in the background areas, on the stage floor, and in the stage curtain.

Although this twelve-year-old's concept of a Polish dance by adult standards would seem immaturely stated, it nevertheless demonstrates a reasonable degree of perceptual skill. Indeed, this painting must be viewed as a serious attempt to make visible a statement of fact, which communicates a valid response to a particular cultural activity.

The abundance of detail, however, could be interpreted to mean several things: first, that it is simply a reasonably accurate account of a stage performance in the school auditorium; secondly, that, having been exposed to similar activities many times before, the pupil is merely bored with the kinesthetic skill of the performers and hence concentrates on the minutest details of the costumes; thirdly, and perhaps less likely at this early stage of development, may be the conscious effort to conceal, or obscure, or compensate for the student's apparent lack of skill in drawing the human figure. The first two assumptions are in all probability more valid than the third.

"The Football Game" (age thirteen). Not unusually creative in organization, nor unique in its concept, is the painting entitled, "The Football Game" (Fig. 8-14), but it possesses other qualities which are of merit and which may be of interest to the reader. For instance, in the above painting an adolescent reveals, with a reasonable measure of accuracy, feelings, and reactions to a professional football game. Through it, he attempts to communicate the feelings of excitement and action on the football field as well as among the restless spectators seated in the bleachers. Although the figures on the field seem massive, they are nevertheless rigidly active as though their activity is restrained by the wearing of strait jackets, rather than football uniforms. The figures of the spectators in the background are treated in a similar fashion; they are rendered inflexible as though they were made of wood. Only their facial expressions and the positions of some of the arms vary. The referee, who is seen in the distance, is taking a leisurely pace across the field. He appears unconcerned about the football game.

Despite this rather average treatment of the human forms, the kinetic aspects of the painting clearly convey a feeling of action and give meaning to this type of activity in this particular setting.

A valiant effort is also made here to indicate relative distances through varied size and value relationships and also through the placement of forms; likewise, through the use of a discreet amount of detail. Hands, feet, and heads, for example, are given some attention but not enough to detract from the massiveness of other parts of the bodies. In a sense, because of this rather limited treatment, the bodies appear more forceful and accent their importance in a football game.

It is interesting to note also that the largest figure in the composition represents a member of one team; i.e., judging from the plainly colored

FIG. 8-14. "The Football Game" (age thirteen).

helmet he is wearing and from the football he is trying to safeguard with his outstretched right hand, he is trying to stop the tackling members of the opposing team. The ram's horn on the helmets of three players symbolically identifies the opposition.

An intimate understanding of the game itself is thus revealed. But, despite all that, the feeling seems strong that this adolescent is not out there on the field playing. Instead, one is inclined to believe that he is seated in the bleachers, cheering alongside his own friends. His perceptively depicted moods of the spectators lead one to think that this assumption is true. These moods are ably expressed in the facial features and in the swinging arms of the spectators. It is interesting to note the details that this young artist stressed here, i.e., the features that he felt were vital in the expression of exuberance or enthusiasm for the game. It seems that the eyes, the eyebrows, the mouths, and the arms, rather than the ears, noses, hair, and even some of the hands, were given more thoughtful consideration. Feeling that the latter were of little significance in a football game, the student relegated these to a minor position. In some instances he deliberately omitted them. The eyes and the mouths, however, were clearly depicted with genuine emotions.

Particularly convincing, also, is the variety of moods which the student depicted in his painting. For example, the faces of those who are presumably interested in the winning team, were made happy; the faces of those who seem to be on the side of the losing team were made sad and angry; the faces of others appear indifferent for one reason or another. Still others appear frightened in anticipation of the unpredictable, which is about to happen at this particular stage of the game. And, in the event that the viewer is somewhat concerned about the possible outcome of this contest in sportsmanship, he may rest assured that the bearer of the ball in this particular football game will never reach his destination. Obviously, the three members of the opposing team will stop him from reaching his goal.

All of the above details attest to this student's keen understanding of what is important in a football game. These also reveal his perceptual skill, and his ability to project graphically the gamut of human emotions. This he has achieved despite the seemingly rigid delineation of human forms or the not overly unique organization of a conceived idea within a given space.

"We Enjoy Dancing after School" (age fourteen). This painting (Fig. 8-15) represents a teenage girl's authentic account of her major interests—boys and dancing. It also reveals a critical awareness of the environment in which the activity takes place. With a keen sense of observation, she depicts with minute detail the interior of a neighborhood store whose proprietor is obviously tolerant of, and perhaps even sympathetic to, the spontaneous outbursts of dancing which occur on his premises periodically—all to the ear-splitting tunes of a jukebox. Judging from the gyrating movements of the girl on the extreme left, i.e., the one whose hair is flowing in the air, whose legs and arms are most active, and whose facial expression is positively ecstatic, it must be assumed that this is a self-portrait of the young artist. The other girl on the dance floor is practically standing still. She is posed in a less buoyant position, possibly a progressive step in this particular dance.

Other details depicted here are: the soda fountain bar, the uniformed clerk behind it, the lonesome customer seated at the bar on one of the typical bar stools; the traditional carbonated drinks and ice cream concoctions, hamburgers, malts, sundaes, and other tempting "delights" which are described in the showcards displayed on the background wall; the essential mechanisms that are revealed through the glazed enclosure of the jukebox, also the treatment of the jukebox exterior; the dress "uniforms" of the teenage girls, i.e., the skirts, blouses, bobby socks and loafers, and ribbons in their long hair; and the uniforms of the boys with whom they are dancing who are wearing the typical T-shirts, sweaters, and blue jeans. From all these, it is evident that this adolescent did not omit any of the all-too-familiar symbols which characterize the teenage world. Indeed, they were drawn with clarity and with authenticity, revealing a keenly perceptive awareness of what constitutes the gamut of meaningful things in the life of a normal adolescent.

Fig. 8-15. "We Enjoy Dancing after School" (age fourteen).

All facial expressions of the figures in this painting seem to have been treated alike. All mouths appear smiling while all eyes are wild with excitement. In general, however, the figures are painted in a more flexible fashion than those which were rigidly delineated in the painting "The Football Game." Indeed, they reveal a clear understanding of the physical differences between boys and girls, a sensitivity to the contours of torsos, size of shoulders and waistlines, length of arms, legs, and feet, sizes and shapes of heads, and type of hairdos. The girls are naturally wearing lipstick; the boys, of course, are not.

A decided interest in perspective is also revealed here. This is particularly evident in the checkered floor, in the varied size relationships of figures, and in the treatment of the furniture in the room. All this undoubtedly indicates a growing maturity in the skill to recognize the relative aspects of forms depicted within a given space.

"Moving into a New Apartment" (age fifteen). The tempera "Moving into a New Apartment" (Fig. 8-16) was painted by a fifteen-year-old high school freshman. Painted from memory or imagination, the composition reveals a maturely perceptive representation of two residential buildings which are located in the heart of an industrial community. Because the building on the right played an important role in the delineation of the student's experience, it has obviously been given much more detailed attention than other buildings represented in that area. But in the treatment of all the structures there is confidently disclosed a high degree of technical skill. Along with this skill there is apparent a clear understanding of the visual forms in the painting and an awareness of the elements involved in a synthesized organization of textural nuances. Also noticeable are the subtle variations that are introduced to create interest in a given space. In addition to this, there is projected the student's sensitive awareness of the environment in which the moving-in is taking place. This is exemplified in the deliberately annotated and all-inclusive particulars seen in the following: the snow-covered brick houses, roofs, and windowsills; the odd assortment of half, or fully drawn windowshades suspended from irregularly shaped windows; lace curtains on some windows with a plant or simply a patch of frost on others; a suggestion of metal guards on the basement windows; factories and their smoke-emitting chimneys seen in the distance; and an accurately drawn moving van in the foreground. Movers are bringing in the final piece of furniture, a heavy living-room chair, through the widely opened space and into the apartment. A "For Rent" sign is carelessly dumped into the trash can on the right of the stairs, indicating that this apartment is no longer for rent. The exact address is 1001. The driver at the wheel of the truck is preparing to leave. The snow-covered ground barely discloses the sidewalk demarcations. There is a fire hydrant in the extreme left corner of the painting.

FIG. 8-16. "Moving into a New Apartment" (age fifteen).

Electric wires are extended from a building on the left to the wooden post in the distant center of the composition.

All of which suggests a highly developed image-forming and image-recording skill. This kind of ability has not been demonstrated to such an extent in any of the previous examples painted by teenagers. It may be recalled that those paintings were selected for study primarily because they more nearly typified the artistic performance of the average student. The artistic performance of this student can obviously be rated as being above average and therefore be placed in the category of the talented or "gifted."

But, despite this fact, the deeply felt convictions which characterized the paintings that have been done by younger students are lacking here. Although by contrast the painting, "Moving into a New Apartment" is seemingly more impressive because of the strong manifestation of technical skill, it nevertheless remains just that. No one can deny that this is a commendable product from a fifteen-year-old student, but to the informed observer, it would appear that moving into a new community or into a new apartment in the same community would, in all probability, evoke a far greater emotional response and spontaneity from an eight-, nine-, or even ten-year-old student than it did from this teenager. Despite the fact that this painting displays a highly rational, fluent, and articulate expression of unusual caliber, it seems utterly devoid of a deeply felt reaction to a supposedly significant event in the life of an adolescent. Instead, it depicts a rather detached, calm, cold, and highly intellectual response to the season of the year, obscuring the all-important event of "Moving into a New Apartment." But, perhaps, this student felt a distinct displeasure at this experience and therefore disdainfully expressed his honest reaction to it.

CONCLUSION

As has been stated previously, and it bears repeating here, the ability to render visible one's particular conception of an idea, motivated by things experienced, seen, remembered, or imagined, often reveals an acuteness of perception that is less likely to come forth through any other means of expression. To the trained observer, therefore, a careful examination of a student's artistic product can disclose many meaningful things which cannot become readily discernable to the average layman. This is particularly true when the criteria for identifying talent in art are unsound; i.e., when they are based upon one single factor, namely, the ability to imitate or copy the creative products of others. It is this erroneous definition of talent or giftedness which eventually leads the unimaginative individual to a dead end.

On the other hand, there are those who place a high premium upon creative values. These individuals live to see a world of infinite possibilities which is exciting, never boring, productive, and most rewarding. A true index to one's perceptual and aesthetic skill is constituted by the ability to be selective or to identify the unusual, to be flexible or experimental, to be observant and analytical; the desire and the determination to explore in depth each possible approach to the solution of an art problem; and the ability to synthesize and organize creative thoughts. The student whose ingenious capacities are greatest, is the most talented.

Though many a youngster's ability to imitate nature, or man, served to awaken his initial interest in art, it is imperative to recognize the need to gradually terminate overly tenacious reliance upon imitative successes. This should be done as early as possible in the life of the individual, in order to encourage complete confidence in one's own inner capacities for inventiveness and uniqueness in the process of self-realization.

At this point, it might be of interest to examine carefully Chart 1. It should facilitate the recognition of the correlative factors inherent in developmental, creative, and perceptual growth. The chart defines *the stages of developmental, as well as creative growth, identifies the characteristics* of each, and establishes *the fundamental needs* for the promotion of creative and perceptual growth of children.

CHART 1

CORRELATIVE FACTORS IN DEVELOPMENTAL, CREATIVE, AND PERCEPTUAL GROWTH OF CHILDREN—CHARACTERISTICS AND NEEDS FROM INFANCY THROUGH ADOLESCENCE

Stages of Developmental Growth	Stages of Creative Growth	Characteristics of Developmental Growth	Characteristics and Tendencies of Creative Growth	Needs for Creative and Perceptual Growth
Infancy to 5 years (kindergarten)	Scribbling stage 1) uncontrolled 2) controlled	1) Gradual development of motor coordination. 2) Uneven development of motor skills; loses one skill while developing another. 3) Skill in the use of large muscles primarily. 4) Active and imaginative play. 5) Short span of interest. 6) Develops friendships with boys and girls.	1) Manifests uncontrolled random movements. 2) Uses media merely as kinesthetic experience. 3) Names his scribbles; often adds significance to what appears to be meaningless. 4) Uses scribbles which often represent lines and shapes and which express mere enjoyment in the use of the materials. 5) Explores using brush, paint, crayon, chalk, and mixing colors for the sheer pleasure of doing so.	1) Tools compatible with child's physical development (those he can control: large brushes, large paper, etc). 2) Simple toys which challenge his imagination; a variety of forms from which he can build or construct new forms by interchanging parts, by adding or removing sections, etc. 3) Freedom to explore the possibilities of every new medium or experience. 4) Comfort when frustrating situations arise. 5) Adult appreciation for his creative endeavors.
Early childhood ages 5–7 (grades 1 and 2)	Symbolic stage	1) Uneven and incomplete muscular development. 2) Develops motor skills slowly. 3) Incomplete hand-eye coordination. 4) Gradually develops sensory-motor equipment necessary for reading. 5) Short interest span which is increasing.	1) Begins conscious creation of forms. 2) Develops symbols which he names to represent human form, animal, tree, or house, etc. 3) Establishes some relationship with reality: uses baseline, skyline, etc. 4) Has better control of medium and attempts to tell a	1) Honest responses to his inquiries so that he may develop image-forming skills. 2) Adult appreciation for his own ideas, at his own level rather than at an adult level. 3) Rewards for creative thinking, for the search to understand the nature of things, for the hunger to learn.

CHART 1 (continued)

Stages of Developmental Growth	Stages of Creative Growth	Characteristics of Developmental Growth	Characteristics and Tendencies of Creative Growth	Needs for Creative and Perceptual Growth
		6) Learns best through activity. 7) Sensitive to criticism. 8) Depends to a great extent upon the approval of adults. 9) Develops friendships of same sex.	story using his invented symbols, such as "circle" for the head, "sticks" for arms and legs, etc. 5) Changes meaning and form of symbols daily, depending upon the importance he attributes to them in a particular context. 6) Exaggerates parts of the human form which he feels are vital to his story. 7) Reveals his active motivations through his drawings. 8) Creates representations which are closely bound up with the self. 9) Appears most ready to build up new concepts.	4) Experiences that satisfy his curiosity and his search for truths. 5) Awareness of his relationship to his environment (playmates, pets, family, school, etc) through creative experiences. 6) Creative opportunities to express feelings and reactions visually and tactually.
Later childhood ages 8–10 (grades 3–5)	Exploratory stage	1) Normally slow in physical growth. 2) Developing small muscles of the hands and fingers. 3) Good muscular co-ordination. 4) Continues to develop hand-eye coordination. 5) Internal changes in body glands and body structure. 6) Boundless energy. 7) A wider range of	1) Becomes gradually conscious of his environment and of order in space relationships; uses baseline and skyline in pictures. 2) Develops active concept of objects. 3) Repeats the concepts. 4) Exaggerates important parts and adds details to human form: fingers, features, etc. 5) Changes from ego-	1) Opportunities for group projects concerning the child's major interests and abilities. 2) Recognition and rewards for his ideas. 3) Less pressure for conformity; more encouragement to have faith in his own creative ability. 4) Many opportunities to communicate ideas creatively using varied media.

		Characteristics	Art characteristics	Opportunities
		interests and a longer attention span. 8) Learning to cooperate; responsive to group activities. 9) Interested in peer gangs and social organizations in the community and in other countries. 10) Competitive.	centric to social, cooperative attitude. 6) Has insatiable desire to communicate ideas. 7) Reacts toward the emotional, rather than to the visual. 8) Enjoys manipulative experiences. 9) Enjoys texture, decorative patterns and mixing color.	5) Opportunities to work independently; to use his unique skills creatively. 6) Strengths emphasized and weaknesses minimized to upbuild his inventive tendencies.
Reflective stage	Preadolescence ages 11–13 (grades 6 and 7)	1) In pubescent period: rate of growth is very rapid. 2) Rapid muscular growth. 3) Restless and awkward. 4) Differs widely in temperament and maturity; is strongly individual. 5) Highly competitive. 6) Needs affection from adults, but prestige becomes more important than adult approval. 7) Marked difference in interests from those of the opposite sex. 8) Often rebellious and uncooperative. 9) Overcritical of self and of others.	1) Feeling of inadequacy in the creative process. 2) Conscious of environment and of details, size and space relationships: foreground, middle ground, distance, inside-outside views, and overlapping of forms. 3) Relates expression to nature. 4) Represents figures in a rigid and inflexible manner. 5) Loses symbolic significance of lines. 6) Uses few exaggerations to express emotional importance, few omissions to indicate lack of importance. 7) Realizes significance of proportion and action; closely related to reality. 8) Emphasizes details on parts that are emotionally significant in animals, people, objects, and buildings.	1) Opportunities to explore new materials, processes, and media and to use them to communicate. 2) Awareness of the importance of quality and depth in performance of creative tasks. 3) Opportunities to test his own ideas and skills. 4) Opportunities for independent thinking through exciting and adventurous projects. 5) Opportunities which will reflect his creative skills and thereby gain the respect of his peers. 6) Help offered as he asks for it.

CHART 1 (*continued*)

Stages of Developmental Growth	Stages of Creative Growth	Characteristics of Developmental Growth	Characteristics and Tendencies of Creative Growth	Needs for Creative and Perceptual Growth
			9) Interested in contrasts of light and dark, large and small.	
Adolescence ages 14–16 (grades 7–9)	The Realistic stage	1) Improved coordination. 2) End of the awkward age; puberty cycle completed in most adolescents. 3) Identifies strongly with admired adults. 4) Anxious to be popular with peer groups. 5) Asserts independence from family. 6) Enjoys serving worthy causes. 7) Frequent changes in emotions and interests.	1) Increasingly critical of his environment. 2) Realizes importance of the final product. 3) Interest in correct proportions, action, gesture, expression, and dramatization. 4) Enjoys experimentation with varied media. 5) Interest in techniques and processes. 6) Interest in vocational possibilities of developed skills. 7) Demands practical justification for learning activities.	1) Appreciation of the purpose behind his creative activity; cognizance of his goals. 2) Opportunities to recognize the possibilities of several solutions in resolving any one problem. 3) Consciousness of social problems; his responsibilities and contributions through art experiences. 4) Opportunities to think critically and independently through challenging art experiences. 5) Awareness of how his unique skills can be directed toward vocational as well as avocational goals. 6) Opportunities to harness emotional energy into creative and adventurous art experiences. 7) Special recognition for outstanding performance.

READING REFERENCES

Alschuler, Rose H., and Hattwick, Laberta W., *A Study of Painting and Personality of Young Children*. Chicago: University of Chicago Press, 2 vols., 1947.

Appel, K. E., "Drawings of Children as Aids to Personality Studies," *American Journal of Orthopsychiatry*, 1931.

Bruner, Jerome S., *The Process of Education*.   Cambridge, Mass.: Harvard University Press, 1963.

Cameron, N., "Individual and Social Factors in the Development of Graphic Symbolizations" *Journal of Psychology*, 5:165–184, 1938.

Eng, Hilda, *The Psychology of Children's Drawings: From the First Stroke to the Color Drawing*.   London: Kegan Paul, Trench, Trubner & Co., 1931, pp. viii–223.

Goodenough, Florence L., *Measurement of Intelligence by Drawing*. Yonkers-on-the Hudson, N. Y.: World Book Co., 1926, pp. xi–177.

Harms, Ernst, "Child Art As An Aid in The Diagnosis of Juvenile Neuroses" *American Journal of Orthopsychiatry* 11:191–209 (Apr) 1941.

Hurlock, E. B., and Thomson, J. L., "Children's Drawings: An Experimental Study of Perception" *Child Development* (June) 1934, pp. 127–38.

Lowenfeld, Viktor, *The Nature of Creative Activity*.   London: Routledge and Kegan Paul, Ltd., 1939, pp. xvii–272.

Munro, Thomas, *Art Education, Its Philosophy and Psychology*. New York: The Liberal Arts Press, 1956.

Torrance, Paul E., *Guiding Creative Talent*. Englewood Cliffs, N. J.: Prentice-Hall, Inc., 1962.

9

The Teacher of Art

If art experiences are to reflect the child's reaction to his environment, then nothing in his existence is outside the realm of interest for him. The ability to express his concepts visually is cultivated through habitual involvement in experiences which foster the growth of his inherent artistic consciousness. The role of the teacher in the creative process is to guide and to inspire the student.

"All he has to do is channel the loved excitement which is bubbling through the blood streams of the normal child into a constructive outlet of creating something of his own instead of crippling his ego by imitation," states Ralph Pearson.

THE TEACHER'S BACKGROUND

The teacher must be professionally equipped to teach art in order that she may strengthen the child's imaginative and inventive thought and behavior. To function effectively, she must understand the following:

1) the home and community which constitute the child's environment, i.e., where his behavior patterns have been nurtured and cultivated;
2) the stages of physical, mental, and creative development of children;
3) the range and type of experiences in which pupils have been previously involved;
4) what is reasonable to expect in the way of creative achievement at each particular age and grade level;
5) the role of art education in the total scheme of the curriculum — its philosophy, its function, and objectives;
6) criteria which constitute a basis for aesthetic judgment, i.e., sensitivity to aesthetic values which are applicable to any work of art, whether it is a painting, a piece of sculpture, an architectural form, or any other visual scheme;
7) various art processes, methods, and materials used in creative problem-solving experiences;
8) how to organize a classroom for any two- and three-dimensional art activity with an absolute minimum of confusion;

9) how to use various methods and audiovisual aids to motivate original expression;

10) how to display finished products of children.

HOW RESOURCEFUL IS THE TEACHER?

Assuming that the teacher of art is adequately prepared to teach, a major concern would still be her degree of *resourcefulness and flexibility* as an individual, especially when she is working under trying circumstances. For instance, in a situation where there are poor classroom facilities, such as a room without a sink, small desks, no art supplies, no bulletin-board areas for the display of art work, no storage space, etc. Under such circumstances does her enthusiasm for teaching remain? Can her resourcefulness help her to overcome these handicaps? What methods would she employ to motivate art activities where none were previously experienced? What type of art activities would she need to promote? How would she cope with large class memberships? How would she allow children to discover or invent unique ways of expressing ideas? The validity and effectiveness of an art program, in any school, will depend upon the way in which these questions are resolved.

"My biggest problem is to know what to suggest for children to paint. I always run out of ideas." This concern is certainly a universal one. The supervisor of art is frequently confronted with this problem to which she often replies that the teacher's task is to help the child select subject matter which is closely related to his own experiences and imagination—interests, thoughts, and feelings. For every art activity, these aspects of the child may be revitalized by the teacher. She may assist the children to recall, to imagine, to invent, to perceive, and to select ideas, tools, and materials for expressive purposes. Together they may formulate and firmly establish the goals for which they may be striving; goals which justify the activity in the eyes of the children, as well as the teacher. Certainly in this process of motivation, the child's interests play a predominant role. No teacher can afford to lose sight of this highly significant generating force without jeopardizing the objectives of an art program.

THE TEACHER'S PRINCIPAL RESPONSIBILITIES

At this point, it is well to examine the principal responsibilities of the teacher in the implementation of a creative art program. A teacher of art must:

1) Recognize the uniqueness of every learner and provide him with opportunities that are geared to individual differences in interests, needs, and capacities. His responsibility implies the use of

various teaching methods and devices and the use of a variety of media, processes, tools, and materials in the expression of two- and three-dimensional ideas.

2) Involve the learner in creative experiences which awaken his responses—real, or imagined thoughts, feelings, hopes, and aspirations.

3) Confront the learner with problem-solving situations which challenge his ability to think independently and critically and which help him crystallize his thoughts in an original manner.

4) Help the learner attain a measure of depth and breadth through sequential art experiences which demand the repeated use of previously acquired skills, understandings, and appreciations.

5) Help develop the learner's self-confidence and inner security through recurring emphasis upon the learner's unique and imaginative thoughts, rather than on those that are prosaic, imitative, and unimaginative.

6) Motivate a strong desire to achieve personal fulfillment through the recognition of the intrinsic values of creative activity, thereby helping to develop the learner's psychic strength and courage to pursue more challenging and more complex creative experiences in the future.

7) Broaden the scope of opportunities for the gifted learner so that he may search for new concepts in order that he may develop to the utmost his perceptual potentialities and insights into areas hitherto unexplored.

8) Promote self-realization of the learner through a synthesis, and a genuinely integrated compatibility of his imaginative, intellectual, emotional, and manual capacities.

TEACHER ATTITUDES TOWARD ART

It has been the experience of the author that many of the difficulties which arise in connection with an art lesson are due primarily to poor planning or to no planning at all. To assume that a teacher of art can conduct an art lesson without preparation for it is entirely wrong. It is a fact that, unless a teacher is well prepared to present an art lesson, she will find the period a dreaded chore instead of the worthwhile and exciting experience that it should be.

The classroom teacher who is not trained in art must first of all become familiar with the content which she is planning to teach. Secondly, she must be familiar with educationally sound techniques in order to transmit that information. Thirdly, she must know how to organize the content of each activity and how to use the materials and tools in connection with each lesson. Furthermore, she must be able to devise simple and flexible methods for adapting whatever knowledge and skill she may possess to the varied capacities and abilities of her students. Lastly, she must have some basic and valid criteria for the evaluation of the completed art products.

Teachers in self-contained classrooms are often unprepared in some or all aspects of art teaching. Yet, they are expected to teach the subject. Consequently, they do face many problems. Therefore, they should make every effort to fill the voids created either by lack of training or by lack of experience in this particular area of the curriculum. To assume that one can teach art without preparation is tantamount to the assumption that teaching successfully in any other discipline without training is possible. Inadequate preparation for the teaching of art, or the use of unsound practices, can do much to harm the inherent creative potentialities of young students.

The teacher who has never taught art and who dreads the experience, would do well to examine her own attitudes toward the subject and make every effort to correct them. Special workshop courses in art, services by the supervisory staff, art education conferences or institutes, literature in the field of art education—all these offer a means of improving one's skill and confidence in the teaching of art.

It seems rather ludicrous, however, and at the same time most unfortunate, that teachers feel embarassed to admit their weaknesses in reading, writing, or arithmetic, but are not embarrassed to admit that they know nothing about art and less about the teaching of art and that they are doing nothing to remedy either deficiency. Presumably, one would expect them to make every effort to fill in the gaps which are due to lack of training. But as it stands, for one reason or another, negative attitudes concerning the importance of art in the life of the individual persist, among teachers as well as laymen. This is indeed unfortunate because the classroom teacher, of all people, should be well qualified—culturally, aesthetically, and intellectually—to administer every aspect of education to our youth. To be sure, the teacher's own attitudes must be properly oriented if she expects her students to develop sound attitudes concerning any area of the curriculum, including that area in which she admits her own inadequacy.

COMMONLY USED APPROACHES IN FOSTERING PERCEPTUAL AND AESTHETIC GROWTH

Charts 2 and 3 represent a graphic analysis of the procedures involved in two accepted methods of developing perceptual and aesthetic growth; the "experience-motivated" approach and the "materials" approach.

A careful analysis of both methods will disclose the thought proc-

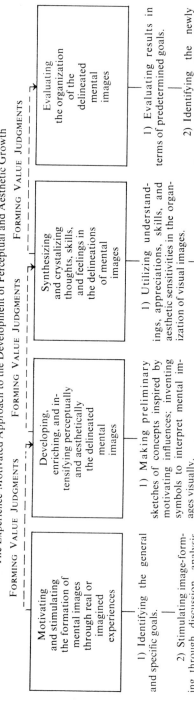

CHART 2

MOTIVATION METHOD I

The Experience-Motivated Approach to the Development of Perceptual and Aesthetic Growth

FORMING VALUE JUDGMENTS   FORMING VALUE JUDGMENTS   FORMING VALUE JUDGMENTS   FORMING VALUE JUDGMENTS

Motivating and stimulating the formation of mental images through real or imagined experiences

1) Identifying the general and specific goals.

2) Stimulating image-forming through discussion, analysis of real or imagined experiences, audiovisual aids, demonstrations, analysis of original works of art or literature in the field, visits to museums, art galleries, art fairs, and school exhibits.

Developing, enriching, and intensifying perceptually and aesthetically the delineated mental images

1) Making preliminary sketches of concepts inspired by motivating influences; inventing symbols to interpret mental images visually.

2) Making choices—accepting or rejecting relevant or irrelevant concepts and visual images.

3) Experimenting with several spatial arrangements of one idea, using variations of art elements (line, color, and texture).

4) Developing a frame of reference, setting, or background for conceived ideas.

5) Experimenting with materials, media, tools, and processes; choosing those that are suitable for the solution of the specific idea.

Synthesizing and crystalizing thoughts, skills, and feelings in the delineations of mental images

1) Utilizing understandings, appreciations, skills, and aesthetic sensitivities in the organization of visual images.

2) Expressing thoughts about and reactions to visual images.

3) Integrating imaginative, intellectual, emotional, creative, and manual capacities.

Evaluating the organization of the delineated mental images

1) Evaluating results in terms of predetermined goals.

2) Identifying the newly discovered insights and skills.

3) Recognizing the means of improving image-forming skills.

4) Appreciating the new level of perceptual and aesthetic growth.

CHART 3

MOTIVATION METHOD II

The Materials Approach to the Development of Perceptual and Aesthetic Growth

FORMING VALUE JUDGMENTS   FORMING VALUE JUDGMENTS   FORMING VALUE JUDGMENTS   FORMING VALUE JUDGMENTS

Motivating and stimulating the formation of mental images through media, materials, tools, and processes	Developing, enriching, and intensifying perceptually and aesthetically the delineated mental images	Synthesizing and crystalizing thoughts, skills, and feelings in the delineation of mental images	Evaluating the organization of the delineated mental images
1) Identifying general and specific goals.	1) Making preliminary sketches of mental images; inventing symbols to interpret images visually.	1) Utilizing understandings, appreciations, skills, and aesthetic sensitivities in the organization of visual ideas.	1) Evaluating results in terms of predetermined goals.
2) Experimenting, discovering possibilities and limitations of materials, media, tools, and processes.	2) Making choices—accepting or rejecting relevant or irrelevant concepts and visual images.	2) Expressing thoughts about and reactions to visual images.	2) Identifying the newly discovered insights and skills.
3) Imagining the possibilities of these in development of originally conceived ideas.	3) Experimenting with varied spatial arrangements and variations of art elements (line, form, color, and texture) in the solution of a specific problem.	3) Integrating imaginative, intellectual, emotional, creative, and manual capacities.	3) Recognizing the means of improving image-forming skills.
4) Selecting the materials media, tools, and method suitable for the solution of a specific problem.	4) Developing a frame of reference, setting, or background for the specific problem.		4) Appreciating the new level of perceptual and aesthetic growth.

esses and activities in the initiating, developing, and culminating stages of an art experience. These procedures are commonly used in the development of creative ideas.

The steps in both charts are similar; the difference lies only in the motivating process. *In Chart 2, the motivating factors are the real or imagined experiences of the student*; while in Chart 3 *the motivation is derived from media, materials, tools, and processes.* Both are valid approaches to creativity. However, Method II does not appear to be practical on the primary level.

READING REFERENCES

Barkan, Manuel, *A Foundation for Art Education.* New York: The Ronald Press Co., 1955.

Beam, Philip C., *The Language of Art.* New York: The Ronald Press Co., 1958.

Conant, Howard, and Randall, Arne, *Art in Education.* Peoria, Ill.: Charles A. Bennett Company, Inc., 1959.

De Francesco, Italo L., *Art Education, Its Means and Ends.* New York: Harper and Brothers, 1958.

Gaitskell, Charles D., *Children and Their Art.* New York: Harcourt, Brace & Co., Inc., 1958.

Gardner, Helen, *Art Through the Ages*, 3d ed. New York: Harcourt, Brace & Co., Inc., 1948.

Jefferson, Blanche, *Teaching Art to Children.* Boston: Allyn and Bacon, Inc., 1959.

McFee, June King, *Preparation for Art.* San Francisco: Wadsworth Publishing Co., Inc., 1961.

Munro, Thomas, *Art Education, Its Philosophy and Psychology.* New York: The Liberal Arts Press, 1956.

Read, Herbert, *Education Through Art.* New York: Pantheon Books, Inc., 1945.

Yochim, Louise Dunn, *Building Human Relationships Through Art.* Chicago: L. M. Stein, Publisher, 1954, Chapters IV, V and VI.

CHAPTER

10

Image-Forming Stimuli; Ideas for Two- or Three- Dimensional Art Activities

This chapter is designed specifically to aid in the solution of the basic problem which faces many teachers of art. Principally, it is the question which deals with the "birth" and development of ideas for two- or three-dimensional art activities. Consequently, a workable list of image-forming stimuli is offered here. The titles are classified according to their relationship to human experience and to internal and external factors which affect human experience or in which experiences occur. These titles act as mental stimuli which may be utilized in structuring two- or three-dimensional forms.

Unless the teacher encourages the organization of thoughts within a specific orientation, background, setting, or frame of reference, student ideas will often remain prosaic and unimaginative. To stimulate growth in perception and imagination, a concerted effort must be made toward the achievement of this goal. "A thought or idea is not an isolated state of mind, but an intermediate response occurring between the original situation which initiates behavior, and the final response that accomplishes an end"[1].

The dominant subjects suggested under a "major classification" will frequently suggest clues to the content of a background, setting, or frame of reference. However, including items that are listed under other "major classifications" will further enrich the total art experience.

For example, let us suppose that the theme, or dominant idea for a painting or for a "3D" form listed under the major classification "People" is "Men Collecting Garbage." The area where this activity occurs (or frame of reference) would of necessity need to be limited to a particular locale, i.e., to a section of an alley, a street, or any other area. The self-imposed limitation will serve as a clue. It will suggest to the student *what* to include in the background space of his composition. That is to say, if the theme occurs in an alley, what will he see in the alley? Will it be buildings, garages, more people, animals, trees, bushes, fences, garbage cans, garbage, fruit-and-vegetable or ice-cream vendors, the umbrella and knife-sharpening man, janitors, coalmen, the junk peddler, delivery boys, cars, trucks, etc.? All or some of these items may be included in the pictorial organization in which the "men who are collecting the garbage" are dominant. They are grouped and placed in the foreground, while all other subject matter related to them is relegated to the background.

In this manner, the teacher of art may generate critical, analytical, imaginative and perceptual thinking about any theme or topic. This kind of teaching approach will tend to "stretch" the imagination of every student. It will place far greater emphasis upon image forming, his perceptual, and imaginative skill, than will the approach which stresses accurate imitation of objects in nature. Altogether, an approach such as this one will lead to a much fuller commitment on the part of the student. (The method described above may be equally useful in developing creative written compositions.)

The following list of image-forming stimuli may be utilized not only to motivate ideas for painting, but also to motivate other two- and three-dimensional art activities. Creative ideas may be expressed through varied media and processes in such activities as: creative stitching, collage, appliqué, felt crafts, weaving, linocuts, woodcuts, silk screening, mono-printing, and other print processes, yarn painting, textile designing, paper batik, cloth batik and other resist processes, paper sculpture, clay model-ing, plaster carving, wire sculpture, wire-and-plaster sculpture, sand casting, metal tapping, copper enameling, and paper or tessera mosaics. Most of these activities will be developed in detail in Volume II.

STIMULI FOR PAINTING AND OTHER
TWO- OR THREE-DIMENSIONAL ART ACTIVITIES
(For all grade levels)

Major Classification: People in a Setting

Self portraits

Family portraits

Portraits of self and pets

Crowds on elevated stations

Crowds at train depots

Crowds shopping

Community helpers: teachers, students, policemen, firemen, grocery clerks, doctors, lawyers, politicians, street cleaners, sales clerks, salesmen, drug-gists, gas station attendants, truck drivers; builders of homes, bridges, tunnels, elevated, roads, sewers, etc.; men working on electric equipment and structures; men planting trees and shrubbery; men collecting garbage; peddlers of fruits and vegetables; the Fuller Brush Man

People in the post office
People in school
People in the library
People in the bowling alley
People in the gym
Attendants in the zoo
Attendants in the circus
Marching men and women
People getting on and off the buses and elevated trains
Nurses in a hospital
People in a lunchroom or restaurant
People in the kitchen
People in the dining room
People in the factory
People in the hospital
People in the church
People in the temple
People in the synagogue
People in the funeral parlor
People in the doctor's office
People in the drugstore
People in the department store

People in the park
People in the circus
People on the train
People on the plane
People on a boat
People on bicycles
People in the mountains
People in the bank
People in the theatre or movie
People in the grocery store
People in the woods
People in the jungle
People in the police station
People in the court
People on the highway
People on the beach
People at an art fair
People at a flower show
People at a furniture show
People at an art museum
People at a science museum
People at a historical museum
People at an automobile show
People at an international trade fair
People at the boat races
People at the horse races
People at the automobile races
People at a swim-meet
People at a stadium, hockey game, football game, basketball game, etc.

Major Classification: Animals in a Setting

Prehistoric (birds, fish, fowl, etc.)
Imaginary
Gargoyle
On a farm
In the zoo
In the jungle
In the northern hemisphere
In the southern hemisphere
Pets in the home

In the circus
In the parade
In the pet shop
In the animal hospital
In the stable
In the neighborhood
In the science laboratory
In the chicken shop
In the store window

In the dime store (birds, etc.)   In the field grazing
At the horse races   In the stockyards
On a ranch

Major Classification: Growth in a Setting

Trees: in the city streets, in the   Fruits and vegetables: vegetable
parks, on roof gardens, in fruit   gardens, fruit orchards, in the
orchards, in the woods, in the   kitchen, in fruit stores, on
parking lot, around the beach   vendor's wagon or truck, in a
area, in the jungle, in the   bowl, on a plate (cut, sliced,
country, in the suburb, in the   peeled, cooked), in a basket
mountains, in the vineyard, in   (upright, turned over, etc.),
the tropics, etc.   displayed at the fair

Major Classification: Rock Formations in a Setting

Mountains   Undersea formations
Rock gardens   On the moon
Quarries   In caves

Major Classification: Imagination and Feelings in a Setting

Warmth of sunlight   A collision
Coolness of the water   An automobile accident
Freezing temperature (cold day)   A happy mood
Noise   Foggy day
Explosion—fireworks   Dreams
A peaceful moment   Ambitions
Tiredness   Desires
Snowstorms   Strength
Floods   Weakness
Surprise   Compassion
An exciting moment   Night
Rainy weather   Morning
Sunny weather   Noon
Rough ocean   Fire
An atomic blast   A force

Major Classification: Undersea Life in a Setting

Fish   Coral   Mermaids
Shells   Rock formations   Lost treasures
Weeds and plants   Divers   Sunken ships

Major Classification: The Sky in a Setting

Birds   Thunder   Sunshine
Planes   Rain   Moonlight
Clouds   Snow   Lightning

Major Classification: Industry in a Setting

Steel mills

Oil wells and structures

Factories

Transportation

Coal mining

Generating electricity

Baking

Highway building

Airplane factory

Clothing industry

Chemicals, drugs

Auto manufacturing

Shipbuilding

Missile base

Commercial fishing

Lumber industry

Masonry

Paper industry

Office workers

Packing industry

Shipping

Power linemen

Major Classification: Machinery in a Setting

Drills

Motors

Flywheels

Steam shovels

Printing presses

Cranes

Bulldozers

Wrecking machines

Fire-fighting equipment

Hardware

Snow removal equipment

Springs and coils

Tree spraying

Engines

Office machines

Drill presses

Jig saws

Potter's wheel

Sanders

Buffers

Lathes

Bandsaws

Punch press

Sewing machines

Washing machines

Household appliances

Farm equipment

Tanks

Major Classification: Amusement in a Setting

Ice shows

Theatre

Movies

Television

Radio

Parties

Dinners

Resorts

Travel

Singing

Dancing

Playing cards, dominos, etc.

Playing instruments

Orchestra

Chorus

Picnics and outings

Amusement parks

Playing games

Sport activities: boating, golfing,
  billiards, playgrounds, gym-
  nasium, beaches, pools, horse-
  back riding, skiing

Major Classification: Emotions in a Setting

| Fear | Sorrow | Sympathy |
| Happiness | Love | Shock |

Sadness	Hate	Anxiety
Pain	Anger	Pity

Major Classification: Tensions and Forces in a Setting

Stresses	Flight	Hunger
Explosions	Propulsion	Pain
Floods	Storms	Pulling
Fires	Tornadoes	Pushing

Major Classification: Religious Subjects in a Setting

Interiors of churches, temples, or synagogues

Exteriors of churches, temples, or synagogues

Ways of celebrating holidays: Christmas, Easter, Passover, Hanukkah, etc.

People praying in church, temple, or synagogue

People praying at home

Ceremonial processions

Baptismal and other ceremonies

Confessional booths

Wedding ceremonies of various cultures

Burial ceremonies of various cultures

Administering of last rites

Heaven and hell concepts

Major Classification: Transportation in a Setting

Planes	Trolleys
Boats	Roller skating
Wagons	Bicycles
Autos	Motorcycles
Trucks	Locomotives
Buses	Box cars
Scooters	Pony express
Elevateds	Sleigh
Subways	Air travel
Horseback	Submarine
Stagecoach	Elevators
Canoe	Lifts
Elephant	Ferris wheel
Camel	Parachute jumping
Ox carts	Swimming
Donkeys	Boat rowing
Chariots	Ricksha riding
Dog sleds	Walking
Monorail	Running
Cable car	Carriage riding

Major Classification: Structures in a Setting

Bridges

Elevated stations

Steel skeleton of buildings

Churches

Schools

Homes

Cabins

Hotels

Motels

Gasoline stations

Drive-in restaurants

Skyscrapers

Ski jumps

Towers

Fire houses

Police stations

Theaters, movie houses

Elevators

Train depots

Harbor structures, piers

Water towers

Lighthouses

Cathedrals

Army barracks

Hangars

Coliseums

Sport arenas

Bowling alleys

Shopping centers

Factories

Airports

Oil wells

NOTES

1. L. Shaffer, B. Gilmer, and M. Schoen, *Psychology and Mental Growth.* New York: Harper and Brothers, 1940, p. 29.

READING REFERENCES

A.S.C.D., 1962 Yearbook Committee, Arthur W. Combs, Chairman, *Perceiving, Behaving, Becoming*, Creativity and Openness to Experience, Chapter 10.

Beck, Otto Walter, *Self-Development in Drawing.* New York: G. P. Putnam's Sons, 1912.

Blake, Vernon, *Drawing for Children and Others.* New York: Oxford University Press, 1944.

————, *The Art and Craft of Drawing.* New York: Oxford University Press, 1952.

Blum, Lucille H., and Dragositz, Anna, "Finger Painting" *Child Development*, 1947.

Boyleston, Elsie Reid, *Creative Expression with Crayons.* Worcester, Mass.: Davis Press, Inc., 1953.

Cole, Natalie Robinson, *The Arts in the Classroom.* New York: John Day Co., 1940.

D'Amico, Victor, *Creative Teaching in Art*, rev. ed. Scranton, Pa.: International Textbook Company, 1953.

Educational Press Bulletin, "Art Education at the Elementary Level," by the Superintendent of Public Instruction, Room 100, Centennial Building, Springfield, Ill. (Sept) 1955, vol. 46, no. 4, whole no. 459.

Edwards, Morton, ed., *Your Child from 2 to 5.* 45 Rockefeller Plaza, New York 20, N.Y., 1955.

Gaitskell, Charles D., *Children and Their Pictures.* Toronto: The Ryerson Press, 1951.

Hoover, Louis F., *A Teacher's Guide for Using Arts and Activities in The Classroom*. Skokie, Ill.: The Jones Publishing Co., 1955.

Randall, Arne W., *Murals for Schools*. Worcester, Mass.: Davis Press, Inc., 1956.

Read, Herbert, *Education Through Art*. New York: Pantheon Books, Inc., 1945, Part III, Chapters 1, 3, 4, 5, 6.

Richardson, Marion, *Art and the Child*. London: University of London Press, Ltd., 1948.

Schaefer-Simmern, Henry, *The Unfolding of Artistic Activity*, 2d ed. Berkeley and Los Angeles: University of California Press, 1950.

Skeaping, John, *Animal Drawing*. New York: Studio Publications, 1937.

Tomlinson, R. R., *Picture Making by Children*. London: The Studio, Ltd., 1934.

11

Developing Fluency and Flexibility through Art Experiences

INTRODUCTION

In his study of four communities of varying social complexity, Mandel Sherman found that "personality traits can be determined by the number and kind of experiences that children have; and that the more complex and varied the experiences are, the more varied and flexible are the resulting personality traits. Also, that children develop significant individual differences only when the environment is relatively complex"[1].

J. P. Guilford, in his article on "The Psychology of Creativity," explains that "potentiality for creative performance is not just one ability; it involves quite a number of different abilities. A person may have much of some, and little of others. A number of those abilities pertain most clearly to creativity." Significant, also, is Guilford's assertion that "creative aptitudes can be developed by virtue of practice" [2].

Art educators have long been cognizant of the relative importance of diligent and persistent effort in the development of creative aptitudes; also, of the operating techniques that are useful in this process. However, much of the evidence has been empirical in nature and depended largely upon the teacher's skill to interpret data from observation. It is indeed reassuring and comforting, to those who are actively engaged in the teaching of art, to know that sociological and psychological investigations of creativity confirm and strongly support the art educator's views and beliefs.

Sherman's and Guilford's findings are particularly relevant to our purpose. These convey implicitly, and most poignantly, the values which

Fig. 11-1. "Spring" (tempera painting by six-year old).

are inherent in, and the multiple outcomes which result from, art education. They call for the realization of the fact that a well planned art
education program develops individual differences because:

1) it recognizes the existence of a "plural number of abilities" in
each learner and individual differences as well;

2) it nourishes those abilities and differences through practice opportunities in the use of varied media, tools, and processes so
that each learner may find his own particular medium for self-
expression;

3) it challenges the learner's varied abilities and aptitudes to the
limit of his intellectual, imaginative, emotional, creative, and
manipulative capacities.

Within this context of diversity, complexity, and multiplicity of
experience, the learner naturally emerges with broadened concepts, insights, and horizons. His novel notions, in particular, flourish freely. He
becomes fluent and flexible in the configuration of mental images. *Idea
fluency* and *flexibility* of personality traits thus emerge as concomitant by-

FIG. 11-2. Self-portrait (tempera painting by seven-year old).

FIG. 11-3. "Fun on Halloween" (tempera painting by nine-year old).

FIG. 11-4. "Winter Fun" (crayon drawing by ten-year old).

FIG. 11-5. "Rehearsing for the Concert" (watercolor
by sixteen-year old).

FIG. 11-6. "Amusement Park" (chalk drawing by thirteen-year old).

FIG. 11-7. "View from the Elevated" (tempera painting by fourteen-year old).

FIG. 11-8. "Banjo Composition" (paper batik by twelve-year old).

FIG. 11-9. Poodle dog (paper sculpture by fourteen-year old).

FIG. 11-10. Collage (by fourteen-year old).

FIG. 11-11. Papier-mâché figure (by thirteen-year old).

FIG. 11-12. Box animal (by twelve-year olds).

products. Collectively these factors lead to a development of open-mindedness in personality growth.

"A creative person is a fluid thinker," states Guilford. "Facility in generating ideas is characteristic of creative people; not necessarily in all fields, but at least in one or two fields—and the person who can come up with more ideas is also likely to bring out more good ideas. There is a positive relationship between quantity and quality of production" [3].

True, it is often difficult, even for the most objective observer to measure accurately the degree to which the learner's artistic value judgments have grown, because such values are often subtle and intangible and cannot be easily measured. However, when these are viewed in the light of the learner's growing skills in bringing his notional concepts to a realization and in terms of newly developed personality traits, or wholesome behavioral patterns, a great deal becomes apparent to the observer.

In Chart 4, entitled "Two- and Three-Dimensional Art Expe-

FIG. 11-13. Swan (paper sculpture by thirteen-year old).

FIG. 11-14. Papier-mâché masks (by fifteen-year old).

FIG. 11-15. Plaster over armature (by thirteen-year old).

FIG. 11-16. Plaster carving (by fifteen-year old).

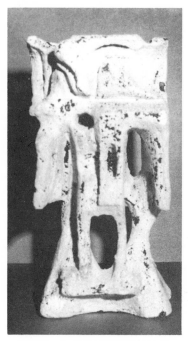

FIG. 11-17. Foamglas carving (by
thirteen-year old).

FIG. 11-18. Clay modeling (by sixteen-year old).

FIG. 11-19. Assemblage (wood by two thirteen-year olds).

FIG. 11-20. Wood carving (balsa by fourteen-year old).

FIG. 11-21. Construction (wood by thirteen-year old).

FIG. 11-22. Construction (wood by sixteen-year old).

riences," are suggested various activities which are not intended to be an end in themselves. Rather, these are intended to serve as a means of fostering perceptual and aesthetic growth, along with idea fluency and flexibility of personality traits. While these objectives can not be realized within one semester nor within one year of intensive art work, a good beginning can be made within this period of time. A firm foundation for creative development, concomitant with physical and social growth, however, can be laid within the framework of eight years; that is, eight years of active participation in creative thinking and doing. *Passive exposure to unrelated and uncoordinated art projects, to uncontrolled experimentation, to undisciplined utilization of materials and media, and to quick and accident-oriented tricks does not suffice. Rather, each creative concept needs to be explored to the fullest degree—in depth and through quality of performance, closely related to the capacities and abilities of each learner.*

The experiences listed in Chart 4 are designed to meet the creative needs of students from kindergarten through the twelfth grade. These

FIG. 11-23. Creative stitching (yarn on burlap by fourteen-year old).

FIG. 11-24. Creative stitching (yarn on burlap by thirteen-year old).

Fig. 11-25. Creative stitching (yarn on burlap by sixteen-year old).

Fig. 11-26. Creative stitching (by thirteen-year old).

Fig. 11-27. Weaving on a board loom (by fifteen-year old).

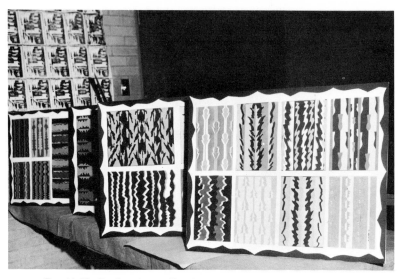

Fig. 11-28. Designs for textiles (by twelve- and thirteen-year olds).

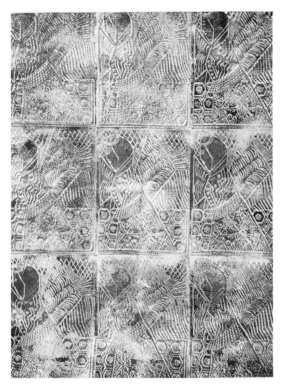

FIG. 11-29. Block printing (linocut by thirteen-year old).

FIG. 11-30. Linoleum-block-printed textile (by twelve-year old).

were arranged in sequential order, bearing in mind the developmental growth of the learner. Skills and understandings gained through each experience will lead the student into subsequent experiences with greater confidence in his own creative abilities.

It may be noted also that the range of experiences prescribed here appears to be wide. However, these can be further expanded, depending largely upon the extent of both the teacher's and pupil's resourcefulness. In this chart, the teacher of art will find a variety of activities from which to select those which are particularly suited to the grade level, temperament, interests, and needs of her pupils. She may experiment with only a few of these during the course of one semester. But, as she gains confidence in her ability to organize a class for these particular art activities, she may add other activities to her limited repertoire.

It should be stated here that, aside from the relative importance of involvement in a variety of problem-solving situations and the use of varied media in the resolution of these problems, there is still another

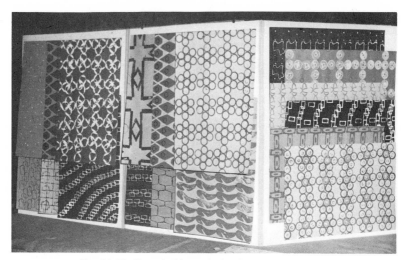

FIG. 11-31. Found-object printing (by twelve-year olds).

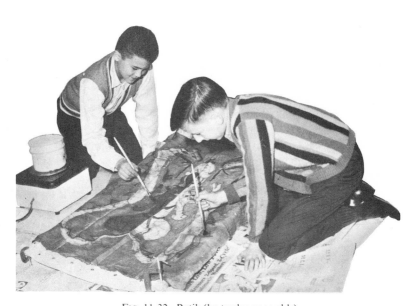

FIG. 11-32. Batik (by twelve-year olds).

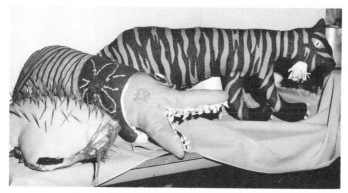

FIG. 11-33. Felt animals (by twelve-year olds).

FIG. 11-34. Paper jewelry (by twelve-year old).

FIG. 11-35. Necklace (porcelain and terra-cotta clay by fifteen-year old).

FIG. 11-36. Rug hooking on a curtain stretcher (by eleven-year old).

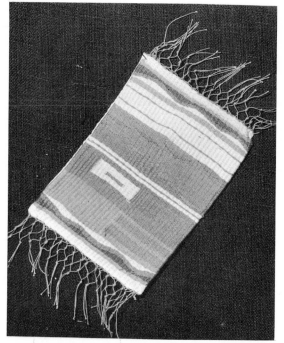

FIG. 11-37. Woven tapestry (by twelve-year old).

FIG. 11-38. "Harbor" (paper batik by fourteen-year old).

FIG. 11-39. Rug hooking (by fifteen- and sixteen-year olds).

FIG. 11-40. Rug hooking (by fifteen- and sixteen-
year olds).

significant factor which must be recognized.   Principally, it is the importance of presenting learning experiences in a sequential order.   This
enables the learner to utilize in new situations, insights, concepts, and
skills which he acquired through previous learning experiences. Further,
he becomes aware of a distinct purpose in learning. Insights, concepts,
and skills lie dormant or are quickly forgotten unless they are reawakened
through learning experiences which demand their constant involvement.

When the content of art experiences is not sequentially oriented, or
when the object is to cover the curriculum guide within a specified period

CHART 4

TWO- AND THREE-DIMENSIONAL ART EXPERIENCES

To Develop Resourcefulness, Ingenuity, Idea Fluency, Flexibility, Perceptual Skill, Originality in Self Expression, and Sensitivity to Aesthetic Values

I Processes or Media	II Art Activities	III Materials and Tools Needed	IV Recommended Grade Levels	V Primary Emphasis

PAINTING AND DRAWING
Applied to paper or to other sheet material or flat surfaces
	Use any suggestions in Chapter 10.	Manila paper
		Newsprint
		Watercolor paper
		Wallpaper
		Wrapping paper
		Construction paper, cardboard
		Paper shelving
		Tempera paints
		Water colors
		Casein
		Finger paints
		Felt pens
		Fountain pens
		Chalk, charcoal
		Inks (black or colored)
		Crayon
		Large or small brushes
		Sticks, etc.
			All grades	*Emphasis and subordination*
				Balance of forms, line, and color
				Color relationships
				Rhythm
				Texture
				Movement, action, direction
				Space relationships
				UNITY
				Variation of
				  lines,
				  shapes,
				  color
				  textures,
				  sizes
				  direction

CLAY MODELING Plasticine Water clay Asbestos-mixture, powder clay, any other clay compound Mounted on cardboard, masonite, plaster, wood.	Tiles Plaques People in bas-relief, in the round Animals in bas-relief, in the round Birds Flowers Insects Nonobjective forms Jewelry: beads, pendants, pins, earrings, bracelets	Buff clay Red clay Talc clay Plaster bat Modeling tools Plastic cloth Synthetic sponge Rolling pin Large can and cover Two strips of wood, $1/4''$ thick Rags	All grades	*Form* *Movement, action, direction* Line *Texture* Color *Space relationships* UNITY Variety Balance

CHART 4 (continued)

I Processes or Media	II Art Activities	III Materials and Tools Needed	IV Recommended Grade Levels	V Primary Emphasis
COLLAGE Applied to cardboard, wood, other flat material	Illustrative compositions Abstract or nonobjective design arrangements	Pieces of cloth Colored felt, burlap Seeds, lentils Corrugated cardboards String Yarn Sandpaper Metallic papers Textured papers Colored tissue paper Paste Scissors	All grades	*Texture* *Space relationships* Shape Line Color UNITY *Harmony of materials used* Variety Balance

PRINT PROCESSES
Using
  beads
  wads of clay
  clay tiles
  vegetables
  plaster of paris
  string and brayer
  monoprinting
  linoleum
  found objects
  silk screening
  chalk and crayon
  stenciling
Applied to paper or cloth
	Greeting cards
	Program covers
	Place mats
	Skirts
	Blouses
	Scarfs
	Collars
	Drapery
	Curtains
	Invitations to home, school, community functions
	Posters
	Pictorial designs
		Printer's ink, water or oil base
		Paper
		Tempera paints
		Cloth
		Plaster of paris
		Cardboard
		Brayer
		String
		Tray or slab of glass
		Turpentine
		Found objects
		Brushes
		Carving or cutting tools
		Rags
			All grades	*Line*
				Shape relationships
				Color
				Movement, direction
				Continuity
				UNITY
				
				Variety
				Texture
				Balance

Activity	Products	Materials	Grades	Concepts
PAPIER-MÂCHÉ SCULPTURE — Mounted on cardboard boxes	Animals, Masks, Puppets, Circus performers, Mardi Gras figures, Dolls, Mobiles, Stabiles	Yarns and scraps, Paper toweling, Newspaper, Paper bags, Balloons, Wheat paste, Brown gummed paper, Masking tape, Coat-hanger wire, Paint (tempera), Cardboard rolls, Shellac, alcohol, brushes	All grades	*Form construction, sturdy and imaginative*; *Movement, action, direction*; Color; Texture; UNITY; Balance; Variety
TEXTILE DESIGNING — Block printing, Batik, Tie and dye, String and brayer, Found objects, Applied to paper or cloth	Scarfs, Doilies, Towels, Napkins, Skirts, Beach bags, Aprons, Place mats, Tablecloths	Newspapers, Construction paper, Linoleum blocks, Linoleum cutting tools, Printer's inks, water or oil base, Turpentine, Burlap, Felt, Muslin, Dyes, Beeswax, Paraffin, Rags, Tray, Cardboard or slab of glass, Paper toweling, Hot plate, Metal container (tin can)	All grades	*Line*; *Shape*; *Color*; *Movement*, direction; *Continuity*; UNITY; Variety
CREATIVE STITCHING AND HOOKING — Applied to burlap, felt, buckram	Rugs, Murals, Place mats, Wall hangings, Beach bags	Buckram, Burlap, Felt, Paper, Raffia	All grades	*Texture*; *Line*; *Color*; *Shape*; UNITY

CHART 4 (*continued*)

I Processes or Media	II Art Activities	III Materials and Tools Needed	IV Recommended Grade Levels	V Primary Emphasis
netting wire screening hardware cloth	Pillows Pincushions School bags Vests Hats Slippers Evening bags Knitting bags	Yarn Beads Sequins Tapestry needles Sewing needles Hooking needles Stretchers (wooden frame) Embroidery hoops Wire screening Cotton roving		Texture Variety Balance of art elements
PAPER SCULPTURE Mounted on posterboard or any cardboard free standing	Dolls Animals Birds Masks Portraits Clowns Floral arrangements Fish Angels Structures People Mobiles or stabiles	Paper bags Construction paper Newspaper Scotch tape Posterboard Scissors Paste Stapler Paper clips X-acto knife	All grades	*Form* *Light and shadow* *Texture* *Line* UNITY *Variety* *Balance*
WEAVING Paper Cloth Basketry	Mats Belts Scarfs Purses Wall hangings Skirts	Warp thread Strips of cloth Paper Yarn, cotton roving Ribbon Lace	All grades	*Line* *Pattern* *Color* *Texture* *Space relationships* UNITY

		String Raffia Reed Tapestry needle Shuttle Cardboard looms Table looms Makeshift looms Threading hook		Variety Balance of art elements
	Ties Baskets Imaginary creatures of reed and raffia			

MOSAICS
Paper
  construction
  corrugated
  metalic
  newspaper
  magazine
Seeds
Beads
Shells
Linoleum
Tesserae
Applied to paper, cardboard, wood, glass, masonite
	Illustrative compositions
	Abstract or nonobjective arrangements
	Functional projects
	  tables
	  murals
	  trays
	  wall plaques
	Jewelry
		Paper mosaics
		  paper
		  scissors
		  paste
		Tesserae mosaics
		  tesserae
		  grout
		  wood or masonite
		  snips (tile)
		  palette knife
		  Elmer's glue
		  rags
		  liquid glass
			All grades
			
			Intermediate and upper grades
				Space relationships
				Color relationships
				Texture relationships
				UNITY
				
				Variety

CARVING Mounted on slab of plaster, wood, cardboard box, or any firm base, depending upon nature and weight of carving	Figures Animals Nonobjective forms Birds Insects, bas-relief, in the round Floral designs Structures	Soap, Firebrick Featherstone Plaster of paris Plaster of paris and sand mixture; or earth vermiculite and plaster mixture Cement, zonolite and sand mixture Balsa, other woods Foamglas Paring knife	Upper grades	*Form* *Movement, direction, action* *Texture* *Line* *Space relationships* UNITY Balance Variety

CHART 4 (*continued*)

I Processes or Media	II Art Activities	III Materials and Tools Needed	IV Recommended Grade Levels	V Primary Emphasis
		Chisels, carving tools Mallet Goggles Vise Sandpaper, rough, fine Linoleum cutting tools X-acto tools		
SCULPTURE AND CONSTRUCTIONS Mounted on bases similar to those for carvings	Geometric Architectural Nonobjective Ornaments Mobiles Stabiles Free forms	Colored tissue paper Toothpicks Balsa wood Wire Wire and plaster of paris Paper-mâché Asbestos, powder clay Wooden beads Elmer's glue Wire cutters Mallet	All grades	*Line* *Space relationships* *Balance* *Texture* *Surface treatment* *Form* UNITY
JEWELRY MAKING Experimental jewelry Enameling on copper Silver	Beads Pendants Necklaces Bracelets Pins Earrings Cuff links Tie clips	Construction paper Cardboard Enamels Sheet copper, 16 or 18 gauge Plaster of paris, quick drying Water clay Wire: aluminum, copper, silver, etc. Files, sandpaper	All grades Intermediate, upper grades	*Shape* *Line* *Color* *Texture* *Form* UNITY

		Jewelry findings: earring, pin backs, tie clip backs, cuff link backs / Asbestos cement mixture / Copper-enameling kiln / Soldering iron / Soft solder and flux / Lumps and threads (glass) / Salt and vinegar solution		
BATIK, PAPER	Any of the suggestions in Chapter 10	Manila paper / Watercolor paper / Newspaper / Tempera paints / Large brushes / India ink	Intermediate, upper grades	As in PAINTING AND DRAWING.
BATIK, CLOTH Suspended on dowels or curtain rods for wall hangings	As above	Paraffin / Beeswax / Dyes, aniline or cold water / Muslin, silk, rayon, etc. / Hot plate / Coffee can or double boiler / Soft brushes, varied sizes / Newspaper / Iron / Large blotter / Drawing board / Colored waterproof inks	Intermediate, upper grades	As in PAINTING AND DRAWING.

of time, much that is of value may be overlooked in the learning process. *Modifications in the number and type of experiences must be continuous, and must be considered valid, so that the learning process may not be impeded.*

In viewing Chart 4, it may be noted that there are five columns:

In *Column I* are listed various art processes and media.

In *Column II* are suggested activities which may be developed with each process or medium listed in Column I.

In *Column III* are offered some possible choices of materials and tools which may be utilized in each of the art experiences suggested in Column II. A selection is made of only those materials and tools which are necessary for each art experience. For instance, different types of paper are listed for painting and drawing. The student makes his own choice of paper.

In *Column IV* are listed grade levels for which the art activities in Column II are suitable and desirable.

In *Column V* are indicated the *primary emphases*, i.e., what to stress in the development of each creative idea. Those elements printed in italics and small caps indicate the need for greater emphasis than those listed in regular type. The consideration of the latter is nevertheless necessary.

The teacher may locate the grade level and find the list of possible activities which appeal to the interests, and parallel the skills, of her pupils. For further information on processes and methods, the teacher may also refer to the selected reading references suggested at the end of this chapter.

NOTES

1. Mandel Sherman and Thomas R. Henry, *Hollowfolks*. New York: Thomas Y. Crowell Co., 1953, p. 213.

2. J. P. Guilford, "Psychology of Creativity," *Creative Crafts*, volume 1, number 1 (April) 1960. Published by Fred de Lidon, Los Angeles, Calif.

3. *Ibid.*

READING REFERENCES

Design:

Emerson, Sybil, *Design: A Creative Approach*. Scranton, Pa.: International Textbook Company, 1953.

Johnson, Pauline, *Creating With Paper*. Seattle, Wash.: University of Washington Press, 1958.

Moseley, S., Johnson, P., and Koenig, H., *Crafts Design*. Belmont, Calif.: Wadsworth Publishing Co. Inc., 1962.

Wolchonok, Louis, *Design for Artists and Craftsmen*. New York: Dover Publications, Inc., 1953.

Painting:

Blake, Vernon, *Drawing for Children and Others*. New York: Oxford University Press, 1944.

———, *The Art and Craft of Drawing*. New York: Oxford University Press, 1952.

Blum, Lucille H., and Dragositz, Anna, "Finger Painting," *Child Development*, 1947.

Boyleston, Elise Reid, *Creative Expression with Crayons*. Worcester, Mass.: Davis Press, Inc., 1953.

Gaitskell, Charles D., *Children and Their Pictures*. Toronto: The Ryerson Press, 1951.

Gezari, Temima, *Footprints and New Worlds*. New York: The Reconstructionist Press, 1957.

Janson, H. W., and Janson, D. J., *Story of Painting for Young People*. New York: Harry N. Abrams, Inc., 1952.

Kellogg, Rhoda, *The How of Successful Finger Painting*. San Francisco: Fearon Publishers, 1958.

Lowenfeld, Viktor, *Creative and Mental Growth*, 3d ed. New York: The Macmillan Co., 1957.

———, *Your Child and His Art*. New York: The Macmillan Co., 1954.

Perrine, Van Dearing, *Let The Children Draw*. New York-Philadelphia: Frederick A. Stokes Company, 1936.

Clay Modeling:

Duncan, Julia, and D'Amico, Victor, *How to Make Pottery and Ceramic Sculpture*. New York: Museum of Modern Art, 1947.

Kenny, John B, *Ceramic Sculpture*. New York: Greenberg Publisher, 1953.

———, *The Complete Book of Pottery Making*. New York: Greenberg Publisher, 1949.

Röttger, Ernst, *Creative Clay Design*. New York: Reinhold Publishing Corp., 1963.

Print Processes:

Baranski, Matthew, *Graphic Design: A Creative Approach*. Scranton, Pa.: International Textbook Company, 1960.

Greenburg, Sam, *Making Linoleum Cuts*. New York: Stephen Daye Press, 1947.

Kosloff, Albert, *Mitography*. Milwaukee, Wisc.: Bruce Publishing Co., 1952.

Stubbe, Wolf, *Graphic Arts in the Twentieth Century*. New York: Frederick A. Praeger Inc., 1963.

Papier-Mâché:

Betts, Victoria Bedford, *Exploring Papier-Mâche*. Worcester, Mass.: David Press, Inc., 1959.

Hughes, Tony, *How to Make Shapes in Space*. New York: E. P. Dutton & Co., Inc., 1956.

Paper Sculpture:

Johnson, Pauline, *Creating with Paper*. Seattle, Wash.: University of Washington Press, 1958.

Johnston, Mary Grace, *Paper Sculpture*. Worcester, Mass.: Davis Press, Inc., 1952.
_____, *Paper Shapes and Sculpture*. Worcester, Mass.: Davis Press, Inc., 1958.

Carving:

Rood, John, *Sculpture in Wood*. Minneapolis, Minn.: University of Minnesota Press, 1950.
Röttger, Ernst, *Creative Wood Design*. New York: Reinhold Publishing Corp., 1961.
Struppeck, Jules, *The Creation of Sculpture*. New York: Henry Holt and Co., 1951.

Sculpture and Constructions:

Duncan, Julia, and D'Amico, Victor, *How to Make Pottery and Ceramic Sculpture*. New York: Museum of Modern Art, 1947.
Lynch, John, *How to Make Mobiles*. New York-London: The Studio Publications, Inc., 1953.
Moholy-Nagy, L., *Vision in Motion*. Chicago: Paul Theobald and Co., 1947.
Read, Herbert, and others, *Gabo Pevsner*. New York: Museum of Modern Art, 1948.

Creative Stitching and Hooking:

Booker, Molly, *Embroidery Design*. New York-London: Studio Publications, 1935.
Enthoven, Jacqueline, *The Stitches of Creative Embroidery*. New York: Reinhold Publishing Corp., 1964.
Karasz, Mariska, *Adventures in Stitches*, rev. ed. New York: Funk and Wagnalls Co., 1959.
Lane, Rose Wilder, *Book of American Needlework*. New York: Simon and Schuster, 1963.
Mochrie, Elsie, *Simple Embroidery*. Peoria, Ill.: Charles A. Bennett Company, Inc., The Dryad Press, 1952.
Nicholson, Joan, *Contemporary Embroidery Design*. New York: Viking Press, Inc.
Phillips, Anna M. Laise, *Hooked Rugs and How to Make Them*. New York: The Macmillan Co., 1925.
Rex, Stella Hay, *Practical Hooked Rugs and How to Make Them*. Chicago: Ziff-Davis Publishing Co., 1949.
Roseaman, I. P., *Rug Making, Knotted and Embroidered*. Leiseden, England, 1958. Distributed by Charles A. Bennett Company, Inc., Peoria, Ill.

Weaving:

Black, Mary, *New Key to Weaving*. New York: Pitman Publishing Corp., 1958.
Brown, H., *Handweaving for Pleasure and Profit*. New York: Harper and Brothers, 1952.
Crampton, Charles, *Junior Basket Maker*. Peoria, Ill.: Charles A. Bennett Company, Inc., 1953.
Davison, Marguerite Porter, *Handweaver's Pattern Book*. Published by the author, Swarthmore, Pa.
Moseley, S., Johnson, P., and Koenig, H., *Crafts Design*. Belmont, Calif.: Wadsworth Publishing Co., Inc., 1962.

Mosaics:

Argiro, Larry, *Mosaic Art Today.*   Scranton, Pa.: International Textbook Company, 1961.

Jenkins, Louisa, *The Art of Making Mosaics.* Princeton, N. J.: D. Van Nostrand Co., Inc., 1953.

Young, Joseph, *Course in Making Mosaics.* New York: Reinhold Publishing Corp., 1957.

Jewelry Making:

Bates, F. Kenneth, *Enameling: Principles and Practice.*   Cleveland: World Publishing Co., 1949.

Martin, Charles J., and D'Amico, Victor, *How to Make Modern Jewelry.* New York: The Museum of Modern Art, 1949.

Murray, Bovin, *Jewelry Making.* Published by Murray Bovin 68–36, 108 Street, Forest Hills, L.I., N. Y.

Winebrenner, D. Kenneth, *Jewelry Making: As an Art Expression.* Scranton, Pa.: International Textbook Company, 1953.

Batik and Tie-and-Dye:

Emerson, Sybil, *Design: A Creative Approach.* Scranton, Pa.: International Textbook Company, 1953.

Krevitsky, Nik, *Batik.* New York: Reinhold Publishing Corp., 1964.

Maile, Anne, *Tie and Dye.* London: Mills and Boon, Ltd., 1963.

12 Design: A Means of Perceiving and Achieving Aesthetic Relationships

INTRODUCTION

Fundamental to the perceptual growth of the individual is the ability to apprehend aesthetic relationships in a work of art; that is to say, to appreciate those subtle qualities and nuances with which spatial, textural, linear, and color relationships have become endowed through the artist's skillful and flexible manipulation of art elements. These qualities are vital in the achievement of artistic products.

In the realm of visual communication, designing constitutes a process through which the creative individual structures and projects his notional concepts in space. An awareness of the design concepts is a means through which an informed and critical viewer perceives with depth and with sensibility the works of the artist.

A number of pertinent factors strongly relate to the designing process. These are clearly understood by the artist and are often by the informed viewer as well. Yet, a reasonable degree of understanding of these factors does not necessarily insure the achievement of designing skill. Much more is apparently needed in the realization of a work of art. These are possibly qualities which reside in the refinement and in the intensification of aesthetic values, qualities which transcend any technical skill, and which bring to the work of art the individual's perceptivity and acuteness of feeling.

The process of designing also demands the acquisition of a significant body of knowledge. This includes: a thorough understanding of various *media*, i.e., their possibilities and limitations; an awareness of many *techniques, processes, and devices* which may be utilized in the structuring of visual forms; and a knowledge of the *unlimited possibilities* inherent in the skillful *manipulation of line, form, color, texture, and space.* Perhaps, even more important in the process of designing is the cultivation of a keen sensitivity to the means through which it is possible to achieve coherence within the total visual scheme. Designing, therefore, is the intellectual structuring of visual elements in space, with due emphasis upon the utilization of perceptual skill and individuality.

THE MEANING OF "DESIGN"

The term "design" is frequently used in a variety of contextual references. But, in the realm of art, it applies mainly to two significant areas, i.e., 1) either to the orderly structuring of art elements in a visual form; or 2) to the decorative treatment of two- or three-dimensional surfaces. In the former, 1), "design" refers to an orchestration of visual patterns in which there is an achievement of coherence, variety in unity, and a harmonious integration of art elements. This definition applies directly to a painting, a piece of sculpture, an architectural structure, or to any functional form. In the designing of any visual scheme, therefore, the creative individual (i.e., the innovator, the artist-designer, the painter, the sculptor, the interior designer) in his own unique way is intensely concerned with structural problems which relate to the achievement of aesthetically satisfying results.

In the latter reference, 2), to "design," the term applies to the enrichment of two- or three-dimensional surfaces. It implies a sensitive use of pattern, of intricate textural effects, or of any other decorative treatment simply or elaborately rendered. In this frame of reference, design involves the addition of interest to some particular area which is in contrast to another plain area in a two- or three-dimensional visual scheme in order to enhance that form.

In either case, the design objectives are borne in mind even where modifications, for practical reasons, appear to be necessary as is generally so in industrial designing.

THE LANGUAGE OF DESIGN

To become sensitive to existing design concepts, it is essential to examine the meaning and the function of art elements. Moreover, it is necessary to become familiar with those considerations, guideposts, or principles (as they are sometimes called) which influence the artist in the designing process. Although these considerations are regarded by some as rather limiting, others believe that these definitely serve as a means of evolving an order out of chaos within a given context. For example, principles of art may be valid, but only so long as they are not considered

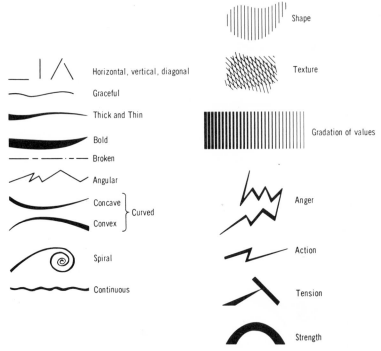

FIG. 12-1. Lines possess a vitality which makes them dynamic and useful in the designing or the structuring of visual forms. Lines may be used for creating shape, texture, or gradation of values. Lines may be used to convey feelings.

binding in the achievement of design goals. True, a conscious effort must be exerted in the realization of balance, rhythm, harmony, and contrast in visual forms; however, often these goals may be achieved intuitively.

Let us examine each art element briefly to see how these function in the process of visual communication. On the following pages line, form, shape, color, texture, and space are simply defined and illustrated.

Line, Its Meaning and Function.   What is a line? A line in mathematical terms is a point which creates a path while moving in any direction from its original source. A line is composed of many dots in close contact with one another. Lines as such, do not really exist in nature. They are a tool devised by the artist to symbolize reality, to represent an edge of a shape, or to delineate a visual form.

Lines in themselves, i.e., without reference to a particular shape or form, can be expressive (Fig. 12-1). They possess a vitality which makes them dynamic and useful in the designing or structuring of visual forms. For example, a line may be bold, graceful, broken, horizontal, vertical, diagonal, spiral, continuous, angular, or curved. It may have color,

Affection   Gaiety   Pathos

Humor   Tension   Strength

Action

FIG. 12-2. Lines can be expressive of feelings when skillfully combined either in illustrative or in abstract shapes or forms.

texture, thickness, opaqueness, or transparency. It also may be a combination of some of these qualities.

Lines may be expressive of feelings. They may be used to express sadness, gaiety, excitement, tensions, action, serenity, strength, or humor (Figs. 12-2, 12-3, and 12-4). For instance, they may express purely whimsical or symbolic notions as they appear to be doing in Miro's paint-

FIG. 12-3. "My Classmate" (ink drawing by sixteen-year old).   Student expresses a passive mood through the use of rippling and flowing lines.

ing, "Figures and Dog Before the Sun" (Fig. 12-5), or they may express boldness as in Picasso's painting, "Pitcher and Bowl of Fruit" (Fig. 12-6).

Lines may express intricately lacy patterns as they do in Mark Tobey's painting, "City Radiance" (Fig. 12-7). So it is in the communication of ideas that the artist or designer uses line in an unlimited manner but appropriately suited to his immediate purposes. The architect, the sculptor, the painter, and the designer—all are intellectually, creatively, and emotionally involved in the proportionate use of line. All are perceptive of the role which line plays in visual communication.

Form, Its Meaning and Function.   In the organization of a work of art, "form" is a structural element whereby the artist's vision is given mass or volume.   Mass is solid, it displaces space.   It is either flexible like clay

FIG. 12-4. "Teenager" (Lillian Desow-Fishbein, conte crayon drawing, courtesy of the artist). A line drawing in which form has been skillfully foreshortened in an unusual pose. Solidity of form has been achieved, and a pensive mood has been created through line alone.

or rigid like stone. A form may be real as it is in a piece of architecture, sculpture, furniture, or pottery. A form may also be illusional as it generally appears in a painting or drawing. Size, shape, direction, color, texture, and depth are other attributes of form. A form may be of a particular structural character, i.e., geometric, organic, transparent, or opaque. A form may also be a volume which encloses space. For example, a pewter pitcher is an opaque volume. A glass vase is a transparent volume.

Shape, Its Meaning and Function. The term "shape" as it is used in the context of designing is applied to two-dimensional areas which may or may not be defined by contours. Or the term "shape" may be applied to illusional, i.e., simulated three-dimensional forms such as may appear in paintings, textiles, weaving, etc. Color, value, size, direction, and texture are attributes of shape.

FIG. 12-5. "Figures and Dog Before the Sun"
(Juan Miro, 1949, Kunstmuseum, Basel). A
whimsical and symbolic treatment of lines and
shapes is represented in this painting by Miro.

The appearance of both "form" or "shape" is significantly influenced by the background spaces which surround them [Fig. 12-8(a)
and (b)]. The relationship between each of these may be subtle, contrasting, or dynamic (Fig. 12-9).

Color, Its Meaning and Function. In the process of designing, color
is used to intensify and to evoke an emotional response from the viewer,
to create illusions of distance or nearness, to express dynamic power or
strength, or to add decorative qualities to two- or three-dimensional
surfaces.

Color has three dimensions: hue, value, and intensity. *Hue* is the
name given to a color; *value* refers to lightness or darkness of a color;
intensity refers to saturation or density, or to the fullness of strength in a
color.

FIG. 12-6 "Pitcher and Bowl of Fruit" (Picasso, oil, 52″ × 64″, 1931, private collection). A bold treatment of space by means of massive line, strong contrasting values, and textured surfaces.

A color chart is a simple method of viewing color in an orderly sequence. One may begin with yellow at the top and proceed clockwise: yellow, yellow-green; green, blue-green; blue, blue-violet; violet, red-violet; red, red-orange; orange, and yellow-orange (Fig. 12-28). This includes the primary, secondary and tertiary hues.

Hue indicates the position of the color on the color wheel and the warmth and coolness of each color. For example; yellow, yellow-orange, orange, red, red-violet are known as *warm hues*; while yellow-green, green, blue-green, blue, blue-violet and violet are known as *cool hues*. The twelve hues on the color wheel are classified into three major categories.

1) The *primary* colors, i.e., red, blue, and yellow. These colors cannot be created by mixing any combination of colors. They are basic natural colors, which must be obtained commercially.

2) The *secondary* colors (green, orange, and violet) are produced by mixing two primary colors together, i.e., yellow and blue = green; red and yellow = orange; red and blue = violet.

3) The *tertiary* colors (yellow-green, blue-green, blue-violet, red-violet, red-orange, and yellow-orange) are produced by combining a primary and its immediate secondary color. For example: yellow and

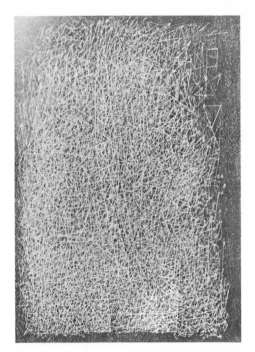

FIG. 12-7. "City Radiance" (Mark Tobey, $19\frac{3}{8}''$ × $14\frac{1}{4}''$, 1944, collection of Mrs. Julia Feininger, New York). A delicate and lacy-patterned composition structured by means of finely webbed, threadlike lines.

(a)   (b)

FIG. 12-8. The appearance of a form or shape is greatly influenced by the background which surrounds it. Although both forms are of similar size, the form in (b) appears larger than the one in (a) due to the apparent difference in the background space which surrounds each.

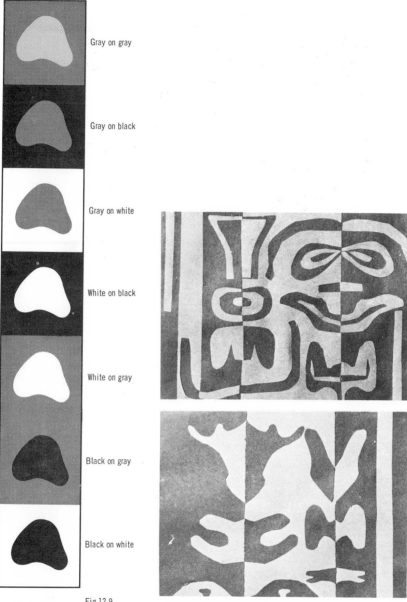

Gray on gray

Gray on black

Gray on white

White on black

White on gray

Black on gray

Black on white

Fig 12-9

FIG. 12-9. The value relationships in each of these vary: some are subtle, some are contrasting, others are dynamic. Each shape is influenced by the value of the background space which surrounds it.

FIG. 12-10. Designs for textiles made by fourteen-year-old boys. Negative and positive shapes were used as an integral part of the design. This is one of many approaches to the designing of space.

Fig. 12-11. Design for creative stitching done by fourteen-year-old girl. The above design illustrates the use of a bisymmetric or formal approach to the designing of space. The paper is folded in half. The design is cut and unfolded. This method is often called Polish paper cutting.

green = yellow-green; blue and green = blue-green; blue and violet = blue-violet; red and violet = red-violet; red and orange = red-orange; yellow and orange = yellow-orange.

The blues, greens, and blue-violets, project a feeling of coolness, depth, and calmness whereas the yellows, oranges, and reds suggest a feeling of warmth, excitement, vigor, and vitality. The cool colors tend to recede, the warm colors tend to advance. The artist-designer whose aim it is to generate a visual mood or feeling or to create depth or nearness is particularly cognizant of this color phenomenon.

However, in order to achieve a satisfying result, color must be disciplined. For instance, when two colors in full intensity (that is to say when they are at their brightest) are placed next to each other, they tend to clash. But, when one of these is grayed, i.e., the intensity is reduced, while the other is left intense, a harmonious and unified relationship is achieved. Example: when an intense red is placed adjacent to an intense green, the result appears discordant; but when the intensity of one is reduced, the combination appears pleasing. The intensity of any color may be reduced by changing its value, either by the addition of gray pigment to it or by the addition of a small amount of its complementary color. [A complementary color is one which is directly opposite any color

FIG. 12-12. Wall hanging (felt, yarn, and burlap designed by twelve-year olds). A theme-in-variation approach to the designing of two-dimensional space was used in this wall hanging. Each student in class contributed his version of the approach to the class project.   Ideas were developed in two colors of construction paper first; then executed in felt. The design was glued onto a burlap background. Lines of yarn were added to unify the individual units.

FIG. 12-13. Textile design (courtesy Chicago Teachers College, North). A theme-in-variation approach to the designing of space was skillfully developed in this linoleum-block-printed cloth. In the design unit the square was used as the theme. Variations of the square (rectangular shapes open and closed, joined, or superimposed) were organized into a design unit. Since two colors were used in this design, two blocks were needed; one for the light color, the other for the dark linear pattern. The units were printed close together in order to achieve continuity and movement.

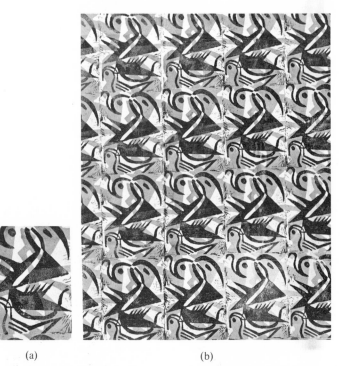

(a)   (b)

FIG. 12-14. Textile design (linoleum block print done in two colors by seventeen-year-old student). (a) A single unit design inspired by bird forms and flight. (b) The unit in (a) was used in the allover-pattern approach to the designing of space.

FIG. 12-15. Silk-screened textile (by Marian Witt). Design was inspired by forms in nature.

FIG. 12-16. Design for wall hanging by sixteen-year old. Decorative treatment of a two-dimensional surface; inspired by the human form.

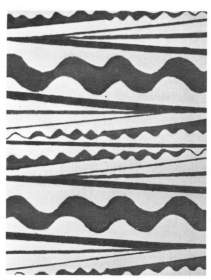

FIG. 12-17. Design for drapery material (by sixteen-year old) achieved through the use of varied types of lines in a dominant direction.

FIG. 12-18. Mexican platter in which the floral theme, and variations of it, were used as surface decoration in combination with linear borders of vertical, horizontal, diagonal, and curved lines.

on the Prang color wheel (Fig. 12-28).] For instance, if red needs to be grayed, green, the complement of red, is added. If orange needs to be grayed, blue, the complement of orange, is added. If yellow needs to be grayed, violet, the complement of yellow is added, and so forth.

A Scale of Values: Tints and Shades. Any color may be changed in value by the addition of white or black. These values are called "tints" and "shades." The values may be compared to the tones in a musical scale. In a scale of values the tints are the lighter tones of a color, and the shades are the darker tones (Fig. 12-32). In painting, the tints are produced by the addition of *white* to any color. The shades are produced by the addition of *black* to any color. The amount of white pigment in a color determines the degree of lightness in a tint, while the amount of black pigment in a color determines the degree of darkness in a shade. Thus may be achieved an infinite number of color values through the addition of white or black to any color.

This procedure offers the artist-designer many possible color variations for the expression of his ideas.

Color Schemes. A number of formal color schemes are known which traditionally the artist-designer utilized in the designing process in the past, and which he still uses to some extent. These color schemes suggest a variety of color relationships and combinations which, with some modification, produce harmonious results. Often, these schemes are used only as a point of departure. More often the color schemes are adapted to suit the artist's intuitive feelings or to serve the immediate purposes for which color combinations are intended. The artist-designer's sensitivity to color, as to all other elements of art, largely determines the aesthetic quality of his product. The creative artist usually searches for new color relationships, for new effects.

FIG. 12-22. "The Prow" (Unitarian Church by Frank Lloyd Wright). Line, form, color, and texture are combined in a unique relationship of materials in this architectural structure of glass, brick, and cement.

6) Triad—a color scheme which forms *an equilateral triangle* on the color wheel. Example: red, yellow, and blue or red-orange, blue-violet, yellow-green (Fig. 12-36).

7) Tetrad—a color scheme in which *four colors* that are *equidistant* on the color wheel are used. Example: yellow-orange, green, red, and blue-violet (Fig. 12-37).

When using any of these traditional color schemes, it is essential to bear in mind that tints, shades, grayed values, black, white, and colors in full intensity offer an infinite range of possibilities through which other unique and harmonious relationships may be developed. In fact, any number of clashing colors, selected at random, may be made compatible by mixing into each a small amount of still another color. The latter then serves as an integrating element. It orchestrates the totally unrelated group of colors selected.

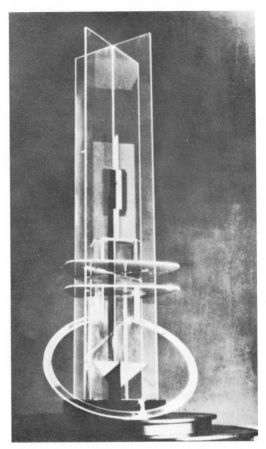

FIG. 12-23. "Column" (Naum Gabo, glass, plastic, metal, and wood, 41″ high, 1923, The Solomon R. Guggenheim Museum, New York). A sculptural form in which geometric, transparent, and opaque planes are combined and interpenetrated, creating a unified organization of elements in space.

Texture, Its Meaning and Function. In the designing process, "texture" is a vital element. The term applies to surface qualities of materials or media which are perceptible to the sense of touch. Surfaces, which feel rough, smooth, hard, soft, metalic, etc., are recognized as possessing qualities of texture (Fig. 12-38).

In a painting, texture refers to the realistic representation of surfaces which create an illusion of "skin," "fabrics," "wood," "foliage," "stone," etc (Fig. 12-39), or it may refer to real texture of paint applied to a canvas in a smooth or rough fashion (Fig. 12-42). But in the treatment of real

FIG. 12-24. "Seme" (Stuart Davis, oil, 1953, Metropolitan Museum of Art, George A. Hearn Fund).   Two-dimensional, geometric, and free-form shapes, circumscribed by precise and rigid contours, are juxtaposed and overlapped to create a unified abstract organization.

forms, such as architectural and sculptural as well as woven fabrics, texture is used to add interest, to enrich, or to achieve a contrast in surface appearances within a given spatial organization (Fig. 12-44).   In this sense, texture is real; it has tactile appeal.

Texture may be achieved through various means.   For example, it may be achieved through the skillful manipulation of tools, as in a wood or stone carving; through the addition of alien or related ingredients such as grog or sand to a clay compound used in sculpture or ceramics; through the use of pattern on an otherwise plain surface; or through the introduction of various types and thicknesses of fibers, i.e., of warp and weft in the weaving of fabrics.   In a room interior, textured surfaces are used to create added interest and character, i.e., rustic, formal, spiritual,

FIG. 12-25. Functional products of Danish design in which line, form, volume, and texture are harmoniously integrated. These objects reflect the integrity of the artist in the use of material.

etc. In any event, textured surfaces become an integral part of the design, and their use in a creative scheme is determined largely by the purpose and function of the design (Figs. 12-20, 12-44, and 12-45).

Space, Its Meaning and Function.   The area within which the elements of design are arranged and within which masses or volumes are organized is called "space." Space may be two-dimensional or three-dimensional in character. While it is the area within which a design is arranged, space is also the area which surrounds the design and which greatly influences the appearance of it. Frequently, the design areas are

FIG. 12-26. "Guernica" (Picasso, oil, 1937, The Museum of Modern Art, New York, on loan from the artist). A two-dimensional treatment of spatial organization depicting the horrors of war. Line, shape, and texture were used in strong contrasting values. The jagged and distorted shapes symbolize human and animal forms which literally shriek with sorrow, agony, and pain. The emotional impact upon the viewer is indeed great, despite the highly abstracted rendition of a realistic theme. It represents an informal balance of art elements in space.

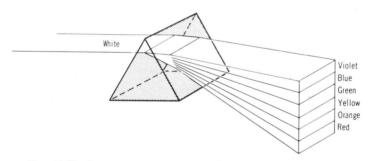

FIG. 12-27. Component colors of a beam of light have different wavelengths. When a beam of white light is passed through a prism, the component colors of light spread out and can be seen as separate colors. This is because each wavelength passes at a different speed and angle through the prism of glass. The result is the separation of the component colors into the spectrum of rainbow-like colors.

described as the positive shapes while the background or open areas are referred to as the negative shapes. In the designing process, negative shapes are regarded as having a function that is similar to "rests" in music. Both negative and positive spaces are an integral part of a design. These must therefore relate to each other, and to the total organization (Figs. 12-10, 12-46, and 12-47). Two-dimensional space may have the attributes of texture, color, opaqueness, or transparency.

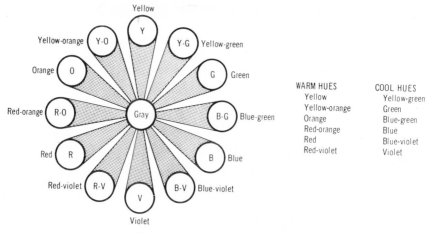

WARM HUES
Yellow
Yellow-orange
Orange
Red-orange
Red
Red-violet

COOL HUES
Yellow-green
Green
Blue-green
Blue
Blue-violet
Violet

FIG. 12-28. The Prang color wheel.

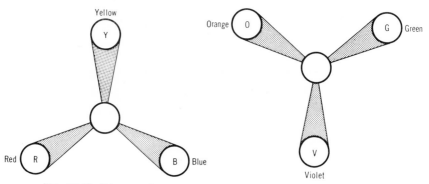

FIG. 12-29. Primary colors.

FIG. 12-30. Secondary colors.

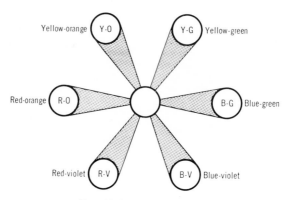

FIG. 12-31. Tertiary colors.

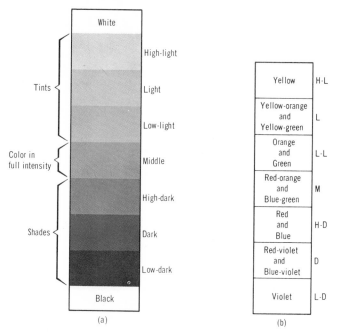

FIG. 12-32. (a) Value scale. (b) Colors relate to the value scale.

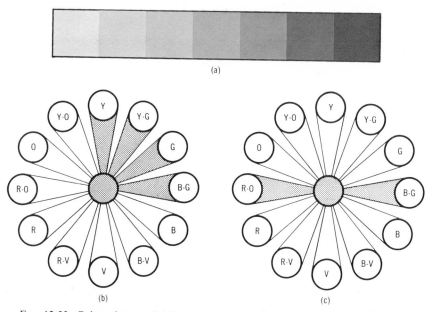

FIG. 12-33. Color schemes. (a) Tints and shades of one color constitute a *monochromatic* scheme. (b) Any three or four colors which are adjacent to each other on the color wheel are *analogous*. (c) Any two colors which are directly opposite each other on the color wheel are *complementary*.

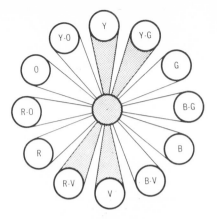

Fig. 12-34. Double complementary. Two adjacent colors and their direct opposites on the color wheel constitute a *double complementary* color scheme.

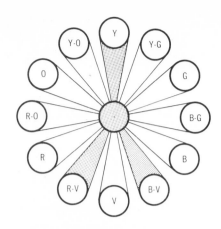

Fig. 12-35. Split complementary. Any color and two other colors which are located on either side of its complement constitute a *split complementary* color scheme.

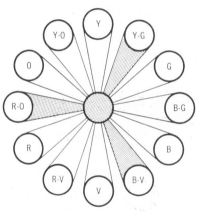

Fig. 12-36. Triad. Any three colors which form an equilateral triangle on the color wheel constitute a *triad* color scheme.

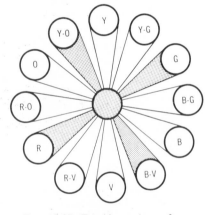

Fig. 12-37. Tetrad. Any four colors that are equidistant on the color wheel constitute a *tetrad* color scheme.

(a)   (b)   (c)

Fig. 12-38. The textural qualities of (a) brick, (b) wood, and (c) woven fabric are all perceptible to the sense of touch.

FIG. 12-39. "Prologue" (Aaron Bohrod, oil, 18″ × 24″, courtesy of the artist). The artist skillfully simulates texture; he renders with microscopic accuracy the characteristic textures of decayed wood, flesh, hair, blades of grass, metal, rubber, and paper.

FIG. 12-40. "Living Still Life" (Salvador Dali, collection of Reynolds Morse Foundation). A symbolic painting in which simulated textured effects of objects found in man's visual world are organized in a surrealistic manner.

FIG. 12-41. A collage (Kurt Schwitters, 1918, in the
A. Mazzota Collection, Milan) in which illusional and
real textured surfaces are organized. Included and combined are shapes of an abstract nature with some which
depict man-made or man-grown objects.

ART ELEMENTS IN THE DESIGNING PROCESS

Having explained some of the elements of design, i.e., their characteristics or attributes, it seems appropriate to examine how these function in the design process and how guiding principles and creative devices
are used in the organization of them. Although few artist-designers today
feel necessarily bound by established principles of art, nevertheless they
do recognize, whether intuitively or consciously, the need for an order in
things and the need for some guideposts that lead to the achievement of
that order.

In the process of designing, therefore, there are at least four major
concerns. They are: 1) to create *interest* in a given space; 2) to achieve a
unity of all the elements or components in a design; 3) to distribute the
interest in order to create a feeling of *balance*, or a state of equilibrium;

FIG. 12-42. "Bay of Naples" (Harry Mintz, oil, 48″ × 72″, 1960, courtesy of the artist). The heavy impasto of oil paints creates a textured quality which adds vigor and luminosity to this painting.

and 4) to create a track of vision, a *rhythm or movement* of art elements within the space.   The above concerns are realized in the following manner:

> *Interest* is achieved through various devices; for example, through variation, i.e., through degrees of contrast, through exaggeration, through alteration, invention, interpenetration, overlapping, enclosure, attraction or proximity, and through a combination of any of these devices.

> *Unity* is achieved through emphasis of a design idea or of a central focus point with all of the components, the dominant and the subordinate, falling into place and contributing to the clarity and to the enrichment of the main idea.

FIG. 12-43. "Triumph of the Egg" (Flannagan, granite, 16″ long, 1937, The Museum of Modern Art, New York). A sculptural piece in which the massive character of granite has been retained. The roughly textured surface adds interest to the simple and compact form.

FIG. 12-44. Ceiling detail of Exhibition Hall, Turin (Pier Luigi Nervi, 1948). A rare treatment of an architectural surface achieved through the use of sculptural and ornamental allover radiating pattern to create a textured effect in the ceiling.

FIG. 12-45. A room interior in which texture was given a great deal of emphasis. The parquet floor, the rough-textured fabric of the drapes, the thick-piled rug, the beamed ceiling, the leather-covered chairs, and the grass cloth on the walls—all add a sense of charm and warmth to the room atmosphere of the dining area in this home.

Balance is achieved through a formal or informal (i.e., bisymmetric or occult) distribution of interest using the art elements and their attributes to achieve an illusional state of equilibrium in a painting or to effectuate a balanced distribution of interest in architecture, sculpture, or any other visual form (Figs. 12-5, 12-20, 12-22, and 12-25).

Rhythm is achieved through the repetition of art elements and their attributes, i.e., through gradation of color; through radiation of line; through alternate stressing and relaxing, as expressed by thinness and thickness of line; through depth and shallowness of

(a)

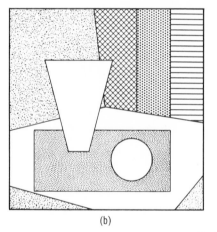

(b)

(c)

FIG. 12-46. (a) Illustrates an illusional treatment of third-dimension achieved through the use of light and shadow in a still-life composition. (b) Illustrates a two-dimensional treatment of the same still life. (c) Illustrates a complete redesigning of shapes, although retaining the essence of the original still-life arrangement.

curves; and through varying the widths or heights of areas contained within contours (Figs. 12-5, 12-6, and 12-19).

DEVICES USED IN DESIGNING

In the realization of design goals, many devices are employed. These are flexible and workable tools in the hands of the artist-designer. They are not intended to serve as formulas; rather, they represent a variety of methods through which it is possible to achieve satisfying relationships of visual elements in the organization of space.

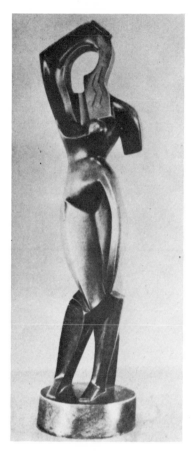

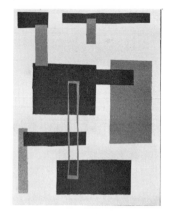

FIG. 12-48. Designing with geometric shapes, using the device of overlapping.

FIG. 12-47. "Woman Combing Her Hair" (Archipenko, bronze, 1915, The Museum of Modern Art, New York). Negative and positive areas in this sculptural design have been combined with well-defined geometric planes to capture the essence of the human form.

FIG. 12-49. Designing with geometric shapes, using the devices of enclosure and overlapping.

However, it must be remembered that the greatest merit lies in the artist-designer's use of his personal approaches to designing, which are a direct outgrowth of his perceptual skill, imagination, and experience and which suit his immediate purposes in the projection of ideas.

Some possible approaches to the treatment of space are suggested here for students.

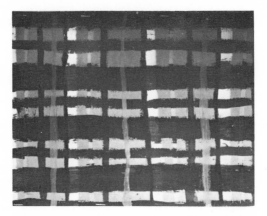

FIG. 12-50. Breaking up space with vertical
and horizontal lines.

Designing with Shapes

1) *Overlapping geometric shapes*, circles, triangles, squares, or any derivative shapes or segments of them (Figs. 12-23, 12-48, and 12-49).

2) *Overlapping free-form or organic shapes* such as are formed by a drop of liquid, an amoeboid, or any free-flowing shape (Fig. 12-14).

3) *Overlapping combinations* of geometric and free-form shapes (Fig. 12-14).

4) *Interpenetrating shapes:* any of those listed in 1), 2), and 3) above (Figs. 12-7, 12-10, 12-19, 12-47, and 12-51).

5) *Sketching many views* of any one object or natural form and overlapping the views to create an original form.

6) *Creating a continuous line* by "scribbling" or by dropping a string on a sheet of paper to suggest a rhythmic pattern.

7) *Simplifying, altering, and eliminating* details from realistic line sketches (Figs. 12-15, 12-16, and 12-46).

8) *Altering shapes by degrees* of elongation or compression to add interest to them and to fit them into a given design area (Figs. 12-5 and 12-6).

Designing with Lines

9) *Breaking up* space with *vertical* and *horizontal* lines; seeking variety in the treatment of lines and in the size and placement of them (Fig. 12-50).

10) *Breaking up* space with *diagonal lines*; seeking variety in the treatment of line and in the size and shape of the areas between the lines.

FIG. 12-51. "Reclining Figure" (Henry Moore, elmwood, 75″ high, 1945–1946, Cranbrook Academy of Art, Michigan).   A sculptural piece in which negative and positive space areas are an integrated part of the total design and in which the smoothly grained surface of the form harmonizes with the free-form contours of the sculptural design.

FIG. 12-52. North Shore Congregation Israel, Glencoe, Illinois (Minoru Yamasaki, architect). A beautiful and inspirational sanctuary, contemporary in feeling and a fusion of Occidental and Oriental design. It represents a synthesis of geometric form and flowing line.

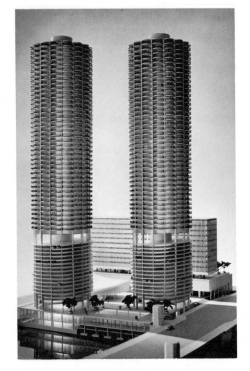

FIG. 12-53. Model of Marina City, Chicago, Illinois (Bertrand Goldberg, architect; Hedrich-Blessing, photo). An architectural structure in which a perforated effect has been achieved through the use of negative and positive shapes and vertical, horizontal, and spiral lines. These create a vibrant textural quality and accentuate the height of the cylindrical forms. While retaining the essence of the cylindrical forms, the negative and positive areas project an airy, rather than a massive, illusion of them.

11) *Breaking up* space with *curved lines;* seeking variety in the treatment of line and in the size and shape of areas between them.

12) *Breaking up* space with *vertical, horizontal, diagonal, and curved lines;* seeking variety in the treatment of line and in the size and shape of the areas between the lines (Figs. 12-17 and 12-18).

13) *Illustrating* an idea in line showing *nearness and depth* of forms through variation in value, color, texture and thickness or thinness of line and size.

14) *Recording* the *rhythmic movements* of dancing, skating, sweep-

ing, birds flying, fish swimming, wind blowing, water running, etc., using line as a basis for abstract pattern.

Designing with Varied Media and Processes

15) *Flowing colors together* as a background for a superimposed linear pattern with the addition of texture for the enrichment of surfaces.

16) *Abstracting facial features and expressions* as suggested by primitive masks, using paper media.

17) *Cutting geometric or abstract shapes of colored paper* and arranging them in pleasing patterns utilizing some of the above methods of designing.

18) *Superimposing* a line pattern over an arrangement of colored paper shapes.

19) *Designing with various shapes of textured materials*, creating pleasing abstract or nonrepresentational shapes or textures associated with people, places, structures, feelings, or moods.

20) *Breaking up the design space* using any of the resist processes.

21) *Breaking up the design space* using any of the stencil processes.

22) *Breaking up the design space* using any of the block-printing processes.

23) *Breaking up the design space* using any of the monotype processes.

Adapting the Design Qualities Characteristic of Other Cultures

24) *Becoming familiar with* the design characteristics of different cultures, i.e., Primitive, Egyptian, Assyrian, Byzantine, Romanesque, Gothic, Oriental, Oceanic, African, etc.

25) *Making adaptations* of any of the above design approaches to capture characteristics of other cultures.

26) *Utilizing* the qualities of opaqueness or transparency in any of the above space-breaking methods.

27) *Utilizing* sheet, mass, or linear materials in the organization of 3-D forms and creating designs inspired by other cultures.

READING REFERENCES

Anderson, Donald M., *Elements of Design*.   New York: Holt, Rinehart & Winston, Inc., 1961.

Arnheim, Rudolph, *Art and Visual Perception*.   Berkeley and Los Angeles: University of California Press, 1954.

Bates, F. Kenneth, *Basic Design*. Cleveland: World Publishing Co., 1960.

Beitler, Ethel Jane, and Lockhart, Bill, *Design for You*.   New York: John Wiley & Sons, Inc., 1961.

Emerson, Sybil, *Design: A Creative Approach*. Scranton, Pa.: International Textbook Company, 1953.

Faulkner, R., Ziegfeld, E., and Hill, G., *Art Today*. New York: Holt, Rinehart & Winston, Inc., 1963.

Fry, Roger, *Vision and Design*. New York: Meridian Books, 1956.

Graves, Maitland, *The Art of Color and Design*. New York: McGraw-Hill Book Co., 1941.

Grillo, Paul Jacques, *What Is Design?* Chicago: Paul Theobold and Co., 1960.

Higginson, Glenn D., *Psychology*. New York: The Macmillian Co., 1936.

Hunter, Sam, *Modern American Painting and Sculpture*. New York: Dell Publishing Co., 1959.

Huxley, Aldous, *On Art and Artists*, New York: Meridian, 1960.

Itten, Johannes, *Design and Form—The Basic Course at Bauhaus*. New York: Reinhold Publishing Corp., 1963.

Johnson, Pauline, *Creating with Paper*. Seattle, Wash.: University of Washington Press, 1958.

Kandinsky, Wassily, *Point and Line to Plane*. New York: Solomon R. Guggenheim Museum, 1947.

Kepes, Gyorgy, *The Visual Arts Today*. Middletown, Conn.: Wesleyan University Press, 1960.

Lippincott, Gordon J., *Design for Business*. Chicago: Paul Theobold and Co., 1947.

Moholy-Nagy, L., *Vision in Motion*. Chicago: Paul Theobold and Co., 1947.

Moseley, S., Johnson, P., and Koenig, H., *Crafts Design*. Belmont, Calif.: Wadsworth Publishing Co., Inc., 1962.

Neutra, Richard, *Survival Through Design*. New York: Oxford University Press, 1954.

Read, Herbert, *The Philosophy of Modern Art*. Cleveland: The World Publishing Company, 1954.

Ruch, Floyd L., *Psychology and Life*. Chicago: Scott, Foresman & Co., 1941.

Sartain, A. Q., North, A. J., Strange, J. R., and Chapman, H. M., *Psychology, Understanding Human Behavior*. New York: McGraw-Hill Book Company, 1962.

Shaffer, Laurance F., and others, *Psychology*. New York: Harper and Brothers, 1940.

Wolchonok, Louis, *Design for Artists and Craftsmen*. New York: Dover Publications, Inc., 1953.

13 Viewing, Perceiving, and Appreciating

ACHIEVING VISUAL LITERACY

"Visual literacy," an attribute which is generally associated with a high degree of perceptual skill, is achieved through constant and judicious viewing, and experiencing through other senses, one's visual world. The visual literate is one who views his world with profound, penetrating, and purposeful intent and who as a result of such experiences grows keenly appreciative of his environment.

Basically, appreciation of one's visual world is determined by one's ability to perceive logical relationships between visual elements. This involves not only personal feelings and reactions to external stimuli, but it also embraces each viewer's previous conditioning, all of which must be translated by the viewer into meaningful and familiar terms to intensify appreciation. Indeed they are valuable skills, the ability to identify relationships, (discords, harmonies, contrasts—proportionate use of art elements) the ability to recognize subtle nuances, and the ability to recognize the imaginative and the ingenious concepts which manifest structural sensitivity. To the viewer these constitute a means of probing into the fantasies, feelings, and apparent reasoning which moved the painter, the sculptor, and the architect to create, as he felt the impact of stimuli. That is to say, these skills represent a way of responding intellectually to the visual world. However, to appreciate a work of art intimately and keenly, as to create a work of art, involves a great deal more than an intellectual response to viewing. The viewer's emotional, spiritual, and aesthetic propensities also enter into the realm of appreciation. Therefore, just as these elements are fundamental to the resolution of aesthetically conceived ideas, so are they basic to the process of viewing and appreciating.

But, despite one's ability to perceive deeply, appreciation often remains an extremely personal matter. For example, there are many to whom the sentimental manifestations of a painting, a piece of sculpture, or an architectural structure seem infinitely more appealing than the quality of the work itself. For them viewing remains a rather limited experience, which evokes responses that are correspondingly limited. Appreciation of visual forms, therefore, demands a degree of aesthetic sensitivity cultivated through active and continuous participation in creative experiences. Because aesthetic sensibility is a direct outgrowth of conditioned responsiveness to subtle relationships of art elements and to the refined nuances in a visual form, a high degree of appreciation is seldom achieved through a sporadic involvement in viewing alone. Rather, it is realized through the persistent application of disciplined yet flexible aesthetic criteria and through the use of discerning abilities to *look* and to *see*; i.e., to *view* and to *perceive* with depth and with critical judgment. As viewing becomes an active and continuous process in which the aesthetic judgment of the viewer is constantly challenged, appreciation naturally grows. Viewing thus emerges as a creative experience, drawing heavily upon aesthetic values and upon the viewer's intellectual, emotional, creative, manipulative, and keenly developed perceptual skills.

Because of the variable factors involved in the process of viewing, the viewer's opinion of a work of art, alone, is not enough, for it frequently reflects his personal taste which may or may not be highly cultivated. But, when he becomes aware of the artist's philosophy, his intent, and the methods which he employed to achieve the intended, the viewer's appreciation broadens. To separate the creative form from the thought processes which led to its creation, or to disregard those elements which motivate the creative act, is to lose sight of the factors which influence the expression of the artist and correspondingly lessen the viewer's appreciation of the art form. Therefore, while each viewer may view a work of art in terms of his own understanding and taste, ultimately it is his *conditioned responsiveness* to the impact which was created by the stirring arrangement of visual elements in space that may bring a sense of deep satisfaction to him.

As the viewer learns to perceive his visual world in depth, the inordinately perplexing mysteries of artistic consequence begin to unfold, generating in him a lively interest in the old, the new, and the experimental.

Today it appears rather difficult for the viewer to establish objective criteria for aesthetic judgment. This may be partially due to the rapidly changing concepts of art and possibly due to the fact that established criteria which once served the viewer so well seem no longer valid or well defined. In the annals of history this has not been an entirely strange phenomenon. Each generation, in fact, has had to face a similar dilemma, to which it frequently directed extremely vigorous protests. But, despite this fact, the new, the novel, and the strange have ultimately become acceptable.

In this frame of reference, it is well to remember that the tendency to change is in itself a significant force. For it reflects the adventurous and intensely exciting pattern of life. It mirrors the dynamic nature of man, who is ever in search for the new and the novel in order to add zest to his life.

The viewer, therefore, must be receptive and responsive to new ideas. He must probe beyond the surface appearances of his visual world. He must be open minded. As Allen Weller so aptly expresses this viewpoint,

> If we can understand the way in which the artist's mind works, if we have a comprehension of the material with which he is dealing, if we can begin to sense the spirit which impels him in the direction he has taken and which underlies the work he has accomplished, we shall know a good deal about contemporary art and also perhaps have a clear comprehension of ourselves and the world we have made for ourselves [1].

GOOD TASTE, THE LAYMAN'S CONCERN

How does a viewer become sensitive to the intrinsic beauty, emotional intensity, aesthetic strength, or weakness in a work of art or in any other tangibly creative scheme? This question often arises. It expresses the layman's natural concern for aesthetic matters which he cannot resolve for himself and for which he earnestly seeks some satisfactory answers. His own, admittedly noticeable, lack of sensitivity is frequently accompanied by statements which strongly affirm his aesthetic illiteracy.

"I often rely upon the taste of the sales clerk," the layman may say, "knowing full well that her major interests lie mainly in her ability to sell —to sell anything—no matter how poorly it is designed. Of course, I know that this isn't right, but, frankly, I have no idea what is right for me, and this is what I resent mostly. Why shouldn't I, as a member of a seemingly cultured society, be able to make my own decisions on matters concerning aesthetic choices? Should only the artist-designer or the interior designer be the sole judge of what is or what is not in good taste for me? Should not every individual in a democratic society be adequately prepared to exercise his own aesthetic judgment and be encouraged to strive for the ultimate in good taste in all matters which concern him?"

These are seemingly valid questions if for no other reason than that they virtually imply a need for cultivating basic skills which may be useful in the enrichment of all aspects of one's life, the temporal and the spiritual as well.

Indeed, none should be deprived of that exalted and ennobled feeling which excites the imagination of one who is responsive to a well-designed visual form. None should be hindered from taking keen delight even in a single passage in the context of a painting or from finding pleasure in the beauty of a single line in the contour of a sculptural form. None should be deprived of experiencing a feeling of sublime grandeur when viewing an imposing or elegant architectural structure or of becoming enchanted with the charm of a well-planned room interior or any other visible and creative scheme.

Taste is a direct result of involvement in the making of choices. But good taste is cultivated through a methodic approach to making choices in matters of artistic consequence, for through this process are developed sensitivities which serve as criteria in selective judgment. Discriminate responsiveness to aesthetic stimuli engenders refinement of taste. With refinement of taste emerges intense appreciation.

CULTIVATING AESTHETIC VALUE JUDGMENTS

Basically, the vital considerations in the process of cultivating aesthetic value judgments, or aesthetic sensitivity, are as follows:

1) *It is of utmost importance to develop a skill in identifying those elements which go into the organic structure of aesthetically conceived notional concepts.* Active involvement in the creative process is undoubtedly the *quickest* and possibly the best method of becoming attuned to aesthetic values. Flexible criteria which are useful in the evaluation of visual elements are acquired through creative art experiences. Being a direct outgrowth of exploration, experimentation, innovation, and implementation, these are meaningful and functional not only in the structuring of visual images, but also in the evaluation of them. Creative art experiences challenge one's capacities to implement thought processes skillfully, and to apply aesthetic value judgments discriminately. Because this challenge persists through every phase, i.e., through the initiating, developing, and culminating stages of an art experience, it penetrates the innermost crevices of every idea, permitting the individual to become critical and analytical and, as a consequence, increasingly more discerning.

Although it is believed by some that appreciation of aesthetic values may be derived from verbal analysis of visual forms alone, yet it is recognized that appreciation is more quickly and more fully achieved through a direct involvement in the creative process, preferably in addition to the verbal analysis. For, even though one becomes well informed about theories, ideological concepts, philosophical orientations, techniques, and methods of procedure through verbal analysis—all of which is extremely pertinent to the understanding of one's visual world—it is nevertheless believed that the practical application of this knowledge is the true test of the individual's understanding. This is particularly apparent when an attempt is made to project an original idea into visual form. In this process the insights gained through verbal communication become clearly manifested. This includes the essential thought processes which enter into the visual structuring of creative thoughts as well as those which challenge the aesthetic values of the individual.

Through this type of involvement an individual learns not only to view but to perform and thereby to perceive in depth the intricacies that go into the birth and the growth of ideas. Appreciation of and sensitivity to aesthetic values thus become the inevitable byproducts of creative expression.

2) *It is essential to recognize that aesthetically satisfying results may be achieved through many and varied approaches and media*; also, that one idea may lead to other equally significant ideas, each having infinite possibilities for expansion; similarly, that one medium may have limitless possibilities in the expression of one idea.

3) *It is necessary to realize that while materials which are used in the creative process decidedly influence the character of design in the visual form, the design in turn may also become the determinant factor in the selection of materials.* Moreover, a design which is intended to be used in a two-dimensional shape may not necessarily be suitable for a three-dimensional form, because each of these usually requires unique treatment. Each demands the use of particular tools, materials, and media which are in keeping and in harmony with the essential character of the material and the purpose of the design. Consequently every design demands a careful analysis of its intrinsic qualities so that, as far as possible, these may be preserved and integrated in the organic structure of the total expression.

4) *It is essential to judge a creative product in its proper environmental perspective.* A visual form needs to be viewed in its indigenous setting and judged in relation to other forms of its time. It must also be seen in the light of creative expressions of other cultures. For example, it is totally fallacious to assess the artistic merits of a sixteenth century Leonardo da Vinci or Michelangelo in the light of contemporary aesthetic concepts since concepts have changed considerably through the centuries. Aesthetic values of the twentieth century do not necessarily parallel those of the sixteenth century. It seems more appropriate to judge the artist of the twentieth century by criteria which evolved in his day and from his cultural milieu.

It must be recalled here that, largely because the sixteenth-century artist mirrored his culture, he remained unique, i.e., distinctly different from the artist of the twentieth century or of any other century. He truly reflected a philosophy, technology, and aesthetic values which were advanced in his particular era. The artist, being a product of his ecology, therefore, cannot escape the sublime, or the cataclysmic, influences which are a part of his culture. In each epoch of art history, the predominating religious, political, social, and philosophical forces have significantly textured the fiber of the creative artist. The sixteenth-century artist was no exception to this phenomenon as he pursued his search for truths. Enchanted with the anatomical structure of the human form, with the creation of three-dimensional illusions through chiaroscuro (light and shade), and with the achievement of illusional depth through perspective, he sought to convey reality in all of its manifestations—through paint, through stone, or through other means.

In these respects the contemporary artist differs greatly from his sixteenth-century counterpart. He feels no longer bound by similar concerns. His interests lie in the explorative fields of unrestrained and illimitable space—in contourless shapes which seem rooted in faintly discernable sources and which yield to languid or vivid masses of color; in vigorous and often violent treatment of line, mass, and color—depicting feeling, tension, forces—which juxtapose, clash, explode, or which simply rest. Although he, too, is concerned with reality, it is a reality of another sort. It is the kind which lingers far beyond the normal scope of vision and which may be revealed through microscopic, telescopic, or x-ray vision. It is the sum and substance of force and matter which captures the imagination of the contemporary artist and which stirs, moves, terrifies, and jolts the artist into action. As Weller states:

> This is creation without illusion, presentation rather than representation
> of something outside of the inner depths of the creative being. The artist
> is less and less concerned with the image of the natural world and more
> and more with feeling for its own sake. Increasingly the artist has no
> outer life, only an inner one. Image becomes feeling, and feeling becomes
> image [2].

A GRAPHIC ANALYSIS OF THOUGHT PROCESSES WHICH ENTER INTO CRITICAL VIEWING AND APPRECIATING

From all indications, it becomes increasingly evident that many elements enter into the formulation of value judgments concerning artistic matters. Also, that it is indeed difficult to respond fully to any visual form or scheme unless one brings to it a backlog of pertinent information based on theoretical and empirical evidence. In this frame of reference, viewing involves all of one's faculties—the intellectual, the emotional, the creative, and the manipulative. A viewer who has been involved in creative experiences is more likely to become sensitive to the artist's concerns than one who has never or seldom been involved. This is because, through such involvement, he sharpens his perceptual powers and becomes attuned to those values which contribute to the highest in aesthetic achievement.

Consequently, unless the viewer is oriented to the cultural and other influences upon the artist—to the designing processes, guiding concepts, methods, and devices, materials and tools employed—he may gain few insights into the thought processes which generate the birth of ideas and which unfold the notional schemes of the artist.

Chart 5 delineates graphically the methodical procedure involved in formulating desirable value judgments concerning artistic matters.

CHART 5

A GRAPHIC ANALYSIS OF THOUGHT PROCESSES WHICH ENTER INTO THE CRITICAL VIEWING OF ART FORMS

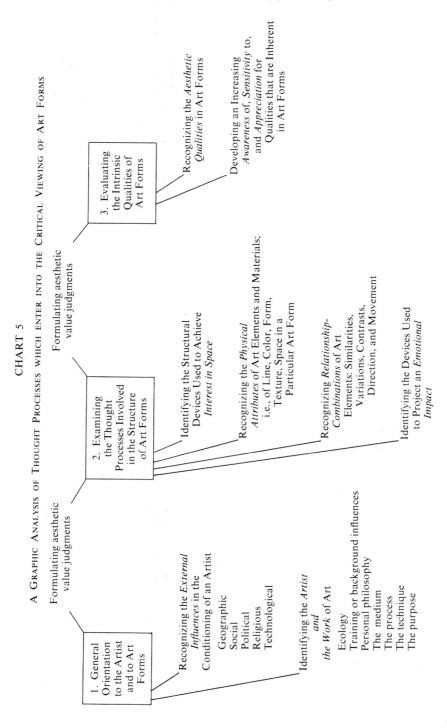

Formulating aesthetic
value judgments

Formulating aesthetic
value judgments

1. General
Orientation
to the Artist
and to Art
Forms

Recognizing the *External
Influences* in the
Conditioning of an Artist

Geographic
Social
Political
Religious
Technological

Identifying the *Artist
and
the Work* of Art

Ecology
Training or background influences
Personal philosophy
The medium
The process
The technique
The purpose

2. Examining
the Thought
Processes Involved
in the Structure
of Art Forms

Identifying the Structural
Devices Used to Achieve
Interest in Space

Recognizing the *Physical
Attributes* of Art Elements and Materials;
i.e., of Line, Color, Form,
Texture, Space in a
Particular Art Form

Recognizing *Relationship-
Combinations* of Art
Elements: Similarities,
Variations, Contrasts,
Direction, and Movement

Identifying the Devices Used
to Project an *Emotional
Impact*

3. Evaluating
the Intrinsic
Qualities of
Art Forms

Recognizing the *Aesthetic
Qualities* in Art Forms

Developing an Increasing
Awareness of, *Sensitivity* to,
and *Appreciation* for
Qualities that are Inherent
in Art Forms

THOUGHT PROCESSES INVOLVED IN THE ORGANIZATION OF ART FORMS

As has been frequently noted, the artist or designer with integrity does not imitate visual forms in nature for the mere sake of imitation. Rather, he is inspired by them. He reorders, or reshapes these forms to suit his own purposes. In this process he also projects his personal commitments and feelings concerning what he sees or what he imagines he sees. But, to express these commitments forcefully, he uses various devices. Among these are: simplification, alteration, reorganization, exaggeration, invention, and adaptation. For example:

1) He alters visual forms in order to project his own aesthetic schemes and feelings into them.
2) He invents new forms to express tangible or intangible ideas.
3) He shifts the shapes, lines, and colors in space and, through distortion, exaggeration, deletion, or addition, he intensifies his statement.
4) He eliminates details and nonessentials in order to simplify and to strengthen the form. He adds detail in order to enrich the surface appearance of the form.
5) He adapts his ideas to the space, the tools, and the materials, or he adapts materials, tools, and processes to a preconceived idea in order to evolve a sincerely executed expression.

The graphic analysis of thought processes constitutes the basic, but general, considerations which the artist or designer takes into account as he aims for aesthetically satisfying goals. There are, however, specific considerations which are equally significant to him. These are listed here and then described in detail in the following paragraphs.

1) Does the total notional scheme, whatever it may be, project a feeling of a unified whole—a totality of a conceived idea? Or does it impart a feeling of chaos and of cluttered confusion?
2) Does the total organization have one dominant unit of emphasis and interest—a form or a group of forms (abstract or illustrative) as the case may be? Or is there a division of emphasis where more than one dominant unit or interest is projected?
3) Are there subordinate units of interest in the scheme which contribute to the main idea?
4) Do the forms within the total expression suggest a movement, i.e., a track of vision; or do they remain static, inert, and isolated against a containing background?
5) Are the forms connected by the usual devices, i.e., by overlapping, touching, intersecting, interlacing, or penetrating; or are they scattered aimlessly without due regard for unity and coherence?

6) Are the forms clearly defined by linear contours or contrasting color; or are they faintly discernable, having no easily identifiable derivative sources?

7) Are the forms contained within defined basic geometric shapes, or are they fluid, free formed, or organic in structure?

CONCERNS PERTINENT TO INTEREST AND UNITY

1) *What devices* are utilized to achieve interest in a particular area?

2) *Which art elements* (line, color, form, texture, etc.) are most suitable in the creation of interest in a particular art form?

3) Which are more effective in the realization of interest and unity— the use of a *number of elements, or the creative use of a limited few?*

4) *Which physical attributes* of the art elements are *most suitable* to a particular visual scheme?

   a) *Lines*—thick, thin, soft, hard, diffused, dynamic, static, forceful, restless, active, humorous, sad, restraining, broken, smooth, graceful, clumsy?

   b) *Shapes*—organic, geometric, articulate, diffused, transparent, opaque, or textured? Are they rooted in imagery, or are they languid and shapeless, devoid of derivative sources?

   c) *Forms*—geometric, or organic; illusional or actual?

   d) *Colors*—contrasting, muted, harmonious, discordant, intense, grayed, cool, warm, textured, or variegated?

   e) *Values*—(i.e., lights and darks) in subtle gradations, or in sharp contrasts, or both?

   f) *Textures*—rough, smooth, shiny, hard, or soft; actual or simulated?

5) Which of the listed elements are *emphasized*, which *subordinated* in the attempt to create interest?

6) Which of the art elements (i.e., color, line, form, and texture) contribute to the unity of the total scheme and which destroy its unity?

CONCERNS PERTINENT TO AESTHETIC RELATIONSHIPS OF ART ELEMENTS

Since every artist or designer is much concerned with relationship combinations, it may be of interest to examine these in the context of visual art forms. Leading questions serve to facilitate this process.

1) Were aesthetically *satisfying form* (color, line, texture) and *space relationships* achieved? Were these elements utilized discriminately? For example, were some combinations used, such as: large and small, thick and thin, wide and narrow, intense and

FIG. 13-1. "Three Musicians" (Picasso, oil, 1921, Philadelphia Museum of Art, E. Gallatin Collection). In this painting line, shape, color, and texture were utilized to create interest and unity. Contrasting values of light and dark patterns and an illusional treatment of the third dimension are projected through a combination of flat shapes and geometric forms.

grayed, cool and warm? Were these combinations varied in size, shape, or color, in order to achieve interest? Were these unified in order to realize a harmonious orchestration of the total scheme?

2) Were aesthetically satisfying *directional relationships* achieved? Which verticals, horizontals, or diagonals were utilized to emphasize a dominant direction or movement? Were the relationships moving, exciting, tranquil, or placid?

3) Were aesthetically satisfying *spatial relationships* achieved, i.e., between the positive and negative shapes or between the foreground, middle ground, and background areas?

4) Were *depth relationships* realized through overlapping, perspective, gradation, intensity, etc? Were any other devices employed to achieve depth relationships?

FIG. 13-2. "Revolt in the Warsaw Ghetto" (Samuel Greenburg, oil, Memorial Museum, Acre, Israel). A powerful manifestation of intense and valiant determination to resist force, heightened through the use of massive and linear brush strokes.

FIG. 13-3. "Spectators" (Lillian Desow-Fishbein, encaustic, courtesy of the artist). A hauntingly somber rendition of shadowlike human forms reflecting the fear, anxiety, and hopelessness of inmates in a concentration camp.

5) Were aesthetic *textural relationships* achieved through patterned or plain surface treatment or through the use of the natural characteristic of the material, i.e., hard or soft, coarse or smooth, etc.? Was the textural treatment real or simulated?

CONCERNS PERTINENT TO EMOTIONAL IMPACT

Did the total organization of art elements evoke tangible or intangible feelings, such as: feelings of horror, sadness, pleasure, distastefulness, disgust, or excitement; or feelings of gentleness, subtlety, kindness, pathos; or feelings of warmth, exhilarating coolness, explosiveness, friction, turbulance, harmonious fusion, or tranquility? Or, does the total expression solicit no response from the viewer whatsoever? See Figs. 13-2, 13-3, and 13-4.

AESTHETIC VALUES CHANGE

No discussion of aesthetic values may be considered complete unless some attention is drawn to the metamorphic nature of elements which concern the concept of beauty. For, through the centuries, this concept has undergone considerable change. Although the classic notion of beauty permeated many cultures for a long period of time, nevertheless it gradually yielded to the changing concepts of beauty in each historical epoch. At first, this concept was modified by the restraining forces of ecclesiastical thought. Later, it was altered by the strident demands of science and technology. Today, the concepts of beauty echo the standards of our own time. The trends in architecture, in sculpture, in painting, and no less in the popular arts reflect an exhuberance which is dynamic in nature and which expresses concepts of beauty uniquely distinguished from those of other historical eras. Principally, it is in Europe and in the United States that the major visual arts and the so-called popular arts (i.e., pottery, weaving, textile designing, metalcrafts, etc.) exhibit a complete breakaway from the notion of what was once considered the highest in aesthetic achievement. In other countries, the status quo is yet retained, particularly where the characteristic and indigenous concepts of beauty have been carefully guarded for centuries. For example, that which may still be considered beautiful in India, Indo-China, Africa, or Guatemala may not be necessarily considered so in other parts of the world, because aesthetic criteria and standards of taste indigenous to each of these cultures remain a direct consequence of native tradition and native orientation. Although the concepts of beauty which prevail in older or primitive cultures have altered to some degree in the course of time, these have not however changed for the better as some would have us believe. The influence of Western civilization and the encroachment of com-

Fig. 13-4. "Job" (Milton Horn, plaster, courtesy of the sculptor). An intensely moving and sensitive rendition of Job. It reflects man's eternal search for the reasons why he must suffer.

mercialism upon the artisan's world have unquestionably modified the design quality of his products. In some instances, this has resulted in a complete loss of cultural entity—a precious commodity in a technologically oriented civilization. Countries such as Mexico, Italy, Japan, and even parts of Africa have tended to yield to the impressive power of the machine, and to the economic and social advantages of mass production.

Admittedly, while these advantages do raise the standards of living— in the underdeveloped countries particularly—yet it will be most regretable if these industrial advances should, in time, completely obliterate the inimitable artistic qualities with which each nation has been endowed through its long and colorful historical past. For, *the beauty which lies*

FIG. 13-5. "The Fishermen" (Tim Meier, oil, oil glazes, courtesy of the artist). Despite the bold and broad-stroke treatment of the content and the use of heavy impasto oil paint, a feeling of contentment or serenity was achieved by the artist.

in aesthetic diversity and novelty is of utmost importance to the spiritual uplift of mankind. It is entirely conceivable, of course, that in time new and universally acceptable standards of aesthetic merit will emerge. These may become no less desirable than were those of the classic era. In that event, such values may possibly serve as a cohesive force for the good of all mankind.

All the same, a cohesiveness which is realized within the context of sameness is perhaps less desirable than the kind that reflects a genuine respect for the veritable and diverse aesthetic viewpoints. For, no matter how valid the reasons may be for achieving the universal, there is always the danger that individuality may be lost in the process.

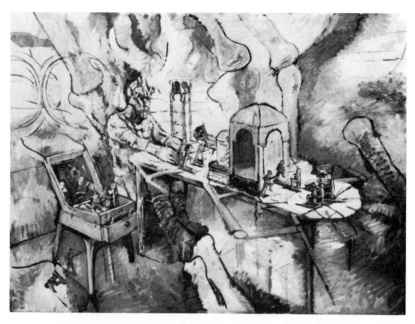

Fig. 13-6. "Attack on the Castle" (Seymour Rosofsky, oil on canvas, 43⅞″ × 61⅝″, 1963, courtesy Richard Feigen Gallery, Chicago). In this painting the artist created an aesthetic synthesis of art elements through which a figure of a seated man, objects, furniture, toys, and bony shapes all fuse into a mood of loneliness amidst chaos and destruction.

THE ARTIST VERSUS SOCIETY

The artist is considered less communicative today than he has ever been in the annals of history. When in the past he has been the object of abusive treatment, it was not his inability to communicate which was assailed. Rather, it was the manner, the technique, the distortion of form and color which were the object of subjective scrutiny. Ridicule, contempt, disdainful treatment of the new, the novel, the unique were then, as they are to some degree today, manifestations of rebellion and resistance to change. Change, in the visual arts particularly, was seldom welcomed with enthusiasm. In the sixteenth century, for example, Rembrandt refused to compromise with the ideals of the Dutch burghers. He found the latter contemptuous of his formal approach to painting. They even scorned his imaginative compositions. His painting, "The Night Watch," was rejected as being incompetently executed. In the nineteenth century, the Impressionists (Manet, Pissarro, Monet, and Renoir) literally created storms with their momentary illusions of light and atmosphere through broken color. Seurat, Cézanne (the Postimpressionists), Braque, Picasso (the Cubists), van Gogh, Gauguin, Matisse (the Expressionists)—

FIG. 13-7. "Time and Space" (William S. Schwartz, oil, Montclair Art Museum).   An impressive rendition of a thought-provoking mood, created through strong contrasts of light and dark values, marked spatial relationships, and distinct textural treatment of surfaces.

all experienced disdainful treatment by their contemporaries.   Neverthe-less, despite the critical attitudes, these late nineteenth-century artists have emerged as giant innovators of profound art movements in the history of art.

While criticisms toward the arts and the artist are no less vehemently experienced today, the circumstances seem somewhat different.   Society is less resistant to change today than it has ever been in the past.   Whereas once it was passionately determined to maintain the status quo, today society welcomes change to a great extent—in industry, in commerce, in fashion, in scientific ventures, and in other areas of human endeavor.   In the main, change has become a desirable and attractive phenomenon in our culture.

But, in the visual arts, acceptance of change has been rather slow. Among other reasons, is one generally attributed to a definite lack of com-munication between the artist and his audience.   More than anything else,

FIG. 13-8. "Prayer" (Jacques Lipchitz, bronze, $42\frac{1}{2}''$ high, 1943, collection of Mr. and Mrs. R. Sturgis Ingersoll, Penllyn, Pa.). Intense and ardent feeling is expressed in this sculptural form; the free-form, positive, and negative shapes contribute to the zeal and fervor of the prayer.

it is this lack of communicative substance which is being deplored. Indeed, it is argued, "After all, should not the artist articulate some kind of moral and philosophical commitment? Is it not his predestined role and responsibility, as that of the writer's, to interpret and to evaluate life? Should not he comment on man's noble aspirations, sufferings, and upon his political, industrial, and social revolutions? What does the artist do instead? He expends his energies upon strokes and drips. He invents devices of handling, processing, and texturing surfaces with total disregard for content and for human values. He is disinterested, detached, and egocentric."

These, in essence, are some of the criticisms hurled at the artist today, as society searches for substance and for clarification of aesthetic truths. But are these criticisms valid? Perhaps some of them are; yet, even these are debatable.

Let us examine, for a moment, how the contemporary artist justifies his goals and what he feels is pertinent for him in his quest for honest expression.

IN DEFENSE OF THE CONTEMPORARY ARTIST

It is generally acknowledged that the creative individual must enjoy absolute freedom in the expression of his fantasies, personal feelings, and reactions to life. But, paradoxically enough, when he is moved to create new concepts in visual form, he is frequently criticized for doing so. Irrespective of this strange phenomenon, it is evident that a clear understanding of the artist's goals must be reached. It must be *recognized* once and for all that to seek out new and unique relationships, to discover the hitherto unexplored functions of line, form, color, texture, and space; to express abstract throughts—i.e., forces, tensions, intuitions, impulses, or whatever else the artist chooses to express visually—is as vital to him today as the traditional organization of the above, in the context of a conventional framework, was to the artist in the past.

Indeed, the artist must be permitted to penetrate all aspects of his visual and nonvisual world, including the intuitive, the spontaneous, and the unpredictable. And this he must express as freely as he has expressed the natural forms of his environment in the past. Therefore, he must be constrained neither by traditional nor by conventional concepts of content.

The artist of today is intensely interested in abstract expressionism (a movement in art of which Jackson Pollock was the major proponent). He finds new and intellectual excitement in forms that are open, fluid, or mobile; in lines that are self-involved—not rooted in imagery—in impulses and in stirring movements. He has a perfect right to yield to this interest. The alluring qualities inherent in the intuitive, unconscious, and spontaneous are of natural consequence to him, as they are to the poet, the writer, the musician, or to the psychiatrist.

There are those, of course, who contend that conscious and disciplined control constitute the only means of aesthetic order. But this assumption is not entirely true, since every work of art has in it some accidental "gems" which come into view by chance and which the artist did not foresee. In the creative process these "gems" often become attributes which remain engaging, inspirational, and challenging to the artist. It should be born in mind, however, that it is the artist alone who determines the degree to which the accidental gems may be exploited and the degree to which these may be integrated into the totality of his notional schemes. Often, it is the accidental, the spontaneous, or the intuitive stroke which serves as a point of departure or suggests a direction, a theme, a configuration; and it is because the artist finds these passages, drips, blots of color, lines, or shapes—forceful, unique, essential, and inspirational—that he utilizes these expediently in the resolution of ideas.

Aside from the effects that the artist achieves from the intuitive or the accidental, there are two universal truths about a work of art to which the contemporary artist heartily subscribes and in which he firmly believes. In essence, they are 1) that every work of art must be uniquely structured, unified, or orchestrated, regardless of the type of shapes or forms included in it and 2) that the intrinsic powers of line, form, and color, rather than imagery, must project a vital and "emotionally-charged" impact upon the viewer. All other considerations must, in his opinion, become subservient to the above objectives. However, although these subservient considerations may appear to be secondary concerns, they are nonetheless significant, but only so long as they permit the artist to intensify his personal expression.

Consideration of the concepts discussed in the preceding pages may facilitate understanding of what the contemporary artist is attempting to convey. The true value of his creative commitments, however, must be seen in the light of historic perspective. For only then will it be possible to assess with objectivity the validity of the goals which the contemporary artist has set for himself. However, as stated by Weller:

> The greater our experience as spectators, the more associations we are likely to be able to make: we see the work, not as an isolated and independent thing, but as part of an organic whole which includes more than itself. A work which is rich in its points of contact with life and with experience at many levels will seem more significant to us than one which exists in an exclusive and walled-in atmosphere. ... But as we come to know such works intimately and personally, as we bring to them qualities of mind and of spirit which are creative in their own right, they emerge as significant facts in our search for the realities of our age [3].

To gain further insight into the thoughts of the contemporary artist, it may be of interest to review some of the briefly quoted philosophical commitments made by living American painters and sculptors. Dorothy Seiberling, art editor of *Life*, describes the paintings of two abstract expressionists, Kline and de Kooning. Other comments were made by the artists.

FRANZ KLINE (painter):

> His paintings dramatize a basic condition of life: the conflict of opposing forces—such as observed in personal relations, in politics, in moral concepts of good and evil [4].

WILLEM DE KOONING (painter, Fig. 13-9):

> His paintings express the explosive images of a dislodged and ambiguous world. Vestiges of realism clash and slide in and out of the paintings—a kind of split-second view of the world—the speed of modern life, the constantly changing scene, the myriad [5].

FIG. 13-9. "Woman" (Willem de Kooning, 1952, The Museum of Modern Art, New York).

THEODORE ROSZAK (sculptor, Fig. 13-10):

> The New Content as it appears in modern art, is shaped organically out of an evolution of forms that have a corresponding bearing upon historic necessity for us today. It arises painfully, yet naturally, out of heaps of fragments and experiments that result from decades of accumulated and visual ideas. It emerges out of a plethora of plastic elements that belong entirely to our contemporary vocabulary, visually revealing bones, nerves, and senses, as well as man's varied state of being.

> Considered in this light, sculpture emerges as a language of visual content in space—not as an "act" sufficient unto itself, nor as a repository for the "object" either lost or found—but as an unequivocal statement charged

FIG. 13-10.   "Golden Hawk" (Theodore Roszak, steel and bronze, 1961, Pierre Matisse Gallery, New York).

FIG. 13-11.   "Ices" (Jacob Lawrence, tempera on gesso panel, 24″ × 30″, 1960, The Terry Dintenfass, Inc., New York).

to fulfill man's awakened sense of his inner reality, upon whose threshold of affirmation stands delineated—a new image [6].

NICHOLAS VASILIEFF (painter):

... to me there is nothing new or dynamic except total individuality of the artist himself. Only when the artist has his own focus and a personal color harmony, no matter which school of art he belongs to, can he create. For the real significance of creativity is in the individual expression of the artist. Only this is new [7].

MARGO HOFF (painter):

My work seems to go in cycles—from subject to no subject, from outer life to inner life. If there is a development I think it must move in a kind of spiral [8].

JACOB LAWRENCE (painter, Fig. 13-11):

I try to observe to my fullest capacity the life and people about me—the pain and misery of those in a free hospital clinic—the drama backstage during a performance—the eagerness and attention of children hearing a librarian reading a story—the teeming main section of a Negro ghetto [9].

MIRKO (sculptor):

Since visual expression is an intrinsic part of society and one of its examinations, it can only exist in its time and is an expression of its time. Considering the age-long arguments about the figurative or nonfigurative situation in art which only appears to be two different aspects of the same substance, it seems to me that these both might be valid. This is a question of function and quality and not of fashion. To use languages and ways of the remote epochs is always false and anachronistic [10].

HANS HOFMANN (painter, Fig. 13-12):

Creative figuration in the visual arts, in the sense of any subject matter, is in no way to be condemned, when achieved through the qualitative and aesthetic substance of every work intended toward such ends.

As an artist I condemn any dogmatism and categorization because the scent of death accompanies every such style [11].

Art is to me the glorification of the human spirit and as such it is the cultural documentation of the time in which it is produced. The deeper sense of all art is obviously to hold the human spirit in a state of rejuvenescence in answer to an ever-changing world. Art is an agent destined to counter-balance the burdensomeness of everyday life—it should provide constant aesthetic enjoyment [12].

KARL KNATHS (painter):

The sensibility the artist has will be apparent in whatever mode is suitable to him [13].

HOLLIS HOLBROOK (painter):

To understand the meaning of contemporary art form is to understand the meaning of contemporary man and his beliefs [14].

FIG. 13-12. "Scattered Sunset" (Hans Hofmann, oil on canvas, 72″ × 84″, 1961, Samuel M. Kootz Gallery, New York).

FIG. 13-13. "Minos in the Labyrinth" (Richard Anuszkiewicz, oil on canvas, 58″ × 52″, 1962, Sidney Janis Gallery, New York).

RICHARD ANUSZKIEWICZ (painter, Fig. 13-13):

> My work could best be explained as a creative approach to the use of optical phenomena in configurations with a primary interest in ambiguous space, color change, and visual movement of shapes [15].

PETER GRIPPE (sculptor):

> Creation is like a never ending stream constantly changing its course and direction until it flows into the great sea of aesthetic purity and truth [16].

TSENG YU-HO (painter, Fig. 13-14):

> A name is given to my painting usually after the picture is born: I am still fascinated with power of mastering the matter, to animate inanimate things [17].

FIG. 13-14. "Mana" (Tseng Yu-Ho, watercolor, dsui mounted on panel, 24" × 32", 1962, Downtown Gallery, New York).

BERNARD REDER (painter):

> Sometimes the form brings out the reason, sometimes the reason brings out the form. And to find out which came first, I do not care [18].

ABBOTT PATTISON (sculptor, Fig. 13-15):

> Cannot the sculptor too comment upon a landscape and is not the landscape itself a magnificent sculpture? There lies the land—convex and concave—enormously varied in texture and stroke, slashing flatness and intricate concentration of detail—all pulsing with life of the present and

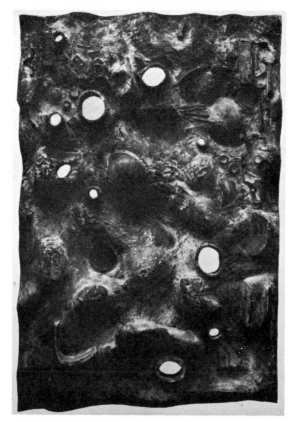

FIG. 13-15. "View of Pittsburgh" (Abbott Pattison, bronze relief, 72"high, 1960–1961, Feingarten
Gallery, New York).

life of the land is gouged out of mountain ranges by the erosion of the
waters [19].

NOTES

1. Allen S. Weller, *Contemporary American Painting and Sculpture.* Urbana,
Ill.: University of Illinois Press, 1963, Introduction.

2. *Ibid.*

3. Allen S. Weller, *Contemporary American Painting and Sculpture.* Urbana,
Ill.: The University of Illinois Press, 1961, Introduction.

4. Dorothy Seiberling, Art ed., Part Two, "The Varied Art of Four
Pioneers," *Life,* November 16, 1959, pp. 74–80.

5. *Ibid.*, pp. 81–82.

6. Allen S. Weller, *Contemporary American Painting and Sculpture.* Urbana,
Ill.: University of Illinois Press, 1963, p. 198.

7. *Ibid.*, p. 149.

8. Allen S. Weller, *Contemporary American Painting and Sculpture.* Urbana,
Ill.: University of Illinois Press, 1961, p. 112.

9. *Ibid.*, p. 113.
10. *Ibid.*, p. 218.
11. *Ibid.*, p. 116.
12. Hans Hofmann, "Hans Hofmann," *Eastern Art Education Bulletin* Vol. 11, No. 7 (Oct) 1954, p. 4.
13. Allen S. Weller, *Contemporary American Painting and Sculpture.* Urbana, Ill.: University of Illinois Press, 1961, p. 108.
14. *Ibid.*, p. 90.
15. Allen S. Weller, *Contemporary American Painting and Sculpture.* Urbana, Ill.: University of Illinois Press, 1963, p. 71.
16. Allen S. Weller, *Contemporary American Painting and Sculpture.* Urbana, Ill.: University of Illinois Press, 1961, p. 72.
17. Allen S. Weller, *Contemporary American Painting and Sculpture.* Urbana, Ill.: University of Illinois Press, 1963, p. 55.
18. *Ibid.*, p. 164.
19. *Ibid.*, p. 214.

READING REFERENCES

Baudelaire, Charles, *The Mirror of Art.* Garden City, N. Y.: Doubleday & Company, Inc., translation by Jonathan Mayne, 1958.

Beam, Philip C., *The Language of Art.* New York: The Ronald Press Company, 1958.

Berenson, Bernard, *Aesthetics and History.* Garden City, N. Y.: Doubleday & Company, Inc., 1948.

Bosanquet, Bernard, *A History of Aesthetic.* New York: The Meridian Library, published by Meridian Books, 1957.

Cary, Joyce, *Art and Reality.* Garden City, N. Y.: Doubleday & Company, Inc., 1958.

————, *The Transformation of Nature in Art.* New York: Dover Publications, Inc., 1956.

Coomaraswamy, Ananda K., *Christian and Oriental Philosophy of Art.* New York: Dover Publications, Inc., 1956.

Edman, Irwin, *Arts and the Man.* New York: New American Library of World Literature, Inc., 1951.

Fiedler, Conrad, *On Judging Works of Visual Art.* Berkeley and Los Angeles: University of California Press, 1949.

Fry, Roger, *Vision and Design.* New York: Meridian Books, 1956.

Kuh, Katharine, *The Artist's Voice.* New York: Harper & Row Publishers, 1961.

Ozenfant, Amédée, *Foundations of Modern Art.* New York: Dover Publications, Inc., 1952.

Panofsky, Erwin, *Meaning In The Visual Arts.* Garden City, N. Y.: Doubleday and Company, Inc., 1957.

Read, Herbert, *The Grass Roots of Art.* Cleveland: The World Publishing Co., 1961.

————, *The Philosophy of Modern Art.* Cleveland: The World Publishing Co., 1954.

Santayana, George, *The Sense of Beauty.* New York: Dover Publications, Inc., 1955.

Sartre, Jean Paul, *Essays In Aesthetics.* New York: Philosophical Library, Inc., translation by Wade Baskin, 1963.

Shahn, Ben, *The Shape of Content.* New York: Vintage Books, 1960.

Glossary

ABNORMAL A psychological term used to describe an individual who deviates considerably from the norm or average, usually in the direction of poorer performance or poorer adjustment to the conditions of life.

ABORIGINAL ART Art done by the earliest known inhabitants of a country, a native race, especially as contrasted with an invading or colonizing race.

ABSOLUTE In a general sense, a term used to describe that which is independent of relations to other subjects.

ABSTRACT ART The term implies either the rendition of the aesthetic essence of form as contrasted with an accurate imitation of it, or concern solely with the use of the elements, i.e., line, form, color, texture, in a composition aesthetically pleasing in itself. In an abstract painting the artist extracts from the form qualities which he uses as a means or as an end, to a lesser or greater degree, depending upon the emphasis and purposes intended. An abstract painting of a figure may depict the organic structure or the dynamic nature of the form, but not necessarily the realistic representation of either, e.g., the work of Picasso, Braque, and others. There are degrees of abstraction. Some paintings are highly abstracted to the end that the content is almost completely lost, but not entirely. When the content is lost completely the painting is then called nonobjective.

ABSTRACT EXPRESSIONISM A contemporary movement in art, which is sometimes called "action painting" and which places primary emphasis upon intuitive and spontaneous treatment in two-dimensional space. Movement in line and color, opposing tensions and forces rooted in ambiguous space are of interest to the abstract-expressionist painter. He finds new intellectual excitement in forms that are open, fluid, and mobile; in lines that are self-involved—not rooted in imagery, in impulses, and in stirring movements. The major proponents of this school of thought are Jackson Pollock, Kline, and de Kooning.

ACADEMIC A descriptive term generally applied to a work of art which has been executed in a more or less traditional style based on established theory and philosophy.

ACTION PAINTING See ABSTRACT EXPRESSIONISM.

ADAPTATION In the creative process, a change in structure or form of an existing idea to fit conditions different from those which inspired the change, emerging as a redesigned and decidedly altered result. Psychologically, a process by which a sense organ gradually ceases to respond to a constant stimulus.

AESTHETIC   An intangible quality in a work of art, a result of a harmonious relationship of art elements orchestrated into a unified organization, evoking an appreciative response from the sensitive viewer. It is the artistic manifestation of a work of art, a criterion for assessing the merit of a work of art.

ALLOVER PATTERN   One method of designing a two-dimensional surface. In an allover pattern a design unit is repeated in a continuous organization, e.g., horizontally, vertically, diagonally, in checkerboard fashion, and in other ways, creating a sense of unity and continuity within a given space.

ANALOGOUS   A color scheme consisting of several colors having a common component. They are located next to each other on the Prang color wheel; example: yellow, yellow-orange, and orange. All of these colors have yellow in them.

A PRIORI   Reasoning which is not based on experience but is presumptive, developed from the conjectures of the individual; that which is known by reason alone in contrast to that which cannot be known except through experience.

APPERCEPTION   Perception that is clear and conscious accompanied by mental activity; characterized by the assimilation of sense data or new ideas and perception into ideas already present in the mind.

APPLIED ART   Art which serves primarily the production of utilitarian objects as distinct from works of art of aesthetic consequence, such as a painting or a piece of sculpture.

APPLIQUÉ   A method of designing in which a pattern created of one material is placed upon another and soldered, glued, or stitched. The method is used in needlework, metalwork, and various other crafts.

APTITUDE   Natural capacity, ability, or tendency to acquire knowledge or skill, as distinguished from developed ability.

AQUATINT   A process of etching which involves the use of particles of resin upon a printing plate which is then etched in order to render tonal effects instead of lines. The effect is similar to water color; hence the name *aqua*, or water, tint.

ARCHITECTONIC   A term applied to a method of painting or sculpture in which a sense of formal order, generally geometric and structural, is projected. The emphasis is upon spaces and forms rather than on subject, e.g., the works of Cézanne and Mondrian.

ARMATURE   Framework or skeleton, usually made of metal or wood, used as a support for the pellets of wax or clay which the sculptor applies to it and around it in modeling forms.

ART THERAPY   Art experiences, particularly painting, drawing, and clay modeling used in the promotion of an active and healthy state of mind of convalescent patients; a branch of occupational therapy.

ASSEMBLAGE   A composition or arrangement which has been created through the use of a variety of two- or three-dimensional materials such as pieces of cloth, wood, glass, photographs, scraps of metal or actual objects such as pieces of furniture, artificial fruit, toy soldiers, or other readymade objects. See COLLAGE.

ASYMMETRY   Balance in a design or composition in which the groupings of shapes or forms are informal and are not identical on either side of the center. See OCCULT.

ATMOSPHERE   In the classroom, an environment conducive to learning and to creative activity; a surrounding influence; a stimulating and inspiring factor in fostering mental activity.

ATTENTION   Psychologically, the selective responsiveness to certain stimuli apart from others; direction of the mind to the particular; selectivity in perception.

ATTITUDE   A disposition of opinion, action, feeling or mood directed toward a person, object, or idea.

BALANCE   A bisymmetric or occult, i.e., a formal or informal arrangement, often clearly devised but sometimes subtly achieved in the distribution of interest within a given two- or three-dimensional space.

BAROQUE   An art movement of the seventeenth century; a reaction to the classic tradition of painting, sculpture, and architecture characterized by unrestrained use of ornamentation—sometimes grotesquely conceived in the treatment of two- or three-dimensional space.

BAS-RELIEF   Sculpture in which the subject matter, carved or modeled, projects slightly or considerably from the background; in low-relief as contrasted with high-relief (*haut-relief*).

BASIC RESEARCH   A term applied to the study of natural, psychic, social, physical, scientific or other phenomena without concern for the possible use of the data discovered. However, when the data are found to be applicable to the solution of a particular problem, it then becomes known as *applied research.*

BATIK   A method of designing fabrics originally practiced by the natives of the Dutch East Indies. The parts of the fabric which are to be protected from the dye are given a coating of wax before dipping. The process is repeated for each color used. The wax is removed by boiling or ironing.

BAUHAUS   A school and research centre founded in Germany by the architect, Walter Gropius, for the training of architects, artists, and industrial designers. It subscribed to the principle of striving for the integration of art, science, and technology. Closed by Hitler in 1932, the Bauhaus moved to Chicago in 1937, expanded its program, and later became known as The Institute of Design.

BEAUTY　The term is relative and a matter of personal taste and opinion rooted in experience. What may be thought of as beautiful at one period of time may not be so considered at another. This change in taste varies from person to person, and from culture to culture. Beauty must therefore be viewed through vision which has been nurtured by varied factors. Beauty may be seen as an aesthetic quality, a sensuous, or spiritual experience. Beauty is created by man and also by nature. It is that perfection which strikes a responsive chord and evokes a feeling of exaltation from the viewer.

BEHAVIORAL SCIENCES　Systematic investigations which center around the origins, conditioning, causes and effects, responses and reactions, interactions, and all the aspects of human behavior. Anthropology, sociology and psychology are the behavioral sciences.

BIOMORPHIC　Forms which are associated with living organisms.

BISCUIT　Unglazed pottery which has been fired once.

BISCUIT FIRING　The first firing of unglazed, thoroughly dried clay objects, i.e., greenware.

BRAYER　A gelatin or rubber roller which is used to apply ink to blocks or plates in the printing process.

BROKEN COLOR　A term used in painting when small strokes of different values are applied to the surface, in contrast to washes or bold long strokes.

BRONZE　Sculpture produced by casting from a mould which has been made from the original clay or wax model created by the sculptor.

BURIN　An engraver's pointed steel tool used for cutting.

BURR　In engraving, the term applies to the rough ridge or edge of metal which has been created by the graver or burin.

BYZANTINE　A period in art history (fourth century, AD) known largely through its mosaic and fresco murals, miniatures, icons, enamels, jewels and textiles.

CALLIGRAPHIC　In drawing and painting, a term applied to a linear, sketchy type of brush technique, such as is used by Henri Matisse in many of his paintings.

CANVAS　Sized cloth which is most commonly used for painting in oils. It is stretched tautly on a wooden frame.

CARTOON　A full-scale drawing done on heavy paper in preparation for a mural; generally transferred onto a canvas, or developed in a mosaic, tapestry, or stained-glass medium. The term is also used to describe drawings of humorous or satirical nature reproduced in newspapers and magazines.

CASEIN　A paint medium which has a milk base; used as tempera paint, water being the solvent. The medium is more permanent than ordinary tempera paint.

CAST STONE   A concretelike material, a mixture of stone dust and a binder, used in sculpture and architecture.

CASTING   The process of reproducing clay forms through the use of molds into which slip clay or various molten metals are poured to duplicate the original.

CENTER OF INTEREST   That area in a composition in which a great deal of interest is created through size, intensity of color, detail, and placement and to which other areas of lesser interest contribute to enhance and to unify the composition.

CERAMICS   The art of creating clay forms including the study of the nature of ceramic glazes, the application of them to bisqueware, variations in the firing cycles, the operation of the kiln, and the use of kiln furniture.

CHASING   The art of ornamenting gold or silver or other metal surfaces by means of embossing or hollowing by means of chasing tools or steel punches; also, the process of polishing and correcting small imperfections on the surface of castings.

CHIAROSCURO   An Italian word meaning *light* and *dark* (similar in effect to *pianoforte* in music, meaning *soft* and *loud*); in painting, drawing, and prints, meaning light and dark values used to create an illusional effect of third-dimension in forms and in space.

CHROMATIC   Pertaining to color or colors.

CHRONOLOGICAL AGE   One's actual age in years and months.

CLASSIC   A term associated with the characteristics typical of works of art produced in ancient Greek and Roman cultures, based on formal principles and methods.

CLOISONNÉ ENAMEL   Surface decoration in enamel in which the designs are outlined with bent wire (usually gold) secured to the background (usually gold). The spaces or "cloisons" between the wire are then filled with various vitreous pastes or enamels of various colors. The process is of Byzantine origin.

COGNITION   A general term covering all the various modes of knowing—perceiving, remembering, imagining, conceiving, judging, reasoning.

COGNITIVE THEORY   A theory of learning and problem solving which views learning as a process of perceptual reorganization, perceiving relationships and principles.

COLLAGE   The term means "a pasting" in French. The process describes a visual organization of unrelated fragments of wallpaper, photographs, newsprint, or any other textured materials synchronized by means of paint, charcoal, or some other medium for the purpose of creating a new reality, i.e., one which is based on the accident and on the unforeseen elements emerging from the basically unlike materials. The Cubists were the first to use this method as a serious form of expression; later, it was adopted by the Dadaists. The Surrealists used this method to express an extreme form of association.

COMPLEMENTARY COLORS Any two colors directly opposite each other on the Prang color wheel are called *complementary*.

COMPOSITION The organization of art elements, i.e., line, color, form, and texture, within space creating a unified whole in which the parts relate aesthetically to each other and to the total organizational scheme.

CONCEPT A mental image of an action or thing; an understanding of the essential attributes common to a class of objects.

CONSTRUCTIVISM A nonobjective painting and sculpture movement of the twentieth century which was originated in Russia by Pevsner and Gabo. Tatlin, Moholy-Nagy, Malevich and others were also involved in this movement utilizing such solid materials as pieces of glass, wood, etc in relief forms and in sculpture-in-the-round. The constructions were purely nonrepresentational, emphasizing geometric form by means of materials which were generally used by engineers and architects.

CONTENT The sum of qualities which make up the work of art as opposed to subject matter. The intellectual, emotional, and aesthetic essence of a work of art which gives it its essential import.

CONTINUITY A quality in a design or composition which manifests a rhythmic organization of elements related to each other and to the total scheme.

CONTOUR The line which represents an outline of a form.

CONVENTIONAL Traditional treatment of visual forms in painting or sculpture; a tenacious reliance upon established rules; hence lacking in spontaneity, originality, or individuality.

CRACKLE A planned not an accidental effect of cracking in the glaze on a fired clay object, produced by the mixture of certain kinds of clay in the glaze. The size of the crackle can be controlled by the type of clay used in the mixture.

CRAZING Accidental separation in the glaze on the fired clay pieces.

CREATION The process of bringing into existence a novel idea which has been conceived either accidentally or through experimentation and exploration of media and processes and projected as a subjective expression.

CUBISM A vital movement in painting and sculpture which developed in France, beginning in 1907, through Cézanne's inspiration. The movement was given impetus by Picasso and Braque. This, together with an influence of African Negro sculpture, prompted the experimentation in the reduction of forms to their basic geometric shapes. At first these were sharply angular. Later the shapes became transparent and intersecting, and still later these were combined into a spontaneously conceived composition.

CULTURE Patterns of behavior, beliefs, values, attitudes, and social structure developed through time, and based upon a heritage and tradition common to a group of people.

DADAISM A French word meaning a *hobby horse*. A movement in art and literature initiated by Hans Arp in 1916. A sort of cultural revolt against the holocaust of World War I. The movement expressed itself by a violent reaction to traditional forms of logic, art, and society in general. Geometric diagrams and fantastic childish fabrications were assembled in compositions using found objects such as buttons, pieces of cloth, paper, bus tickets, wire, etc. The movement was in a sense a cultural counterpart of political anarchy, e.g., the "Mona Lisa with the Moustache," or the so-called "Fountain" (a urinal) by Duchamp.

DECORATIVE ART Art which is used primarily to enhance or enrich the plain surface of an object such as that of a book cover, a piece of pottery, a textile, a rug etc., as distinct from art which represents the actual form, an end in itself.

DELINEATION In art, a term used to describe a process in which an idea, an object, a shape, a form, or a design is rendered by means of lines primarily.

DESIGN a) The aesthetic relationships of line, color, form, texture, values, planes, and subject arranged in space and formed into an organically unified whole. b) A term also used to describe the enrichment of a plain surface.

DISTORTION A device used by the artist to exaggerate shapes or forms in order to give expression to his concept of the ideal, rather than for the imitation of forms in nature; to place emphasis upon, or to dramatize a particular shape or form.

DOMINANCE A term used to indicate emphasis upon a particular shape or form in a two- or three-dimensional composition. Dominance is achieved through placement, through size, through direction, through detail, and through contrast in values and color.

DRYPOINT A method of engraving, or intaglio process, in which a graver or needle is used directly on the surface of a metal plate without the use of an acid. Using a dauber, the incised lines are filled with ink. The excess ink is wiped away and the plate is printed on paper.

DYNAMIC Changing, brought about as a result of forces within a system; in a work of art, manifested tensions created through value and color, through varying degrees of depth, through varied directions, giving an effect of vitality and exhuberance.

DYNAMIC UNITY Created through diverse elements in a work of art, but maintained in a state of equilibrium; a projection of contrasts in feelings and in tensions, in values and colors, in depth and in varying directions which, nevertheless, contributes to the organic unity of a design.

FIGURATIVE PAINTING A term in art used to describe paintings which have recognizable subject matter in them, in contrast to paintings which are nonfigurative, i.e., abstract or nonobjective; e.g., a painting by Renoir in contrast to a painting by Jackson Pollock.

FLEXIBILITY A term used to denote an individual's ability to adapt his behavior to the changing forces of his environment; also, to the skillful use of his intellectual creative and manipulative resources in the resolution of problems.

FORM A term used to describe the structured totality of art elements within a two- or three-dimensional area.

FORMAL The term describes the organization of art elements in space according to generally accepted procedures, often balanced in symmetrical or nearly symmetrical order.

FOUND OBJECT A term used to describe objects found in one's environment and utilized in the aesthetic creation of new art forms, arranged in two- or three-dimensional space.

FREE FORM A shape which is not bound by geometric contours such as in the square, triangle, or circle but which has a contour that is fluid and devoid of sharp edges; essentially biomorphic.

IONIC One of several architectural orders created by the Greeks. Its chief feature is the capitol which consists of spiral scrolls. The column is more slender than those in the Doric or Corinthian orders.

KAOLIN A white china clay which is composed of a decayed felspar rock and a fusing agent. Kaolin is used in the manufacture of porcelain.

KEYSTONE The central stone of an arch against which other stones are arranged to create the arch. Often the central stone is highly embellished.

KILN A furnace or oven used for drying, hardening, or firing clay products. Ceramic kilns are used in the firing of bisqueware and glazed pottery. Enamel kilns are used in firing enamelware.

KINESTHETIC Related to the sense of muscular effort. The receptors for this sense are in the muscles and joints.

KINESTHETIC RESPONSE Consciously directed muscular effort toward perceptual stimuli.

KINETIC Pertaining to motion.

KINETIC SCULPTURE Sculpture which has the added dimension of movement. This type of sculpture was first introduced by the Constructivists (Gabo, Pevsner, Moholy-Nagy). The objective was to express the relationships of volumes in movement. Alexander Calder is known for his mobiles or "plastic forms in motion," sculptures which use materials not as solid mass, but as vehicles for motion.

LACQUER   A painting medium which gives a hard and lasting surface. It is obtained from the sap of a sumac tree.

LAISSEZ-FAIRE   A type of leadership which lacks leadership responsibility; A policy of noninterference—tantamount to no leadership.

LAMINATE   Materials which have an affinity of structure, i.e., homologous, bonded by glue, heat, and pressure to create a tough material such as plywood.

LAW OF PRÄGNANZ   A psychological theory of perception which infers that a person tends to perceive a stimulus pattern in as "good form" as stimulus conditions permit.

LAYOUT   A term applied to the arrangement of pictures and words on a page. The term is generally used in printing and in commercial art.

LEADERSHIP   The process of initiating, guiding, and coordinating group activity.

LEARNING   The process through which, as a result of practice or experience, knowledge or skill is gained and by which a relatively enduring change in behavior occurs.

LIGHT AND SHADE   A method by which the artist achieves the effect of third dimension in two-dimensional space, giving volume to shapes.

LINE   Line as such does not exist in nature. Line is used to symbolize reality. By varying the thickness of lines it is possible to suggest recession, projection, and interrelation of planes. Line is sometimes used without reference to any form. Because it possesses a rhythmic vitality of its own, it provides the interest in works of a purely abstract nature.

LINE ENGRAVING   A method of producing prints from a metal or hardwood plate upon which an image has been incised with a graver or burin.

LINTEL   A horizontal architectural member supported at ends by piers or walls, generally of wood or stone, used to span openings.

LITHOGRAPHY   The art of making a drawing on a lithographic stone or metal plate so that ink impressions can be taken from it. The drawing is made with a greasy crayon, ink, or paint. The stone is then saturated with water. The printing ink when applied adheres only to those portions which are covered with the greasy medium.

MAGIC-REALISM   Twentieth-century painting in which the artist reproduces nature naturalistically or photographically with an added touch of emotional tension and a sense of suspense.

MAJOLICA   A species of pottery which is coated with a fine enamel on which the decoration is painted and then fired. First imported from Majorca, Spain, into Italy.

MANNERISM   A constrained or affected style, a distinctive characteristic often exploited to cover the absence of originality in a work of art.

MARQUETRY   Inlaid work done with woods of varying colors and grain or with other materials such as tortoise shell, ivory, metal, or mother-of-pearl.

MASONRY   Structures made from materials such as stone, brick, tile, and plaster.

MASS   In painting, mass refers to any large area of color, shape, or shapes, or light and shade. It is the subject matter or content in a painting in contrast to the background space.

MATURATION   The process by which an organism completes its growth and development. Involved in maturation are both heredity and environment.

MEAN   The *average*, derived from the division of the sum of the scores by the number of scores.

MEDIEVAL   The Middle Ages in history during which the Romanesque and Gothic styles of architecture were developed—the period between the sixth and fourteenth centuries AD.

MEDIUM   The material which the artist uses to express his ideas. In a technical sense, medium refers to the liquid with which pigments are mixed to render them fluid and workable.

MENTAL AGE   The level of performance on an intelligence test that is typical of persons of given chronological age; a unit for measuring intelligence.

MOBILE   Sculpture of metal, plastic, or other materials in which the component parts move to create a design in motion.

MODELING   The act of molding or shaping a model in sculpture using some plastic material such as clay or wax. In painting and drawing, the use of colors and values (light and shade) to achieve a three-dimensional effect.

MOLD   A form in which anything is cast or shaped to be reproduced in quantity. Many commercial products, including pottery, are reproduced through this method.

MONOCHROME   The art of painting in different values of one color only (usually black or dark brown).

MONOTYPE   A method of producing one print of a painting or drawing which has been done on a sheet of glass or metal with oil paint or slow-drying ink. By placing the paper on the glass plate and applying pressure by rubbing, the image is transferred. The plate must be re-painted to a certain extent if several copies are to be taken. Variations in color and design in each print may thus be achieved.

MONTAGE   A form of COLLAGE in which sections of photographs are combined to create a unified organization.

MORDANT   The term refers to the acid which is used in etching in order to eat away the exposed portions of the metal plate. It also refers to the adhesive film used for fixing the gold leaf in gilding. In dyeing, a chemical used to fix the color.

MOSAIC A method of inlaid design executed by imbedding colored stone, metal, glass, or enamel in a ground of stucco or mastic. It is the recognized form of mural decoration in Byzantine architecture, usually associated with Early Christian art.

MOTIF A leading idea or conception; an element in a work of art.

MOTIVATION External or internal stimuli which generate a change in behavior, and lead to action.

MOTOR SKILLS Skills which involve movement through muscular control.

MOVEMENT The direction of the lines in a composition. ACTION refers to the attitudes or postures of objects and figures in a composition. The terms are to some extent interchangeable.

MURAL Generally applied to the decoration of walls by painting, using such media as oil, egg tempera, etc. However, this term may also be applied to a collage, montage, bas-relief, or mosaic joined to the wall.

NATURALISM In art, a style of painting or sculpture which completely resembles the object or scene depicted.

NEGATIVE CARVING A method of carving in stone or wood in which the design is hollowed out instead of being left in relief.

NONOBJECTIVE OR NONFIGURATIVE Both of these terms are frequently used in reference to abstract painting or sculpture, i.e., art which has no recognizable subject matter but deals with only the harmonious relationship of art elements—line, form, color, texture, and space.

OBJECTIVE Term applied to painting or sculpture in which there is recognizable subject matter. The antithesis of NONOBJECTIVE.

OCEANIC ART A general term used to describe the art of the South Pacific which includes Australia, Polynesia, Melanesia, and Micronesia.

ORGANIC Pertaining to the structure of interdependent parts found in living organisms.

ORGANIC UNITY A functional relationship of interdependent parts which contribute to the completeness and unification of the whole.

ORGANISMIC GROWTH A term applied to the concept which deals with the whole child, i.e., when all factors are seen as being interdependent in his development—intellectual, emotional, physical, social, etc.

ORGANIZATION The harmonious structure of interrelated parts. The relation of parts to each other and to the whole.

ORIENTATION The process of realizing the relationship of oneself to external factors.

ORNAMENT The embellishment or decoration which enriches the surface of a form or structure.

OUTLINE Man's earliest device for recording his visual experiences.

OVERGLAZE PAINTING The application of decoration after the glazing of ceramic pieces.

PALETTE Not merely the board, porcelain, or glass upon which the artist lays and mixes his pigment, but also the selection and combination of colors which the artist typically uses.

PALETTE KNIFE A flexible tool which the artist uses mainly to mix the colors on the palette. It is also used by many artists as a means of applying the pigment to the canvas or the masonite.

PASTEL A soft colored crayon (bound by gum arabic) delicate in color. PASTEL is also used to describe colors which are light in value.

PATINA The surface corrosion found on metal objects, copper or bronze, produced by the action of the atmosphere or by application of acids. Most typical is the bluish green of bronzes. The effect is quite often simulated on modern sculpture.

PATTERN The repetition of one or more motifs in a regular scheme as applied to textiles or any other two- or three-dimensional surface.

PERCEPTION The faculty for recognizing the significance of aspects of the visual world. The process of receiving knowledge of external things by the medium of the senses.

PERSONALITY The individual's characteristic ways of reacting and the dynamics which cause them.

PERSPECTIVE A term applied to the representation of space in a painting or drawing by the application of the principles of perspective. These are based on the commonly accepted phenomena that objects tend to appear smaller as they recede and that receding lines tend to converge to one or two vanishing points.

PIETÀ A term applied to any religious painting or sculpture which represents the Virgin mourning over the dead body of Christ.

PIGMENT Any coloring matter, usually in powdered form, which is combined with oil, gum, or an emulsion to produce paints, dyes, etc.

PLANES In art, used to describe two-dimensional areas, the surfaces of objects which, according to their position in relation to the source of light, reflect light in varying degrees modifying the color and tone values.

PLASTER OF PARIS A white powdered substance which hardens when combined with water. The mixture is used for molds in casting sculpture or ceramics.

PLASTICINE A clay which has an oil base; therefore it does not harden. It is used for modeling.

POINTILLISM A method of painting of which Seurat was a proponent. The technique consisted of applying paint in small dots or "points" to the canvas in order to effect an optical mixing. This resulted in colors which were more luminous than those mixed by the usual methods.

POLYCHROMATIC SCULPTURE Sculpture to which color has been added to achieve a higher degree of naturalism.

PORCELAIN The finest variety of clay used in ceramics. It is fired to a high temperature, producing a beautiful ware that is translucent when thin.

POSTIMPRESSIONISM   A general term used to identify the tendencies of artists such as Cesanne, Van Gogh, Gaugin, and others to depart from the Impressionist naturalist movement. The emphasis was on the formal aspects of painting such as the control of form, space arrangement, permanence of effect rather than the spontaneous and the transitory; the turning toward the spiritual and the emotional content.

PRÄGNANZ   See LAW OF PRÄGNANZ.

PRIMITIVISM   An element of interest in modern painting, sculpture, prints, etc. It is an attitude adopted by many painters of this century inspired by primitive, peasant, or child art.

PROBLEM SOLVING   A method of learning in which thought processes play an important part.

PROJECTION   Seeing others as possessing the feelings, desires, fears, etc. that we find in ourselves.

PROPORTION   The ratio among parts of an object, figure, nonobjective forms; the relation of parts to the whole.

PUNISHMENT   As a training method, the administration of a painful stimulus following the response.

READINESS   The sum of all of the factors, i.e., psychological, emotional, physical, intellectual which enter into the individual's ability to perform within a given experience.

READYMADE   A Dadaist term used to describe a machine-made object selected by the artist as a work of art by virtue of the fact that it is his perception that endowed it with aesthetic quality; the art of selection in this case is being considered a form of creative activity.

RECEPTOR   Any structure by means of which an organism receives stimulation (stimuli) such as the rods and cones in the eye, or the pain receptors in the skin.

RIGIDITY   Lack of pliability, inflexibility, resistance to change.

RELIEF   Sculpture which projects from the surface of wood or stone and is part of the main piece. It is used mainly in architectural decoration. The sculptural piece can be in high or low relief depending upon the degree to which it projects from the background to which it is attached.

RELIEF PRINTING   A process of printing done from a raised surface.

RENAISSANCE   The great rebirth in art and learning during the fifteenth and sixteenth centuries. It was a period in which the dignity of the individual was held in high esteem and in which the achievements of the Classical Age were studied.

REPETITION   The use of line, form, color, or texture more than once and in one or more directions.

REPRESENTATIONAL   A term used to describe the kind of art in which the artist attempts to reproduce to an appreciable degree the physical appearance of the object or person he views; this is in contrast to non-representational art.

RHYTHM   The recurrence or sequential order of art elements in space resulting in continuity or movement.

SATURATION   The measure of color or hue in proportion to the amount of gray or white in a color.

SCHEMA   An individual's way of symbolizing a concept or situation which influences his perception and remembering, leading to reconstructions in the light of this view.

SCULPTURE   The term describes the forming, modeling, carving, constructing, assembling, forms in wood, stone, ivory, clay, and metal in the round or in relief.

SELECTIVE PERCEPTION   The process of perceiving those aspects of a situation which are closely aligned with our own attitudes and beliefs to the exclusion of incongruent aspects.

SERIGRAPHY   Term used to describe the silk-screen process when used to reproduce fine art.

SILK-SCREEN PRINTING   A method of printing in which silk-organdy screens are used, to which stencils or profilm are adhered or in which tusche is used, to block out areas that are not to be affected by color. Using a squeegee, the color is forced through the uncovered areas of the silk screen, printing the stenciled design on paper or cloth.

SKETCH   A rapid drawing or painting lacking in detail, conveying a general impression of an object or scene.

SLIP   A creamlike consistency of a mixture of clay and water; used in casting ceramic pieces and in surface decoration of ceramic forms. In surface decoration it may be applied as a complete covering by dipping and then be incised to reveal underlying clay, or it may be applied by brush.

SPACE   The whole surface of a painting upon which masses are arranged or the volume in which masses exist when depth is represented. Space is negative mass and may be considered to have the same function as rests in music.

STABILE   A term applied to static abstract sculpture as distinct from mobiles, which are forms in motion.

STATIC   Pertaining to bodies at rest or in equilibrium, without motion.

STILL LIFE   The use of inanimate objects as subject matter for paintings, e.g., flowers, fruits, vegetables, vases, etc.

STIMULUS   Any external environmental factor capable of exciting or arousing a receptor or sense organ.

STIMULUS-RESPONSE THEORY   A theory of learning which regards learning as a change in stimulus-response relationships.

STONEWARE A coarse kind of pottery baked hard; One of two main types of pottery, the other being EARTHENWARE. The clay used for stoneware contains a flux so that in firing the material fuses resulting in a vitreous and nonabsorbent piece. The glaze is added for decoration only.

STRUCTURAL The organization or construction of an art form rather than surface treatment or other details.

STYLE The characteristic or distinctive manner of approach in a painting or a piece of sculpture, not the content.

SUBJECT MATTER Anything which is represented in a painting or a piece of sculpture, e.g., figures, animals, birds, flowers, landscape, etc.

SUBJECTIVE In painting or sculpture, a highly personal expression or interpretation of an idea.

SURREALISM A movement in art the aim of which was to overcome the barriers which exist between the conscious and the subconscious mind. Paintings of this movement were based to a large extent on Freudian psychology. The works are generally characterized by a flawless technique (Dali).

SYMBOL Any word, image, event which stands for something else. In painting or sculpture a symbol stands for something, rather than imitates something.

SYMBOLISM In painting or sculpture, the term describes the expression of an idea in terms of line, mass, and color or the representation of an object by means of a simple formal equivalent. Symbolism is found in much primitive art, and in modern Expressionism (Paul Klee, Wassily Kandinsky). In its Freudian sense, symbolism is largely the basis of Surrealism (Dali, Tanguy).

SYMMETRY A form of balance in which the parts on one side of the center are exactly like those on the other side of the center.

TACTILE VALUES The textural qualities of a work of art which engender ideas associated with the sense of touch; roughness, smoothness, softness, etc.

TAPESTRY Weaving which permits the production of complex designs with an unlimited range of colors.

TECHNIQUE The method of executing a work of art. Mastery of technique is desirable but it does not compensate for a lack of originality.

TECTONIC The formal or structural qualities in architecture or other work of art.

TEMPERAMENT That aspect of an individual's personality which has to do with his prevailing or usual emotion state.

TENSION Stretching, straining, or pulling forces, attributed to forms, colors, lines, etc; in architecture, the straining forces of architectural elements.

TERRA-COTTA   A fine quality of ceramic clay used for sculpture, vases, tiles, etc; characteristic color is brownish red.

TESSERAE   The small units of glass, marble, etc, used in the designing of mosaics.

TEXTURE   In painting, the simulated surface treatment of forms, i.e., skin, cloth, etc. In architecture, sculpture, fabrics, the actual surface quality or physical characteristic of the material which appeals to the sense of touch.

THROWING   In pottery, the act of shaping a vase or bowl on the potter's wheel.

TONE   The strength of a color expressed in terms of lightness or darkness. Every color has its tonal value.

TRACERY   The ornamental carvings or built-up segments of carvings on windows and panelling—a distinctive feature of Gothic architecture.

TRADITIONAL   Implies that the work of art has been rooted in tradition; not new or novel.

TRANSFER OF TRAINING   The effect of having learned one task on the learning of a second task.

TRIAD   A color scheme of three colors forming an equilateral triangle on the color wheel, e.g., red, blue, and yellow.

TRIAL AND ERROR   A method of learning which is characterized by variation in response, a gradual reduction in errors, and an increase in probability of correct responses.

TRIGLYPH   An integral part in the frieze of the Doric order; a rectangular projecting block which alternates with a METOPE in the frieze.

TRIPTYCH   Three hinged panels, paintings or bas-reliefs, generally designed as a single composition.

UNDERGLAZE PAINTING   In ceramics, decoration applied directly to the biscuit or porcelain before covering with transparent glaze.

UNITY   In a painting or piece of sculpture, a harmonious relationship of line, form, color, textures, and space adapted to a single purpose.

VALUES   In painting or drawing, the relationship of two or more tones. Values range from white to black, from light blue to dark blue, etc.

VARIETY   In the process of designing, painting, sculpting, or building, the difference or variation in color, form, line, texture, and space.

VITREOUS   A term applied to high-fire ceramics, nonporous, e.g., porcelain.

VOLUME   In painting volume is achieved through the use of light and shade; a method of expressing a feeling for three-dimensional form.

WARP   The lengthwise threads in a woven fabric. Before weaving begins, the warp threads are strung on the loom.

WASH   In water color or tempera painting and in drawing, the thin application of transparent color.

WAX PAINTING   A method of painting in which pigments are mixed with melted beeswax.

WEAVING   The process of producing a fabric through interlacing flexible materials at right angles.

WEFT   The crosswise threads in a woven fabric, sometimes called FILLING or WOOF. They are interlaced with warp threads in weaving.

WITHDRAWAL   A means of self-defense in which the individual retreats from an overwhelming, trying, or threatening situation.

WOOD ENGRAVING   Wood engraving is done by the use of various kinds of gravers on the very close end grain of boxwood. Very fine detail is achieved through this process. The prints are made from the engraved surface.

WOODCUT   A woodcut is done on the side grain of a softwood (pear) with a knife. The design is done in relief. A graphic print is made from the block.

Indices

INDEX OF SUBJECTS